Reforming a School System, Reviving a City

Other Books by Gene I. Maeroff

School Boards in America (2010)

Building Blocks (2006)

A Classroom of One (2003)

The Learning Connection (2001), editor, with Patrick M. Callan and Michael D. Usdan

Imaging Education (1998), editor

Altered Destinies (1998)

Scholarship Assessed (1997), with Charles E. Glassick and Mary Taylor Huber

Team Building for School Change (1993)

Sources of Inspiration (1992), editor

The School Smart Parent (1989)

The Empowerment of Teachers (1988)

School and College (1983)

Don't Blame the Kids (1981)

The Guide to Suburban Public Schools (1975), with Leonard Buder

Reforming a School System, Reviving a City

The Promise of Say Yes to Education in Syracuse

Gene I. Maeroff

REFORMING A SCHOOL SYSTEM, REVIVING A CITY
Copyright © Gene I. Maeroff, 2013

First published in 2013 by PALGRAVE MACMILLAN® in the United States—a
division of St. Martin's Press LLC, 175 Fifth Avenue, New York, NY 10010.

Where this book is distributed in the UK, Europe and the rest of the world, this is
by Palgrave Macmillan, a division of Macmillan Publishers Limited, registered in
England, company number 785998, of Houndmills, Basingstoke, Hampshire RG21
6XS.

Palgrave Macmillan is the global academic imprint of the above companies and has
companies and representatives throughout the world.

Palgrave® and Macmillan® are registered trademarks in the United States, the United
Kingdom, Europe and other countries.

ISBN: 978-1-137-34965-1 (paperback)
ISBN: 978-1-137-34682-7 (hardcover)

Library of Congress Cataloging-in-Publication Data is available from the Library of
Congress.

A catalogue record of the book is available from the British Library.

Design by Scribe Inc.

First edition: November 2013

10 9 8 7 6 5 4 3 2 1

To my wife, Joyce Maeroff,
for her forbearance, support, and love
through my many books.
It's not easy to share life with an author.

Contents

Preface

This book tells the story of school reform in Syracuse, New York. The individual elements of this project can be found in many places, but seldom have they been assembled in one locale as in this instance. Furthermore, the venture—unlike most others that are limited to individual schools or groups of schools—involves an entire district. The details should have resonance everywhere, providing experiences and lessons that will enrich efforts to improve elementary and secondary education in America.

Of particular note in Syracuse is the desire to link school improvement to the revival of the city. Big cities like New York, Chicago, Dallas, and Los Angeles can thrive even without school systems that distinguish themselves. But smaller- and medium-sized cities cannot as readily get by with public schools that are failing enterprises. Syracuse has become a demonstration model to test the idea that a resurgence of public education will make real estate more attractive, draw business and industry, bolster the tax base, and lead to urban rejuvenation.

The story ought to interest reformers, educators, students of education, policymakers, lawmakers, parents, and all who follow public affairs.

Say Yes to Education Inc., a nonprofit foundation based in New York City, initiated this reform project after carrying out endeavors on a smaller scale with limited cohorts of students in several cities in the Northeast. Say Yes invested millions in its experiment in Syracuse. More importantly, because no single foundation is apt to provide all the resources, Say Yes leveraged backing at various levels of government and obtained contributions from a wide range of donors.

In this regard, too, the effort in Syracuse is noteworthy. Usually, the levels of government and the entities that deal with children go their separate ways, having little to do with the public schools or, sometimes, even with one another. Say Yes has shown how they can collaborate and make the lives of children more fulfilling.

Say Yes attracted much attention for promising college tuition scholarships to all the graduates of public high schools in Syracuse. Students may choose from among at least one hundred institutions of higher education that joined a Higher Education Compact. But this grand gesture was only one feature of the reform effort that Say Yes urged on the Syracuse City School District.

It is too soon to pronounce the experiment in Syracuse a success, though surely many more students attend college now than would have if the much-heralded scholarship offer had not been implemented. Student performance in the city's elementary and secondary schools has barely improved, however, and the innovations fostered by Say Yes have had mixed results. But a superintendent who took office in 2011 has, with the assistance of Say Yes, taken many steps that should bear fruit in the next few years. Hopes are high, and there is a new can-do spirit in the schools and in the city.

There is much to learn from this attempt at educational and civic betterment. The tale is fascinating, and it underscores the many difficulties of trying to change educational outcomes in an urban setting, particularly during the depths of a grievous and lingering recession.

I began watching Say Yes's venture in Syracuse in 2009, when I accepted the task of gathering information for a report on this unusual undertaking in school reform and civic revival. The Ford Foundation provided support for the report. Later I was commissioned by Cross & Joftus, an education consulting group that had Say Yes as a client, to write a book building on the report. In other words, Say Yes paid Cross & Joftus and Cross & Joftus paid me. I accepted the assignment and turned my full-time attention to it on the strict condition that I—not Cross & Joftus, not Say Yes—would have ultimate authority over the manuscript that I produced. I am using the book to widen my purview and place the Syracuse effort in a national context. I appreciate the fact that Say Yes, in its embrace of transparency, understood the need for independence in my writing.

I traveled to Syracuse to conduct interviews and to observe life in the classrooms. In addition, I made extensive use of phone and email conversations to supplement the interviews that I had in person. I read thousands of pages of documents and relied on the Internet to obtain additional materials. I searched books and research journals for pertinent scholarly articles. Citations throughout this book give credit to the many sources that informed my work. In almost all instances where I have used quotations without providing sources, those words came from interviews that I conducted.

Many people—inside and outside the school system—assisted me by responding to my inquiries. I am grateful to the teachers who opened their classrooms to me, and I appreciate the candor of the school personnel in Syracuse who shared information with me. I spoke with public officials and with Syracuse residents who care and are knowledgeable about the school system. People were forthcoming and willing to volunteer information.

The Syracuse City School District has gone through some trying years, and student outcomes have not been encouraging. It is a tribute to the city and its people that they accepted Say Yes's intervention as openly as they did and readily spoke of their hopes and dreams for the children of the city. The interviews I had with recent graduates of the school system—especially important in informing the chapter on remediation at the summer bridge program that Say Yes sponsored—open a window on the struggles and aspirations of the city's young people.

I cannot possibly acknowledge the many people to whom I am indebted for their assistance. But I do want to single out three representatives of Say Yes who were instrumental in my being able to carry out this work. They are Mary Anne Schmitt-Carey, president of Say Yes; Gene Chasin, chief operating officer of Say Yes; and Patrick Driscoll, executive director of the project for Say Yes in Syracuse. This book could not have been written without their cooperation.

Given my gratitude to these representatives of Say Yes and the affinity for the program that I acquired over years of viewing the efforts up close, I still maintained a distance that allowed me to be a critical friend of Say Yes and its efforts in Syracuse. I requested that my book royalties be paid to Say Yes, but I made it clear that my writing would be objective and that I would not shy away from dealing with shortcomings as well as with successes. Those who would emulate this program—or at least parts of it—need that kind of detached view so that the descriptions and findings are worthwhile to them.

I have been a professional observer of American education since the 1960s, making a living by chronicling many aspects of schools and colleges. This is the fifteenth book that I have written, cowritten, edited, or coedited. It is my fifth book for Palgrave Macmillan, and it is an honor once again to have a book published by that esteemed house. My work in Syracuse was enriched by my experiences researching previous books about education.

Through the years, I have seen the nation's public schools become objects of mounting dissatisfaction, especially in such urban settings as Syracuse. Well-meaning people have initiated reform after reform, mostly to no great advantage for the students. School systems and the cities in which they are lodged cannot and should not be regarded as separate. Their destinies are entwined, as Say Yes emphasizes.

Say Yes to Education in Syracuse is not a panacea, but it provides many elements in a cohesive package that will redound to the benefit of the city's students, who deserve something beneficial to happen to them. Say Yes hopes to see its model widely replicated, particularly in small- and medium-sized cities struggling to adjust to new realities in a postindustrial world. The country will benefit if such experiments succeed. And if they don't . . . the consequences are too dire to imagine.

—Gene I. Maeroff

1

The Stakes

Syracuse, a postindustrial urban hub of 145,170 in central New York State, placed an ambitious bet on its future during the first decade of the twenty-first century. Unlike other locales where sparkling casinos and tax incentives for business represent the best hope for uplift, the gamble in Syracuse revolves around a hunch that sending its young people to college en masse will alter the city's fortunes. At the heart of the multimillion-dollar wager is a guarantee that qualifying graduates of the city's five public high schools will be eligible for free tuition at more than one hundred colleges and universities in a Higher Education Compact. Getting students into college is the costliest but easiest part of the bargain; preparing them to succeed is the more challenging aspect.

This bold attempt to resuscitate a troubled city by reforming its entire school system of almost twenty thousand students is a test that holds promise for small- to medium-sized cities throughout the country. School districts in such locales have become enveloped in urban blight, viewed as hapless symbols of city-wide failure. These cities have been swallowed up in a downward spiral that has consumed their public schools and the hopes of their young people as the national economy sputtered to a halt, jobs disappeared, and homes fell into foreclosure.

The effort in Syracuse was initiated and carried out under the aegis of Say Yes to Education Inc., based in New York City. This nonprofit foundation pursued similar ventures in other cities in the Northeast but never on the scale that it undertook in Syracuse, where it sought to reform an entire school system while transforming the economics of a beleaguered city.

Say Yes began planning for its venture in Syracuse in 2007 and officially launched in 2008, rolling it out in one of the school district's four quadrants each fall thereafter. Say Yes officials knew that the program they took to Syracuse had to grow local roots to lend the program the character of a native species. This meant cultivating support in places that would prop up the delicate seedling as soon as it went into the ground. Toward this end, leading figures in government, business, and education were courted as the original backers.

The effort excited people who thought Syracuse, where the population peaked at 220,000 in the 1950s, could never reinvigorate itself. This once vibrant city thrived from the mid-nineteenth century to the mid-twentieth century. Its convenient location—at first smack-dab on the Erie Canal, then on important railroad lines, and finally at the nexus of major highways—attracted business and industry.

But with suburbanization after World War II, Syracuse lost its hold as a center of commerce, and by the 1970s, manufacturing faltered badly. Then there was disinvestment in the city for more than two generations, impacting the public schools profoundly. The story is a sadly familiar one in cities of similar size throughout the United States and especially in the Northeast. "Syracuse was melancholy and felt like a dying city," said Marie Perkins, formerly a principal in one of the city's elementary schools and now a central administrator. "Then you have something like this come in and—I hate to say it—it can keep us from dying."

The marriage between school improvement and economic development consecrated by Say Yes is meant not only to bolster education but to fortify the tax base by making a once proud city a place that can retain and draw middle-class families who select their living arrangements by the quality of public education. Say Yes's approach amounts to a test of whether school improvement on a large scale can drive economic development. Everything came into play—the relationship of educational quality to home prices, property tax revenues, the caliber of the local workforce, and the strength of the city's commercial base.

The notion of better schools leading to a better community, while usually not stated so explicitly, is not a new one. "Reforming the public schools has long been a favorite way of improving not just education but society," David Tyack and Larry Cuban remind us in their history of school reform.[1]

Syracuse proved an eager patient for rehabilitation. Its average household income of $30,075 is considerably below comparable figures for the rest of Onondaga County and for the entire state of New York. Like similar small- and medium-sized cities, where economic opportunity has been elusive, Syracuse has become a relatively inexpensive place to reside. The average rent is $668 a month, and the cost of living is less than half that of New York City.

The population of Syracuse is 57 percent white and 28 percent black, almost the reverse of the public school enrollment: 53 percent black and 28 percent white. The growing Latino enrollment of 12 percent is roughly twice the group's representation in the population at large. Say Yes's efforts are driven in part by the goal of making Syracuse's public schools a more desirable option as middle-class families consider where to educate their children.

Slowing or altogether ending white flight will benefit the city and its minority students. A body of research maintains that minority youngsters fare less well in schools that suffer racial isolation. "Our estimates revealed that between 1972 and 2004, increases in school segregation corresponded to significant increases in the black-white and Latino-white test score gaps," says one study of national trends.[2] A separate study concludes that "the evidence points to racial segregation as the leading culprit" in widening the black-white test score gap.[3]

When Gerald Grant wrote his penetrating tale of the decline of public schools in Syracuse, he said, "[Y]ou don't get good schools by simply pouring money into institutions that have become repositories of the city's poorest citizens."[4] He called for measures that would breach the walls that prevent blacks from attending public schools in the white suburbs.

Poverty is a common denominator among many of the students' families. The link between family poverty and educational outcomes for children is not a difficult one to establish given that county figures show that only 20 percent of welfare recipients in Syracuse had high school diplomas. The recession exacerbated an already troubled situation. Finances in Syracuse deteriorated so much that by 2012 the mayor raised the prospect of declaring urban bankruptcy.

And so a vast partnership coalesced in Syracuse to provide influence, guidance, expertise, and financial assistance to Say Yes. It includes not only government and business but also the most important parts of the school system. The superintendent, heads of the teacher and principal unions, and leadership teams of teachers in the city's schools all assumed roles. Major businesses like Raymour & Flanigan invested in specific aspects of Say Yes, as did foundations.

City hall, members of the Common Council, and the county executive positioned themselves solidly behind Say Yes, a bulwark of local interests lending support to a newcomer while it was still taking baby steps. The business community saw the renewal of the schools as a device to attract companies and solidify Syracuse's unstable fiscal underpinnings. The teachers' union bought into the plan as a vehicle for unleashing the full potential of its members. It is a modus operandi that proved so successful in Syracuse that Say Yes was able to use a similar approach when it took on Buffalo as its next site.

Everything points toward making postsecondary education a reality for children who never before saw college as an option. The feature that initially got the most attention and continues as a significant selling point for Say Yes is its pledge to provide a tuition-free postsecondary education to high school graduates who qualify for specific institutions of higher education.

Years after the program started, some residents still did not understand that Say Yes was about a lot more than scholarships. Say Yes intends to make postsecondary schooling affordable and—just as important—give students the grounding and aspiration to keep them there, once admitted, thereby leading to the completion of degrees. The program, urged on the school system by Say Yes, has to do with social workers, health clinics, and legal assistance for entire families as well as a longer school day and school year and beefed up staff development for teachers aligned with the Common Core State Standards Initiative. These are curriculum standards developed nationally and adopted state by state to clarify what students should learn for success in college and in their future careers.

Obstacles to Improvement

Ultimately, though, all the interventions in the world will make little difference if they don't translate into higher achievement in the classroom. The challenge is huge. The principal of one elementary school in Syracuse, speaking off the record, said, "A lot of these kids don't have the dream. They have lost hope. Everything seems out of reach to them. I'm still hoping that Say Yes will do it for them. We have to hook the kids and motivate them. They're smart. They just don't put the same kind of effort into it that other kids do. They have to be inspired."

Hope can be the catalyst that produces favorable results in the face of adversity. It can help young people envision a better future and keep them engaged in their studies even when they see others despairing. It is a matter of believing in individual efficacy and the idea that tomorrow can be better than today. When Gallup polled almost one million of the country's fifth through eighth graders from 2009 to 2011, the organization found that hope accounts for about 13 percent of the variance in students' academic success.[5] Youngsters with the least amount of hope are among the more than one million who drop out of high school annually.

Much of the concern across the country for academic achievement focuses on the achievement gap, a phrase signifying the nationwide separation among students by race, ethnicity, and socioeconomic class. The circumstances of students' lives in Syracuse, or almost anywhere else in the United States, go a long way toward determining their academic outcomes. Of the students who entered the ninth grade in Syracuse in 2007, for example, the percentage of students graduating four years later was 34.3 percent for Hispanics, 46.7 percent for blacks, and 57.1 percent for whites.[6]

The National Assessment of Educational Progress and the Gap

The National Assessment of Educational Progress (NAEP), the federal government's report card on schools, offers a picture window through which to view gaps in achievement. NAEP conducts assessments in various subjects at the fourth, eighth, and twelfth grade levels and issues periodic reports on the results. NAEP showed gaps in achievement in the fourth grade between whites and blacks—in both reading and math—in all the more than forty states for which results were available.[7] A separate report found that the achievement gap between white and Hispanic students in both math and reading did not change significantly from the early 1990s to 2009.[8]

One of the most recent reports from NAEP, "Vocabulary Results from the 2009 and 2011 NAEP Reading Assessments," sharpens the focus from several perspectives. Analyzing scores on the reading tests from two separate years, the report zeros in on the ability of students to understand the meaning of words in context, which is pretty much the basis of reading comprehension.

The average vocabulary scores of fourth graders, who have reached the point in their education when they must make the transition from learning to read to reading to learn, varied by race and ethnicity. Scores in 2011 were 232 for Asians, 229 for whites, and 201 for both blacks and Hispanics. Similar gaps in vocabulary showed up for eighth graders. Whites scored 273, and Asians scored 271, while Hispanics scored 249, and blacks scored 247. Filtering the scores through economic differences among students' families reveals much the same results. The average scores of eighth graders in vocabulary, for instance, were 277 for those from families with incomes too high to qualify for federally subsidized meals but 249 for those with incomes low enough to qualify.[9]

This phenomenon stretches across subjects. Average NAEP scores in math reported in 2011 for fourth graders were 256 for Asians/Pacific Islanders,

249 for whites, 245 for students of mixed races, 229 for Hispanics, 225 for American Indians, and 224 for blacks. For eighth graders, average math scores were 303 for Asians/Pacific Islanders, 293 for whites, 288 for students of mixed races, 270 for Hispanics, 265 for American Indians, and 262 for blacks. Eighth graders not eligible for subsidized meals scored 296, those who qualified for reduced prices but not poor enough to be eligible for free meals scored 279, and the poorest students, those eligible for free meals, scored 268.[10]

The pattern manifests itself in other subjects. For example, NAEP released civics results in 2011, and the scores reconfirm that the gap forms early in a child's education. Average scores for fourth graders were 167 for whites, 164 for Asians/Pacific Islanders, 143 for blacks, 143 for American Indians, and 140 for Hispanics. Looked at another way, only 13 percent of whites and 18 percent of Asians/Pacific Islanders had scores below the basic level, but 38 percent of blacks and 42 percent of Hispanics were below basic level.

The achievement gap that appears in elementary school generally does not close as youngsters move through the grades. Average scores of eighth graders on the civics examination were 160 for whites and 135 for blacks. The 25-point gap between the two groups on the test in 2010 was not statistically different from the score gap in either 2006 or 1998. The gap continues as well among economic groups. Scores of eighth graders in civics were 163 for those from families that did not qualify for subsidized meals, 148 for those who got reduced-price meals, and 133 for students eligible for free meals, the most economically-disadvantaged youngsters.

The gap persisted right up until the time students had almost completed high school. Scores on the 2010 civics assessment for twelfth graders were 156 for whites, 153 for Asians/Pacific Islanders, 137 for Hispanics, 134 for American Indians, and 127 for blacks. The gap between whites and Hispanics narrowed between 1998 and 2010, but the gap between whites and blacks in 2010 was not statistically different from what it had been in 2006 or 1998.[11]

Confronting the Achievement Gap

It is not because students are black or Latino or poor that they falter in school but because so often those attributes are enmeshed with circumstances that—like placing a concrete block on the shoulders of a runner—hamper their progress. One report on the achievement gap lists three types of conditions that inhibit students. They are school factors (rigor of the curriculum and teacher preparation, for example), factors related to the home-school connection (opportunities for parents to volunteer, for example), and factors beyond the school's purview (low birth rate, excessive television watching, and family mobility, for example).[12]

"The most difficult thing we face in the classroom is the lack of skills that kids come to school with," said Jeannie Aversa, who has taught at both elementary and secondary schools in Syracuse. "Many times we can't meet expectations because of those levels. We scramble and scramble to get them to where our expectations should be for them. It becomes a balancing act and hinders where we can go. It's pretty challenging."

Factors affecting the achievement gap also contribute to a social gap that transcends race to include students of all races and ethnicities who are not the children of the elite. This is especially so in urban settings. Robert Putnam, the renowned social scientist at Harvard University, described his work in progress at a gathering called the Aspen Ideas Festival at the end of June 2012. He warned in a speech titled "Requiem for the American Dream?" that the vast advantages that accrue to the offspring of the wealthy are undermining social mobility in America.

The children of the moneyed class have greater access to tutoring and SAT preparation. They enjoy enriching experiences after school, during school vacations, and over the summer that are worlds away from other youngsters. Their parents regard them as investments to be nurtured, pampered, looked after by nannies, and set on the road to privilege. Americans are so convinced of the promise of upward mobility that they don't recognize that social class is becoming more and more of a divider in their country.

What was already a troubling situation was made worse by the recession, which cost Americans jobs and income, crippling the poor and many in the middle class as well. In New York City, for instance, the number of poor increased by one hundred thousand from 2010 to 2012. This raised the portion in poverty by 1.3 percent, making them 21 percent of the city's population.[13]

Despite America's persistent dream of equal opportunity, those at the bottom and those at the top of the family income ladder, like statues frozen in place, are apt to stay on those rungs as adults. Forty-three percent of Americans reared in the bottom quartile of family income remain stuck at the bottom as adults, and only 30 percent of them ever rise above the middle. Furthermore, blacks are more apt to be stuck in the bottom and more likely to fall from the middle than are whites.[14]

Say Yes may not be dispensing tickets guaranteed to transport the young people of Syracuse to the middle class, but its program creates opportunities that would otherwise be unavailable to the typical student in the city. When one reflects on the social mobility that Putnam says is threatened, the assurance of a higher education is at least a step up toward an uncertain future.

The Role of Good Teaching

One would assume that skillful teachers—as well as the leadership exerted by able principals—make a difference in the education of students who are on the wrong side of the achievement gap. Discussions of how to improve outcomes for the neediest youngsters often circle back to the quality of instruction. Good teachers not only help students attain higher test scores but also have a long-term effect on their rates of college attendance and adult earnings, according to a study of 2.5 million students over a period of twenty years. This study attempted to gauge the value-added impact of teachers.[15]

One problem, though, especially prevalent in urban schools, is that some students do not have good teachers. Studies such as one in the Los Angeles Unified

School District hammer home this point. In this case, Education Trust–West found that a low income student is more than twice as likely to have a low-value-added English language arts (ELA) teacher as a higher income peer and 66 percent more likely to have a low-value-added math teacher. "These patterns are even more pronounced for students of color, with Latino and African American students two to three times more likely (in math and ELA, respectively) to have bottom-quartiles teachers than their white and Asian peers," the report states.[16]

Similar findings emerge in two studies presented in conjunction with the annual meeting of the American Educational Research Association in 2013. A study of ninth graders at 730 high schools found that in low-performing schools special education students and those in low-level courses are one-third less likely to have qualified math teachers. A separate study found that math teachers of students in high-poverty schools are less effective than teachers of students of all income groups in low-poverty schools.[17]

Teacher expectations also may affect student outcomes. A body of research shows that all students—and especially minority and economically disadvantaged youngsters—may achieve less when their teachers don't expect them to perform at higher levels.[18] Ronald F. Ferguson of Harvard University, a pioneer in studying the achievement gap, writes that there is "evidence for the proposition that teachers' perceptions, expectations, and behaviors interact with the student's beliefs, behaviors, and work habits in ways that help to perpetuate the black-white test score gap."[19] He says that cajoling teachers with such admonitions as "all children can learn" is probably a waste of time but that good professional development can make a difference.[20]

Say Yes proceeded in Syracuse with an understanding that the role of teachers is arguably the single most important element in producing improved outcomes for struggling students. Say Yes's endeavor revolves around the supposition that outside supports for students and their families, along with extended learning time and the lure of college attendance, should be combined with good teaching and a more rigorous curriculum. With this approach, fundamental to the way that Say Yes advocates that education operate in Syracuse, the organization looks to foment change that will last even if the money runs out and enthusiasm languishes.

Reforms have marched through schools across the country like bands at a parade for more than two decades during the latest cycle of school improvement. Generally, the reformers are well intentioned. Through it all, school systems in urban settings of all sizes have barely improved. Few of these districts have been able to make themselves as desirable as the school districts in the suburbs that surround them. The University of Chicago Consortium on School Research found in 2011 that twenty years of reform efforts and programs focused on low-income families had done nothing to close the performance gap between white and black students.[21]

In New York City, after the Bloomberg administration had spent a decade trying to improve the schools, Merryl H. Tisch, chancellor of the state board of regents, questioned the value of a diploma from the city's high schools. She wondered about the accuracy of test scores showing improvement and accused the city of making it too easy for students who fail courses to make up the credits.[22]

School improvement, in Syracuse or anywhere else, is a fragile enterprise, always risky and without any assurance of success. Say Yes relies on research to set its agenda, but unlike what occurs when scientists mix chemicals in identical quantities under identical conditions, the outcomes can vary wildly. Human behavior is unpredictable. Teachers, parents, students, and others do not conduct themselves in a prescribed manner. School reform is messy work and sometimes resembles the toys in a toddler's room, seemingly all over the place. Usually, improvements are barely noticeable even after picking up the pieces.

Two Chronic Trouble Spots

Illustrating the difficulty of change in urban settings are attempts to upgrade public schools in two long-troubled spots: Camden, New Jersey, and Hartford, Connecticut. Both places exemplify the disparate efforts to find solutions to lagging student achievement. These cities are in two of the most bifurcated states in the country. Each state has, on the one hand, very affluent suburbs with high student achievement and, on the other hand, a collection of small cities afflicted by severe poverty and low student attainment.

Officials in both locales deserve commendation for their desire to deal with what have until now been intractable situations. Yet one wonders what ultimately will make a system-wide difference in such school districts—of which there are many throughout the country. There are implicit reminders here for reformers everywhere of the obstacles they must surmount.

Camden, New Jersey

Camden City Public Schools struggle to educate 13,600 children amid a plague of violence and corruption that has inevitably soiled the educational fabric. Camden is one of America's poorest and most dangerous cities, having eclipsed its own one-year record for homicides in 2012. Across the Delaware River from Philadelphia, it is the locale where three recent mayors went to prison for assorted misdoings. In 2006, authorities investigated school officials for allegations of abetting cheating on state examinations and falsifying data. In 2008, Camden had the highest crime rate in the United States. The state deemed 23 of the system's 27 schools subject to state overhaul. Forty-two percent of the city's adult residents have not completed high school, as compared with 14 percent in the state at large.

As if to demonstrate that the city's school system could barely care for itself, the 2011–12 school year saw thieves strip more than one-third of Camden's schools of heating, ventilating, and air conditioning units. The equipment probably yielded little profit to the looters who presumably sold it, but the impoverished school system had to find $750,000 for replacements.[23]

The school board commissioned consultants to develop a five-year strategic plan that asserted, among other findings, that the system had no board-approved curriculum, no coherent vision for improvement, insufficient financial management processes, and a school board that disenfranchised the community. The plan was unveiled in 2012 with five objectives: (1) transform the central office, (2) use best practices in finance and operations, (3) follow effective board governance, (4) improve teaching and learning, and (5) hire effective educators.[24]

In 2012, the state considered new ways to help the Camden schools including closing some buildings, taking control of the school board, appointing a new superintendent, opening more charter schools, assigning the operations of some public schools to for-profit companies, and providing scholarships for students to attend nonpublic schools. The superintendent and her senior staff did not even share the news with the school board when the state education department concluded an accountability review. All this in a school district that spends the state's second-highest amount per pupil, $22,306, according to the New Jersey Department of Education.

There was also the prospect, approved by the school board after much bickering, of Camden being New Jersey's first city in which a private, nonprofit group would build and operate schools under the state's new Urban Hope Act.

Then, as the 2012–13 school year opened, three mothers filed a class-action complaint asking that their children be allowed to transfer out of the system because they were not getting the "thorough and efficient" education the state constitution mandates. An administrative law judge ruled that the parents had failed to prove that the schools caused the youngsters "irreparable harm," a questionable ruling if ever there was one. Finally, in 2013, the state seized control of the Camden City Public Schools, setting the groundwork for a new chapter in the district's sorry history.

Hartford, Connecticut

In Connecticut, Governor Daniel P. Malloy assembled a package of legislation to aid the state's lowest-performing schools, particularly in Hartford, the state capital. Like Camden, Hartford has seen better days, but the social infrastructure remains stronger than in the New Jersey city. Hartford retains its reputation as the insurance capital of America. Thirty percent of its residents, however, live below the poverty line, and the city and the school system struggle to absorb a surging Latino migration that has greatly altered Hartford's demographic character.

Under the influence of the statewide teachers' union, the Connecticut Education Association, legislators poured water into orange juice, seriously diluting Governor Malloy's proposals. The measures that remained would add to preschool enrollments, enlarge charter school enrollments, and introduce turnaround teams to support strategies for change but would not provide the sweeping changes that the governor originally sought.

"Our state has the dubious distinction of having the largest achievement gap in the nation," said Stefan Pryor, Connecticut's education commissioner. "This situation cannot be remedied through patient rationalization and modest tinkering."[25] It remains to be seen whether the governor's watered-down program will be more of the modest tinkering that has failed to save the Hartford schools as they have sunk deeper into despair.

Hartford's public school students struggle to meet achievement objectives on the Connecticut Mastery Test. In reading, for instance, only 26.9 percent of third graders, 18 percent of fifth graders, and 44.9 percent of eighth graders reach the goals for their grades. In contrast, in the state at large, 57 percent, 61.8 percent, and 73.3 percent of students at these grade levels meet the goals.[26]

Moving forward, students who entered third-grade classrooms in 2007 and completed the eighth grade by 2012 improved most years in math, reading, writing, and science. But they had difficulty sustaining the improvements at the sixth and seventh grade levels.[27] Students' shortcomings in reading in advancing from third to fourth grade were of great concern, given the expected transition at this point to reading to learn.

By 2012, the city's students enjoyed their fifth consecutive year of overall gains on state tests. The gap between youngsters in Hartford and those in the rest of Connecticut shrank at a rate of 1.8 percentage points per year. Yet students in the Hartford public schools still trailed the state average by 22 percentage points, and at their rate of progress—if they can sustain it—it would take 12 more years to close the achievement gap.[28]

***

Camden and Hartford are just two of the many urban districts where it remains to be seen if results will match the ballyhoo. Elsewhere, New Haven is betting on better evaluations of its teachers. Newark hopes that charter schools, magnet schools, and merit pay for teachers tied to their performance will make a difference. Indianapolis has embraced the idea that charter schools, performance pay for teachers, and a less powerful teachers' union will redound to the success of the city's schools.

At least one report maintains that the country's very future is at stake in efforts to improve education. A task force operating under the aegis of the Council on Foreign Relations in 2012 portrayed the condition of education as a national security crisis, a situation not unlike that depicted in the *Nation at Risk* report of 1983. The Foreign Relations report identified five threats to national security related to shortcomings in the nation's elementary and secondary schools: threats to (1) economic growth and competitiveness, (2) the country's physical safety, (3) intellectual property, (4) global awareness, and (5) American unity and cohesion.

These threats exist, according to the report, because the schools do not harbor high enough expectations for students when it comes to science, technology, foreign languages, and creative thinking. The loss to America is seen in the diminution of the human capital needed to confront and deal with the threats to national security.[29] This report came just a year after another report, this one from the Organization for Economic Cooperation and Development, deploring the outlook for competitiveness. It found that the United States is the only one of the world's leading economies in which incoming workers are less educated than retiring workers.[30]

Whole-District Reform

Whole-district reform of the type pursued by Say Yes in Syracuse depends on the kinds of policies that underlie the efforts. There are *right drivers*, which will produce improvement, and *wrong drivers*, which may sound good but won't necessarily lead to positive outcomes for students. Scholar Michael Fullan, who writes about these drivers, favors capacity building, practices that cause whole-system improvement and that show a clear case that strategy x produces result y, as in any proper algebraic equation. To be effective, he writes, a driver or a set of drivers must do the following:

- foster the intrinsic motivation of teachers and students
- engage educators and students in the continuous improvement of instruction and learning
- inspire collective or team work
- affect all teachers and students[31]

Say Yes in Syracuse

Say Yes's work in Syracuse seems largely in tune with Fullan's propositions. The tuition scholarships certainly are motivators. Superintendent Sharon Contreras has made it clear that she is in pursuit of continuous improvement. The district recognizes that it should encourage teachers to collaborate. All the teachers and students will eventually be affected by the interventions proposed by Say Yes. This reflects the optimism surrounding Contreras's appointment in 2011 to a position in which she saw great possibilities despite the district's many difficulties.

"What really drove me to come to a city with 180 inches of snow a year was learning of the collaborative governance and the Say Yes model," said Contreras, who gave up the job of chief academic officer in Providence, Rhode Island, to make the switch. "Educators all over the country seek this kind of support. I never before saw anything like what's here. I wouldn't have come if not for Say Yes." The magnitude of the cooperation impressed Contreras when she began considering a move to Syracuse. "I had never before seen a mayor, a higher education president, and others come together like that, problem solving together in the same room," she said. "It was quite remarkable."

Say Yes limited its prior attempts to improve education in other locales to individual schools or groups of schools and never before tackled a whole district. George Weiss, the founder of Say Yes, had not previously pursued anything so ambitious. Around the middle of the first decade of the 2000s, Weiss assembled the leaders of his various school programs for a three-day retreat outside Philadelphia. Weiss took a vow of silence, announcing that he would simply listen and absorb what these leaders had observed in the various programs. They were charged with describing what had gone right and what had gone wrong. Many ideas for the future emerged from the discussion.

Above all, someone at the retreat offered the intriguing observation that Say Yes was fomenting jealousies. Participating students were taking field trips, attending football games, and even going to events at the White House. Siblings of the participants felt left out, and family members thought the programs should have a direct impact on their lives, not only on their sons and daughters to whom Say Yes promised tuition scholarships for college.

Weiss knew what he must do. He had to embrace entire families and reach more young people. He charged the new president of Say Yes, Mary Anne Schmitt-Carey, with taking the organization to the new millennium. Say Yes reached some 986 kids in its three separate programs at the time. Schmitt-Carey at first shocked Weiss by proposing that as its next step Say Yes take on an entire school system. One of her main considerations was to find a city in which leaders would put aside political differences and place elementary and secondary students first. Weiss has not been disappointed. "What has happened in Syracuse," Weiss said, "is beyond my wildest expectations. The citizens of Syracuse get it. There's an excitement in the city that is creating national attention."

Turnaround for School Change

While whole-system reform is still unusual, there are efforts under way in groups of schools that could be scalable to entire districts. One such venture is the Denver Summit School Network (DSSN), which encompasses ten schools in the far northeast corner of the city. The network took form in 2010 with the hiring of new principals and a redeployment of teachers. It predicated itself on five core strategies: (1) excellence in leadership and instruction, (2) increased instructional time totaling the equivalent of 37 extra days, (3) a no-excuses culture of high expectations, (4) frequent assessments to improve instruction, and (5) daily tutoring in critical areas.

DSSN pays its 77 full-time tutors $21,000 each, provides them with health benefits, and makes them eligible for bonuses of up to $4,000. Blueprint Schools Network, a nonprofit organization with roots stretching to Harvard University's Educational Innovation Laboratory, operates the Summit School Network. A tutor—many of them college students or retirees—meets with small groups of students at a time to deliver individualized instruction in math. The tutoring program focuses only on students in the fourth, sixth, and ninth grades, where officials determined that students must transition to the most new material.

The tutor plans in collaboration with the student's classroom teacher, communicates with the student's family, and enforces students' compliance with rules of behavior. This turnaround initiative employs tutors with fluency in a dozen languages besides English. The Network added an hour to its school day, and tutoring takes place during an extended block for math, when for half the period tutors instruct their students in groups of four or five. Voices fill the room as students and their tutors vocalize the mysteries of math.

Does the Summit School Network work? A report released in February 2012 showed that during the first semester of that school year, 30 percent of the program's students improved in math by as much as a grade level.[32] Since then, according to Allen Smith, who heads the program, increasing numbers of students have made larger gains than their peers in the district and in the state. The level of success has been so high that the district offered voters a tax levy that they approved to hire 274 additional tutors to begin work at schools outside the network in fall 2013. A concern in Denver is whether and how to take the program to scale while making it financially sustainable. Say Yes entered Syracuse with plans already in place for taking its reforms to scale and making them fiscally sustainable.

Some experts on school turnarounds argue that a district-wide approach coordinated across the entire system, such as the one Syracuse attempted with the aid of Say Yes, is essential and that an approach such as Denver's does not reach enough youngsters. Those espousing this position go on to say that the district itself must build the capacity for taking on this kind of reform, which Say Yes's experience in Syracuse shows can be a daunting task.

Furthermore, some of these same experts call for the sort of extensive collaboration that Say Yes fostered in Syracuse. "[D]istricts cannot do this job alone," says a commentary from the Annenberg Institute for School Reform. "[T]he solution is to build a district's capacity to support its schools, use data to inform its decisions, and involve the community and other partners."[33] The effort to win this local buy-in was a key part of the Say Yes strategy.

A Debate over What Approach Is Best

A debate among reformers revolves around the extent to which factors outside the classroom affect the achievement of American schoolchildren. Reformers on one side, like those in Denver, focus on steps they can take inside the schools to improve performance. Reformers on the other side maintain that results depend on society doing more to offset poverty's impact on children and their families. Admittedly, this summation is somewhat simplistic, and both sides acknowledge that ultimately improved outcomes depend on what occurs in schools and outside of schools.

Two organizations—a Broader, Bolder Approach to Education (BBA) and the Education Equality Project (EEP)—came into existence in 2008 to promote these positions. They approach the issues from the sometimes opposing sides that I have just described. BBA says that EEP ignores the impact of poverty on schoolchildren's learning, and EEP says that BBA makes excuses for the failure of schools. Say Yes largely steered clear of this sometimes acrimonious debate, staking out a middle ground and borrowing from the best of both arguments. Say Yes holds that upgrades in both teaching and learning are required and that society needs to pay more attention to a child's life circumstances.

At the heart of BBA's campaign for school improvement is a belief that schools alone cannot eliminate the effects of poverty on academic achievement. Adherents of this approach point to reports by economists, sociologists, and others to bolster their stance. One such report in 2011, a book from the Russell Sage Foundation titled *Whither Opportunity: Rising Inequality, Schools, and Children's Life Chances*, maintains that from early childhood parental investments in education affect achievement in reading and math. Some parents are far more able than others to make these investments.

The book says that opportunity has been disappearing for some children since the late 1970s and that education as a springboard to opportunity has lost much of its bounce since then. During the thirty years between 1977 and 2007, for instance, family income at the twentieth percentile rose a scant 7 percent, while it increased by 34 percent at the eightieth percentile—five times the rate for families in the lower income, adjusting for inflation.[34]

Sean F. Reardon of Stanford University, the author of one of the chapters in the Sage Foundation book, writes that "the relationship between parental education and children's achievement has remained relatively stable during the last 50 years, whereas the gap between income and achievement has grown greatly. Family income is now nearly as strong as parental education in predicting children's achievement."[35]

By contrast, EEP takes the position that schools bear prime responsibility for raising test scores and improving academic outcomes for students. Those on this side of the debate say that schools must work with students as they are, regardless of their life circumstances, and provide solid classroom experiences that equip them for something better.

In its statement of principles, EEP says that policymakers should redesign school systems to place student learning first and foremost. This means, according to EEP, putting more effective and higher-paid educators in schools, giving parents a voice by letting them opt for charter schools, creating accountability at every level, and making decisions about who is employed and how money is spent based solely on what is best for students.

Paul E. Peterson, director of the program on education policy and governance at Harvard University, became a leading critic of Broader, Bolder Approach to Education. He wrote that "any inference that might be drawn from a simple correlation between achievement and poverty is problematic." Peterson says that the changing structure of the American family has more to do with the growing achievement gap than social and health factors that affect educational outcomes.[36]

Putting the positions of these two organizations aside, the achievement gap is real enough, whatever its causes and whatever it might take to close it. The gap is a phenomenon that Say Yes in Syracuse set out to address in order to attain its goal of making all students college ready.

The George W. Bush administration made the attack on the achievement gap the foundation of its educational policy. The passage of the No Child Left Behind (NCLB) Act by Congress in 2001 required school districts for the first time to report test results by subgroups of students. Districts had to disaggregate scores by race and ethnicity as well as for students in special education and for English language learners.

The challenge to educators is undeniable, and the failure to close the gaps led to requests by states for waivers and for delays in deeming individual schools in need of improvement. By 2012, many states used the waivers to lower achievement goals for subgroups of minority students and those from poor families. Officials in those states decided that expectations were simply too high for these students. The question becomes how long the country can bear up under lower standards for some of its citizens.

Anyone who doubts the stakes associated with the urgent imperative for school improvement has only to examine the nation's demographic statistics. In Texas, for example, from 2000 to 2010 the Hispanic population of the city of Houston grew from 37.4 percent to 43.8 percent, and Hispanics in Dallas increased from 35.6 percent to 42.4 percent of the city's population. The sobering part of this transformation is that 50.9 percent of Hispanic adults in Houston and 56.4 percent in Dallas did not have high school diplomas.[37] This fact alone raises troubling questions about the economic future of these cities, the very questions for which Say Yes is searching for answers in Syracuse.

Children reared in households where parents have a minimal education generally fare poorly in school. The future of the nation depends on schools shattering this link through high-quality education. "What I fundamentally believe—and what the president believes," said President Barack Obama's education secretary, Arne Duncan, "is that the only way to end poverty is through education."[38]

And so it was that when President Obama journeyed to Syracuse on August 22, 2013, to describe his proposal for containing college costs, he used the occasion to laud Say Yes to Education. Speaking to an overflow crowd of more than 1,300 in the gymnasium of the city's Henninger High School, the president, dressed casually in an open-neck sport shirt with the sleeves rolled up, said, "I wanted to come to Syracuse because you're doing something fantastic here with programs like Say Yes . . . This is a community effort. All of you coming together and you have declared that no child in the city of Syracuse should miss out on a college education because they can't pay for it. And so we're hoping more cities follow your example because what you're doing is critical not just to Syracuse's future, but to America's future."[39]

2

Say Yes to Education

Say Yes spent a quarter of a century rehearsing for its prime-time performance in Syracuse, running programs in four other cities with small groups of students in a few schools to make them college ready, and then providing the wherewithal for them to pursue higher education. But Say Yes, the brainchild of the University of Pennsylvania's Norman Newberg and financier George A. Weiss, who remains a fiscal angel, never before climbed the big stage to accept the challenge of remaking an entire urban school system.

The story of what amounts to a demonstration model in gritty Syracuse may serve as a blueprint for school renewal in old factory towns throughout the United States. Though the tale is still unfolding and the results have yet to be determined, the lessons learned so far may instruct those who want to pursue similar goals. Say Yes in Syracuse provides a test of whether school improvement on a large scale can be wed to economic development.

Much of what Say Yes did before planting its flag in Syracuse prepared the organization for this task. Say Yes learned while working with smaller cohorts of students in urban settings about their needs and the efforts required to alter outcomes. The organization formulated a vision of reform and came to recognize that it had to start early in a youngster's life and offer an array of supports for entire families. Say Yes also saw that it needed a carefully crafted financial plan to carry the program through its start-up years and to sustain it as the organization's direct involvement waned. Toward those ends, Say Yes set out to accumulate pledges for millions of dollars in Syracuse, especially to support the college tuition scholarships it promised to students.

As its mission, Say Yes seeks to increase high school and college graduation rates for students from the inner city. At various times since 1987, it has carried out projects with cohorts of students in Philadelphia, Pennsylvania; Cambridge, Massachusetts; Hartford, Connecticut; and the Harlem section of New York City.

Say Yes to Education has evolved into the wraparound program that it exhibits today in Syracuse. It strives to fill the gaps in children's lives. In addition to scholarships and services for students, the program offers adults legal clinics, the expertise of family support specialists, and access to health insurance for their children.

George A. Weiss

For Weiss, getting involved with children early in their school experience is the initial step in a lengthy journey he hopes will overcome barriers and lead to college degrees for people of all backgrounds, not just those who can afford it. Education is empowerment in his version of what it takes to succeed. Personal experience shapes this view. His father, a scientist who earned a PhD, graduated at the top of his class at the University of Vienna. But because he was Jewish, Weiss's father could no longer get a job in the 1930s. The family fled to the United States, and his father's words are indelibly printed on Weiss's memory: "The Nazi's could take everything you owned, but couldn't take your brains."[1]

And so as the Weiss family started over amid freedom, even young George was sent out to work at the age of 11, becoming perhaps the youngest member of an organized labor union. By the time he attended Brookline High School near Boston, he waited tables at a hotel and received advice that he should study business in college and attend the University of Pennsylvania's prestigious Wharton School.

It was as a sophomore at the University of Pennsylvania that Weiss played host at a Christmas party his fraternity held as a service project for about a dozen inner-city kids who were six or seven years younger than he. They lived in a tough area in South Philly, and during the remainder of his undergraduate years, Weiss made it his business to learn about their lives—their older brothers who were in jail and their sisters who were getting pregnant. He encouraged the boys in their studies, and all the members of the group ended up graduating from high school.

He kept in touch with the group, and the boys stunned him when they said that they persisted in high school because they felt they could not otherwise look Weiss in the face. It was that experience, he recollected, that led him "to make a pact with God" that if ever he had the money, he would use it to make a difference in the world, particularly through a venture involving education.

When George Weiss got his degree in 1965, he didn't know it yet, but he had found his calling. Even as he went on to be a stockbroker in Hartford, Connecticut, and then started his own investment firm, George Weiss Associates, which now manages more than $2 billion, he continued to dedicate himself to lifting the fortunes of needy young people.

His first attempt came when he began shepherding 112 fifth graders at Philadelphia's Belmont Elementary School in one of the city's poorest neighborhoods. By Weiss's estimate, as many of these students ended up in prison or suffered violent deaths as the number who continued on to college. Many of the girls were derailed by pregnancies. Though the results of his venture were mixed, certainly more of the students got on the right track than their peers who were not among the original 112. This led him to conclude that Say Yes must work with children earlier, before they reach the upper elementary grades.

Learning as he went along, Weiss launched programs at schools in other cities, mostly out of his own pocket, as for many years he felt uncomfortable asking others to contribute to the fulfillment of his vision. George Weiss was not an absentee landlord in the organizational structure he built to benefit the children to whom he committed his backing. He set up an 800 phone number and encouraged "my kids" to call him when they needed help, providing personal mentoring in some instances. He delights in interacting with the students, freely dispensing advice, and is known to visit some of their homes. Weiss credits "Jewish guilt" for his drive to help the youngsters. "I never feel that I have done enough," he says. For their part, the students just want to give hugs to this avuncular man who they believe has done so much for them.

Weiss even put himself at risk by going into tough neighborhoods at night to assist children in the program, which may have prodded him to become the martial arts expert he now is. Weiss was well into adulthood when he earned a black belt and honed his skills, particularly in Tae Kwon Do. In 2003, at the age of 59, he represented the United States at a World Cup event. The next year he competed in the Olympics. He no longer has the back pain that used to plague him.

Of the hundreds of children that Say Yes has served, 75 percent of those no longer in elementary or secondary school received a high school diploma or its equivalent, and more than half of those graduates got a postsecondary credential or are still enrolled in college. Other programs—the Harlem Children's Zone and the "I Have a Dream" Foundation, for instance—share characteristics with Say Yes, but none have attempted to change an entire school system as Say Yes wants to do in Syracuse.

Say Yes refined its practice of collaborating with partners in each of its venues. The organization entered Syracuse with an understanding that offering to pay for a youngster's education after high school is usually insufficient in the face of crushing needs that must be met as a student moves through elementary and secondary education. So the program retooled itself to reach the youngest schoolchildren and bolster them as they advance through the grades by monitoring their progress, involving families, creating system-wide assistance, providing legal aid, coordinating services, and helping to extend the hours, days, and weeks for learning. The research-driven nature of Say Yes means that it employs the lessons absorbed from previous ventures. Weiss considers the work in Syracuse a breakthrough: a chance for an entire city to help its young people and, in turn, for the educational benefits to bolster life in the city.

He is sensitive to critics who charge that urban education is beyond salvation. It is a proposition that he vehemently rejects. He believes that "the playing field is uneven" and that such programs as Say Yes are about tilting the field to produce higher expectations for urban students. A story he tells to illustrate the disparities has to do with a young woman who attended a Philadelphia high school. She complained bitterly to Weiss that she was in the fourth year of Spanish, a point at which students should be deep into Spanish literature and fluent conversation, and yet her teacher was still teaching students to count to ten. An exaggeration, perhaps, but you get the point.

Such experiences are neither new nor unusual in urban schools. I found out more than twenty years ago in conducting research on schools in big cities for the Carnegie Foundation for the Advancement of Teaching[2] that some districts designated the small portion of high school students who performed at grade level as honor students. The label was certain to leave the young people surprised by the competition they faced if they reached college. In more recent times, Jalen Rose, a retired National Basketball Association player, said that he funded a charter school in Detroit after he met promising students who had been told by their high schools that they were "A" students but were unable to score higher than a 14 out of a possible 36 on the ACT college entrance exam.[3]

When negotiations on a federal budget reached an impasse late in President Obama's first term, Weiss—as a financier—was among a group of money people invited to address an unofficial gathering of some members of Congress in Washington. During a break, he spoke with a former U.S. senator who was one of the hosts. The politician made a snide remark about urban communities that offended Weiss, but he feigned politeness and did not challenge him. Finally, after allowing the comment to stew, Weiss offered a sharp rejoinder to the former senator. "He was helping perpetuate a message of no hope," the offended Weiss recalled.

Weiss's commitment to education as a vehicle for changing lives knows few bounds. His allegiances in this regard have extended beyond Say Yes to his alma mater, the University of Pennsylvania, where it all began. He became a trustee of the institution in 1988 and more recently chaired its $3.5-billion fundraising campaign and, in true George Weiss fashion, provided his own $20-million donation. "I was too poor to fully enjoy a lot of the aspects of Penn," he reflects on his undergraduate years, "but I felt it was a second home to me, and Wharton afforded me the opportunity to be successful." His two daughters followed his path in graduating from UPenn.

The Say Yes Theory of Change

Say Yes predicates its work on ameliorating four main barriers that tend to block the progress of urban students: (1) academic risk, (2) social and emotional risk, (3) health risk, and (4) financial risk. To the extent possible, Say Yes leverages the support of the community to overcome barriers to student success. At the pinnacle of its efforts is the organization's contribution, on its own and in conjunction with partners, toward college tuition scholarships. Providing students with the financial backing to attend the institutions, though, would be insufficient without the preparation to thrive in college. Otherwise, they would be set on an unfulfilling journey that might leave them with a sense of betrayal.

Thus the schools play a central role, and unless the district carries out its part of the bargain, Say Yes's theory of change will not work. This means, as in the case of the Syracuse City School District, that it must do the following:

- allocate resources in strategic ways that support educational goals
- foster site-based accountability and learning autonomy based on a belief that lasting change does not come top down
- support professional development that enables educators to act in behalf of new expectations and responsibilities
- provide rigorous curricula that have been proven to work with similar groups of students

- promote data-informed decision making using a student monitoring and intervention system developed under the auspices of Say Yes
- recruit, develop, and retain effective teachers and administrators who have incentives to do good work

Say Yes maintains that adherence to its theory of change, like taking the medicine that a doctor prescribes, will yield benefits for the school system and its students and for the city and its residents. As seen in Syracuse, however, progress can be slow, and Say Yes has only limited control over the process. In one of its internal papers titled "Delivering the Promise of the Five New Pillars of Education," Say Yes identifies the pillars as the following:

1. Early childhood initiatives
2. Better standards and assessments
3. Recruiting, preparing, and rewarding teachers
4. Promoting innovation and excellence
5. Quality higher education

None of the pillars were fully erected during Say Yes's first five years in Syracuse. All of them remained wobbly. The experience in Syracuse demonstrates that the kind of change to which Say Yes aspires takes time and patience and can be readily thwarted by a host of factors.

Expanding the Vision

In the process of expanding Weiss's vision, Say Yes seeks to make the impact of its intervention sustainable. Say Yes, for example, had to stretch what it accomplished for fewer than four hundred children in Harlem to cover some twenty thousand students in Syracuse. Say Yes used 24 benchmarks to monitor its progress in Harlem, specifying down to the tiniest level how much time representatives should devote to, say, a family interview. How many minutes, though, could someone give to the same kind of activity with so many more families in Syracuse?

Say Yes proposed a system to measure each student's progress in Syracuse against benchmarks across three domains: (1) health and wellness, (2) social emotional development, and (3) academic achievement. The monitoring aimed to draw on information from student records, reports from outside groups commissioned to gather data, and teacher and parent surveys. After feedback from two focus groups, Say Yes streamlined the process it put forth for Syracuse, making it more efficient by scaling down the benchmarks from 24 to 13, each of which went into greater depth than previously. This system sought to ensure that every student remained on track to thrive and be ready for postsecondary education, but for reasons mostly beyond Say Yes's control, it was not fully implemented.

It fell to Mary Anne Schmitt-Carey to start thinking about such matters as benchmarks when she joined Say Yes as president in early 2006. The idea of whole-system reform gestated for almost a year as she oversaw the national program of Say Yes and weighed how and where to take a giant leap into a place yet to be determined. Gradually, she and her colleagues set the following five nonnegotiable criteria for the due diligence that would guide their investigation of what city best suited their proposed project:

1. Community willingness to set a goal of postsecondary completion
2. School district willingness to partner with higher education
3. School district willingness to partner with government and the private sector
4. Transparent accountability in which the school district uses data to discuss what works and does not work
5. Transparent and sustainable fiscal management that commits the locality to fully fund the program by the sixth year and beyond

Say Yes knew it wanted to situate its demonstration model in New York State. In 2003, the state's highest court had ruled in a suit brought by the Campaign for Fiscal Equity (CFE) that the state did not fund the public schools of New York City adequately—given the poverty of its students—and that a new infusion of money was legally required. The state proposed to provide this assistance not only to New York City but to upstate cities as well. Say Yes viewed these funds as a potential reservoir from which its projected program could draw sustenance in one of New York's beleaguered smaller cities. In Syracuse, for example, four out of five students qualify for federally subsidized lunches, while the rate is less than 3 percent in all but two of that city's suburbs.

In applying its five criteria of due diligence, Say Yes discovered that several potential locales did not have the political and civic leadership that the organization deemed essential to the program. In some upstate cities, it was a game of Where's Waldo? Say Yes could not even find the sort of leaders with whom to discuss such a program. Finally, based on its process of due diligence, Syracuse emerged as the best candidate on which to place a bet.

Talks began with officials in Governor Eliot Spitzer's administration about creating a demonstration model to drive the strategic deployment of these new CFE funds. The idea was to ensure effective use of funds and measurable educational and economic development outcomes. Say Yes pushed the notion of a pilot that it could replicate elsewhere. State officials eventually embraced the idea. As a result, Say Yes to Education in Syracuse is a little-known legacy of a Spitzer administration cut short by scandal. The governor's office continued to back Say Yes through the Paterson and Cuomo administrations.

In 2006, when Say Yes was still figuring out how to embark on its program in Syracuse, it commissioned Schoolhouse Partners and American Institutes for Research to produce a planning document that would ease the process. The 73-page confidential report examined such critical issues as Say Yes's central objectives in Syracuse, the work of other organizations that already provided some of the services that Say Yes contemplated delivering to the city's schoolchildren, and the financial requirements of the endeavor.

The consultants reviewed Say Yes programs in other cities to draw lessons for the work in Syracuse. They also examined the "I Have a Dream" model for assisting low-income children to find similarities to and differences from Say Yes. The summary of the document offered ideas for evaluating the work in Syracuse and a timeline for that research.[4]

In looking at what it had to accomplish in Syracuse, Say Yes placed its objectives in the national context. This meant recognizing the insidious effects of the achievement gap. Say Yes studied statistics showing that high school students in low-income families drop out of school at six times the rate of their peers from high-income families. And finally, with its goal of postsecondary completion in mind, Say Yes acknowledged that 11 percent of children from the poorest families earn college degrees as compared with 53 percent from the most affluent families. Despite good intentions, the challenge was staggering, like David taking on Goliath.

Say Yes would be attempting to help bring change to a city in which 31 percent of the residents lived in poverty, a place where more than 80 percent of the students qualified for federally subsidized lunches. This was a school system in which fewer than half of the ninth graders got diplomas four years later. What lent confidence to Say Yes and put a stone in its slingshot was knowledge gleaned from years of working with similar students in other locales. Say Yes knew that it had to start with kindergarteners and build up. Say Yes saw early literacy development as the core of all learning.

The organization already recognized that the normal school day and the ordinary school year did not provide enough time for learning, and the Syracuse public schools would have to extend the day through the afternoon and the school year into the summer. Say Yes saw the need to go beyond the student and reach into the family to overcome obstacles that might otherwise divert students from the task at hand. And Say Yes knew that it could not operate alone or in a vacuum. It had to engage all elements of the school system and of the community.

Similar Programs

Three leading programs that share commonalties with Say Yes are the Harlem Children's Zone, "I Have a Dream," and Strive. They, too, address the needs of youngsters from families of limited means. They also rely extensively on private dollars. The similarities and differences, as compared with Say Yes, provide yardsticks against which to measure what Say Yes does in Syracuse.

Harlem Children's Zone (HCZ) resembles Say Yes in that it tries to make its involvement in the lives of participating youngsters all encompassing. It, too, is concerned with social-emotional influences as well as with the child's family. Its wraparound program extends learning time as Say Yes's does. While HCZ is not a district-wide program, it has identified an area of 97 blocks in central Harlem as its zone of operation. It serves ten thousand children and their family members on a budget of $75 million.

While Say Yes has encouraged the Syracuse public schools to expand preschool offerings, HCZ has taken a more hands-on approach to early learning. It sponsors what it calls a Baby College in which the parents of children age three and younger attend workshops to learn methods of reading to their tots, which they are encouraged to do at least five times a week. Moreover, there is HCZ's Harlem Gems for four-year-olds, a program emphasizing school readiness.

HCZ students receive the bulk of their education through the New York City school system, but Harlem Children's Zone keeps closely connected to that education by operating charter schools that, like charter schools everywhere, receive public funding. This puts HCZ closer to the students' day-to-day learning than Say Yes can be as an exogenous organization. There is not a guarantee of a college tuition scholarship after high school, as Say Yes offers, but HCZ says that about 90 percent of the graduates continue on to higher education, many with scholarships and grants that are directed their way by the organization.

One of the biggest differences between Harlem Children's Zone and almost every similar program is the president and chief executive officer, Geoffrey Canada, the charismatic founder of HCZ whose fingerprints seem everywhere in the endeavor. Unlike George Weiss, he has not put millions of his own money into the program, but his rock-star personality permeates almost every facet of the Harlem Children's Zone and has enabled him to raise large sums of money for the program.

There is also a dominant personality behind "I Have a Dream," but the program is far more decentralized than Say Yes or HCZ. The founding father is Eugene Lang, who, somewhat like Weiss, found his way into such an undertaking in 1981 by promising to pay for college for a class of impoverished sixth graders at his alma mater, Public School 121 in East Harlem. Lang made his fortune as a pioneer of licensing and technology transfers for small American manufacturers so that they might establish business connections in markets abroad.

Unlike Say Yes or Harlem Children's Zone, the "I Have a Dream" (IHAD) Foundation operates akin to a franchising agency, recognizing individuals or groups of people around the country who wish to follow Lang's example by sponsoring a class or entire grade level of students in a particular school or a group of children of about the same age who live in a housing project. These sponsored groups generally consist of fifty to one hundred children. IHAD has 29 affiliates across the country, some led by executive directors who find and work with sponsors who wish to provide the funds for a particular group of children.

Much like George Weiss, Lang learned that a promise to pay for college was not sufficient without support mechanisms to assist children from economically deprived homes along the sometimes difficult route through elementary and secondary education. But "I Have a Dream" does not offer the depth or breadth of supports that Say Yes and HCZ provide.

One of Say Yes's distinguishing features in Syracuse involves the collaborative approach it took to get elements of the community to put aside their separate agendas so that they might cooperate for the public good. A similar, lesser-known undertaking that runs this way and shares many attributes with Say Yes operates in Cincinnati and its two neighboring Kentucky cities across the Ohio River,

Newport and Covington. School districts, colleges and universities, social service organizations, levels of government, and business and industry joined forces in a partnership to create Strive.

When representatives of these sectors met in Cincinnati in 2005 to explore ways to increase the college readiness of students coming out of area high schools, the conversation quickly gravitated to the idea that efforts ought to begin before children even enter kindergarten. Three hundred local organizations eventually fashioned a plan that features five goals for youngsters in the three participating cities: (1) prepare for school, (2) support in and out of school, (3) succeed academically, (4) enroll in college, and (5) graduate and enter a career. Anyone familiar with Say Yes would find resonance in these goals. The four pillars that support Strive are (1) a shared community vision, (2) evidence-based decision making, (3) collaborative action, and (4) investment and sustainability. Say Yes launched its work in Syracuse at about the same time, guided by similar precepts.

Strive established success factors, monitored progress toward goals, made the results public, and continually reset the success factors. By 2013 Strive was able to state that of 34 measures of student achievement that it tracks, 81 percent trended in the right direction, as compared with 74 percent a year earlier and 68 percent two years earlier. These measures include high school graduation rates, fourth-grade reading and math scores, and the number of preschool children prepared for kindergarten.

Say Yes and Strive share two fundamental beliefs: (1) that changing scholastic outcomes depends not just on working with the school system but on mobilizing an entire community and (2) that meaningful change stems not from addressing just one issue at a time but from confronting a whole gamut of issues. Scholars writing in a journal published at Stanford University call this approach "collective impact." They point out, "These leaders realized that fixing one point on the educational continuum—such as better after-school programs—wouldn't make much difference unless all parts of the continuum improved at the same time."[5] Strive went on to establish a national organization to use the framework of the lessons learned in Cincinnati and to help other communities create their own local "cradle-to-career" partnerships. Fifteen locales were making progress in this direction by early 2013.

So all three programs—Harlem Children's Zone, "I Have a Dream," and Strive—cultivate the aspirations of participants and point them toward postsecondary education. These programs, like Say Yes, are dedicated to changing life outcomes for young people by opening doors to opportunities. All of which is to say that Say Yes is not unique in its aims but has some very special ways of realizing those goals for the students it serves.

There has also been a collateral benefit as the result of the leadership of George Weiss, Eugene Lang, and Geoffrey Canada. Their examples inspired a number of wealthy individuals, especially hedge fund executives, to take out their checkbooks and emulate them. Charter schools have been particular beneficiaries of this largesse. It has become fashionable among those of means to lend a philanthropic hand to charter schools that serve children from impoverished families. While these ventures do not have all the supports that characterize the programs just described, they do open possible routes to a better life for some children.

Say Yes's Earlier Ventures

As mentioned, Say Yes unknowingly prepped for its work in Syracuse by operating programs in other locales. These programs informed the how-to manual of the mind that provided the organization with experiences to shape the agenda for whole-district reform in Syracuse. Say Yes drew on prior programs to determine what to do and not do in Syracuse. Even with those insights, however, Syracuse provided a learning experience in its own right, and certain parts of the whole-district program had to be revised as it unfolded, not unlike fixing an airliner in flight. This is all to say that school reform has so many imponderables that any plan must be flexible and subject to rejiggering.

Say Yes in Harlem

Say Yes's Harlem chapter differs somewhat from Say Yes in Syracuse. The chapter began in 2004 with 385 kindergarteners at five elementary schools, three in East Harlem and two in West Harlem. Say Yes announced a $50-million gift to support the program. The inaugural event was a gathering in the famed Apollo Theater for the children and their parents. As in Syracuse, Say Yes promised the youngsters scholarships. The program focused solely on that group of children, a single cohort, as they moved through the grades. The Harlem program did not expand, as occurred in Syracuse, to include new pupils as they entered the five schools.

The Harlem chapter of Say Yes, under the direction of Lidia Torres, is based at Teachers College, Columbia University, operating in conjunction with the college's National Center for Restructuring Education, Schools, and Teaching (NCREST). Originally, Say Yes expected that the various departments at the college would contribute expertise to the program, but the college never really engaged the faculty in the effort. An exception was Jacqueline Ancess, codirector of NCREST and a former New York City public school administrator, who was an especially active partner with Say Yes.

Ancess helped George Weiss identify elementary schools in which to house the project, not an easy process in a part of the city with a paucity of eligible schools. "It's hard to do this kind of work in schools that aren't functional," Ancess said. It was the first time that Say Yes began the project in multiple schools, unintentionally providing a small-scale model for Syracuse. Ancess and NCREST helped Say Yes develop a monitoring system for the Harlem students and, as the years passed, contributed to the students' transition into middle schools and high schools.

By the 2012–13 school year, members of the original group attended middle school, and because the New York City public schools allow for wide choice at the secondary level, they scattered to fifty different buildings. They were in the eighth grade by this time except for 41 students still in the seventh grade because they had been retained earlier.

At the center of the Harlem chapter's work are five monitors from Say Yes, each of whom carries a case load of almost eighty youngsters and meets with every student at least twice a week at their schools. When a Say Yes student is the only one attending a particular middle school, the monitor meets one-on-one with the child. The monitor might gather with the students as a group in a school that several of them attend. When the participants were concentrated in five elementary schools, Say Yes could base monitors in each building and pinpoint support services at each locale. This was not possible once students scattered to more than four dozen middle schools. Then Say Yes monitors had to travel to different schools every day.

Say Yes in Harlem monitors student progress, observing such indicators as attendance, tardiness, and grades. This process amounts to an early warning system that—like the bedside beeping device for a hospital patient—can signal the need for intervention. Advisory sessions in the schools offer settings in which to deal with a range of issues related to academic progress, social-emotional development, and college readiness. The monitors have master's degrees and backgrounds in counseling or in secondary education. They place college readiness at the forefront of their concerns and cultivate the students' habits of perseverance and resiliency. Say Yes also partners with a company to provide tutors for students when they request help with their schoolwork.

Say Yes has little connection to classroom instruction at the middle schools and gets involved with what occurs in classrooms only occasionally. This happened, for example, when Say Yes students at one middle school received marks in math that seemed lower than they ought to have been. By interviewing the students and their families, Say Yes discovered that a particular teacher wasn't grading the students objectively. Meetings with the teacher and the principal rectified the situation.

On many Saturdays during the school year, Say Yes students go to the Teachers College campus, on the edge of Harlem, for sessions that run from 9 a.m. to 3 p.m. During the morning they may choose to study two academic electives from among those available in language arts, math, science, and the humanities. The work in each elective is based on a project that students pursue in a team arrangement. After a half-hour lunch in the classical setting of the college's cafeteria, the students spend the afternoon in talent development and may select among electives of a less academic bent, including such activities as art, cooking, drama, and sports. Say Yes structures its summer program similarly.

Say Yes mostly put aside the regular Saturday program in Harlem during the first half of the 2012–13 school year as students began preparing for the examinations and auditions that would determine their admission to the various special high schools in New York. The city's neighborhood high schools, especially those near Harlem, have poor reputations, and students who expect to attend college try to avoid those schools. Thus fall afternoons on Saturdays found the students practicing for high school entrance exams and learning test-taking skills. Those interested in applying to high schools specializing in the arts and performance prepared for auditions and assembled portfolios.

Say Yes in Philadelphia

While the Say Yes eighth graders in Harlem were preparing for high school admissions tests, the twelfth graders in Philadelphia's Say Yes Bryant program, which began four years earlier than the Harlem chapter, were getting ready for SAT exams. These tests would help determine their college admissions prospects. The program in Philadelphia, like others, involved support for a single cohort of students as they moved through the grades. William C. Bryant Elementary School in West Philadelphia was the original site of the program, which began when Say Yes randomly selected fifty children coming out of Head Start and entering kindergarten. Say Yes got enough space in the building for a parent resource room, a learning lab in which to tutor children in math and reading, and an administrative office.

Every Say Yes group has its own story to tell, and the program at Bryant was marked by conflicts that inundated the school and almost sank the program. Bryant, one of the city's worst schools, had abysmal test scores and no continuity in leadership as six principals revolved through the position in five years. It became a place that the central administration designated for possible takeover by a private educational management organization.

The Philadelphia Federation of Teachers fought such takeovers, and ultimately, Bryant was not turned over to an outside organization. But an aura of hostility infected the building as the union battled to keep the school from passing out of the district's direct control. The mood was not helped by jealousy over the services and support that Say Yes provided to students in its program. Some teachers and non–Say Yes parents resented this "special treatment" even though Say Yes spent tens of thousands of dollars to deliver some of its services to the entire enrollment. "We were seen as adversaries," recalled Maisha Sullivan, the Say Yes director in Philadelphia.

Say Yes extricated its students from this mess by arranging for them to leave Bryant early and transfer as fifth graders to a charter school run by the KIPP group, officially the Knowledge Is Power Program, known around the country for its work with inner-city students. After completing the eighth grade at KIPP, the students split off into two high schools, where Say Yes staff met with them regularly. What emerged in Philadelphia over the years was a program with the attributes of an extended family, as the parents in many cases looked out for each other's children, and the students leaned on each other through their successes and failures. Say Yes headquarters in a suite of offices adjacent to the University of Pennsylvania campus took on the character of a den in a family home, a place where students gathered for programs and assistance after school, on weekends, and during the summer.

Say Yes extended services and support from the outset to siblings of students in the Bryant program who were born by the year 2000 when the organization began the program. Siblings were even eligible to receive up to $25,000 to defray college costs. Another group of children, not relatives of the participants but cousins and neighborhood chums, known as "friendlies," informally availed themselves of parts of the Say Yes program, especially during the summer.

Parents of Say Yes students, too, got assistance. Among them was Natasha Brooks-Clarke, who took advantage of the support—while working full time—to obtain a high school diploma and an associate's degree from Community College of Philadelphia. She said that she wanted to be a role model for her son.

Success in Philadelphia could be seen in figures showing that 45 of the original 50 youngsters remained enrolled in what turned out to be the senior year of high school for most of them and 36 graduated on time in 2013. This was a remarkable statistic given that 39 percent of the school system's students do not graduate in the requisite four years. Furthermore, only one of the male students was known to have fathered a child, and only one of the females gave birth (and remained enrolled in school), also noteworthy given the numbers of inner-city kids whose educational careers are cut short by parenthood.

Say Yes in Hartford

Hartford had two iterations of Say Yes, the first one successful and the second one less so. In 1990, when Say Yes first went into Hartford, it adopted 76 fifth graders and proceeded to follow them through the grades as a single cohort at what was then named the Annie Fisher elementary school. The students got their high school diplomas and went off to college with Say Yes scholarships, tracing much the same pattern as other cohorts. Two Hartford families, the Handels and the Bermans, joined George Weiss in funding the program through Say Yes. So far, so good.

Then in 2008, when Say Yes launched its whole-district program in Syracuse, it started another venture in Hartford, this time working with a full school rather than a single class. Say Yes intended to make Syracuse and Hartford matching experiments of a sort, hoping to compare outcomes in a whole-system approach with what it could accomplish in a single school. The school, Global Communications Academy, was new, and Say Yes planned to work with all of its students as new grades were added each year.

Say Yes hired additional personnel for Global, and the organization assumed the same role as in Syracuse and the other cities, including the promise of eventual financial aid for college. These personnel involved themselves in social-emotional supports, extended day and extended year activities, and assisting families. As a result, the school provided students with features distinctive to Say Yes and not ordinarily found in the city's other schools.

A new school superintendent assumed her duties in 2011, and the district's commitment to Say Yes waned. Hartford, as pointed out in the previous chapter, is a troubled system, and the needs of Say Yes's one school increasingly got lost amid the magnet schools and various choice programs with which it had to compete for attention. Demands within the system were prioritized as the district sought to implement a five-year plan to raise test scores and reduce dropout rates across the city.

Mayor Pedro Segarra was critical of the selection process that led to the hiring of Superintendent Christina Kishimoto, previously the assistant superintendent.

He was so much at odds with the school board that in January 2012 he appointed five new members, including himself, to the nine-member board. This new board rescinded bonuses that the superintendent wanted to award to top administrators. It also rejected the superintendent's proposal to renew a $100,000 contract with the College Board for free SAT tutoring for high school students. Say Yes's connection to Global Communications Academy remained a tiny blip on the radar screen, a Piper J-3 Cub circling in the vastness, as the district descended into chaos.

The coup de grâce came later in 2012 when Superintendent Kishimoto announced the creation of a promise program in Hartford to pay for college tuition for all the system's high school graduates. She took this action without notifying Say Yes, which was, of course, already running its own program of college tuition scholarships and had expertise on such matters.

Say Yes became a jilted suitor, seeking a graceful exit from a Hartford in which its courtship had been rendered incidental. Say Yes announced that it would continue the promise of scholarships to students already attending Global but would otherwise end its involvement at the school in 2013, when its five-year agreement with the district would be up for renewal. As a show of goodwill, George Weiss made a $500,000 contribution to the new city-wide program of tuition scholarships, which still had to raise tens of millions of dollars.

It is clear in the wake of the demise of the Hartford chapter that a program that depends on instigating school reform from the outside, Say Yes's modus operandi, must be in sync with the superintendent, the school board, and the city administration to have any chance for success. It is not surprising that Say Yes assumed a major role in the superintendent searches in its work in Syracuse and Buffalo.

Say Yes in Cambridge

When Anne Larkin, a professor at Lesley University in Cambridge, Massachusetts, set about creating a chapter for Say Yes, she deliberately sought a local school where the children were needy and the neighborhood was struggling. So it was that the program started in 1991 with three third-grade classes at the Harrington School, now known as King Open School. Most remarkably, half of the 69 students were classified for special education, according to Larkin. As with the youngsters in Philadelphia and Hartford before them, Say Yes promised those in Cambridge full tuition scholarships for college, a goal that at the outset seemed as distant as another universe.

A great strength of the chapter turned out to be that Larkin, the director, and the two people she hired to work with her—Jose Ribeiro as project coordinator and Barbara Ulm as administrator—stayed in those roles until 2008, when the program ended. The students and their parents came to know the three of them well and found they could rely on them. Ribeiro, a native of Portugal and a long-time psychologist in the school system, spoke five languages, a distinct advantage with children at a school known as "a world in a schoolhouse." Four couples volunteered to assist the paid staff members, acting as mentors to the students throughout their education.

Lesley University designated the Harrington School as a professional development school, assigning a faculty member to the school and pouring in services for the entire building, not just for the chapter's students. Harrington got help with team teaching, inclusion, English as a second language, and interdisciplinary instruction. Larkin, a special education expert, ensured that a Lesley University representative sat in on conferences to develop individualized education plans for the many disabled students in the Say Yes program.

The Cambridge chapter thrived even as more than twenty of the students' families moved out of the school district, four of them leaving the country altogether. Larkin said that she and her colleagues established contact with the schools to which the students transferred and arranged for the youngsters to get whatever support services they needed, allowing them to remain part of the program. A measure of the program's success is the fact that 62 of the 69 students received diplomas either by completing high school or by passing the equivalency examination. Furthermore, 45 of the students entered postsecondary institutions.

When they went off for higher education, Larkin contacted their institutions to make officials aware of the students. Two colleges were so impressed that they offered free room and board to the students in addition to their Say Yes tuition scholarships. Moreover, Cambridge Say Yes arranged for someone at each college to act as a liaison to every one of the students so that they would receive needed services. Say Yes expected the students to visit the learning centers at their colleges regularly for tutoring.

In most locales, Say Yes terminated scholarships four years after the completion of high school. Larkin persuaded George Weiss to extend the offer for two extra years so that Cambridge students who took a break after high school and those who needed longer to complete college might still benefit from the financial support. Thus students in the Cambridge chapter had two extra years of eligibility for the tuition scholarships, resulting in half of those who attended colleges earning their degrees.

"I knew going into this," Larkin said in retrospect, "that if you do this in a school like the Harrington, you can convince people that any child can succeed if you build the right supports." And as if to demonstrate the continuing influence of Say Yes in lifting aspirations, several of the students who had not attended college enrolled in pursuit of degrees in the years following 2008, knowing they would have to pay on their own.

Say Yes's Hidden Contributions

Many of Say Yes's contributions to students' development and to school improvement remain out of sight, not because the organization tries to hide its involvement but because it exerts influence behind the scenes, especially on individual youngsters. Even in Syracuse, where Say Yes has focused more directly than in its earlier ventures on reforming the schools, the organization doesn't install people in the central office, hire principals, or teach the classes. But Say Yes offers advice and recommendations to help schools operate more effectively and more efficiently.

This guidance often arises from audits and studies conducted by consultants hired by Say Yes on behalf of the school district.

A good example of this process could be seen in the resource mapping that Education Resource Strategies (ERS), a nonprofit group devoted to developing plans to transform schools, provided in a report to the Syracuse City School District. In this case, ERS sought ways that the system could use time, people, and money in a manner aligned with strategic goals. First, ERS set the stage for its recommendations by pointing out that revenues in Syracuse were declining and spending was increasing.

Resource practices, according to the ERS report, would have to be more equitable and based on needs and priorities. There would have to be trade-offs to prioritize the impact on student achievement, and the district would have to base allocations on evaluations and contributions to student achievement. These measures would require seven key transformational strategies in Syracuse:

1. Ensure equitable, transparent, and flexible funding across schools
2. Restructure the teaching job
3. Support schools in organizing people, time, and money to maximize learning
4. Ensure access to aligned curriculum, instruction, assessment, and professional development
5. Build school and district leader capacity
6. Redesign central roles for empowerment, accountability, and efficiency
7. Partner with families and communities

ERS offered steps to monitor and assess progress in each area. For example, in terms of alignment, the school system could explore whether the curriculum was aligned to state standards for all grades and subjects. It could look at whether teachers used regular and aligned formative assessments. It could see how much money was spent on professional development.

And so it is that Say Yes evolved to promote school reform in the Syracuse City School District. Say Yes makes itself a catalyst for change by quietly helping people see shortcomings in the school system and pointing the way to improvement. In other words, Say Yes precipitates action by others—educators, board members, elected and appointed officials, and members of the community—by making them uncomfortable with the status quo. Change generally does not occur in the midst of satisfaction—when the bed in which one lies is too familiar to give up, even if the mattress is lumpy. The problem, though, with complacency in urban school systems is that too many children receive something less than a meaningful education.

3

Elements of Collaboration

Say Yes was shrewd when it came to winning support from Syracuse's Common Council, the mayor, the county, and the state legislature. Influence and money were at stake. Even the federal government figured in the deliberations. Say Yes wanted to persuade elected and appointed public officials to view its efforts in Syracuse not simply as an educational endeavor. Lawmakers could more readily justify extra funds for a pursuit in economic development than for education, which already consumed large portions of the city and state budgets.

The Challenges in Getting City Support

Urban school systems, even smaller ones like Syracuse, face American education's greatest challenges. They account for a disproportionate share of economically disadvantaged students, as well as minority members, those who reside in homes where English is not the first language, and the disabled. Such characteristics mean that city districts of all sizes, given the needs of their students, must spend more on each pupil than many other school systems in the country. Furthermore, such schools are often islands amid crime, violence, and poverty. Unemployment is rife in the inner city in the best of times, and in recent years, it has been endemic.

In New York State, the school systems of the five largest districts, which serve more than 40 percent of the state's pupils, are known as the Big 5. This designation includes Buffalo, New York City, Rochester, Syracuse, and Yonkers. State law does not give these districts independent taxing authority, thereby rendering them supplicants dependent on their city governments to finance education. Elementary and secondary schools consume more than half of the budgets for these cities.

The years since Say Yes arrived in Syracuse have not been good ones for a school system in this position of dependency. The five largest cities in New York State, as most of their counterparts elsewhere, suffer under severe financial constraints that are exacerbated by urban poverty. These circumstances throw the schools into direct competition with payments for police and firefighters, maintenance of roads and bridges, garbage removal, and a host of other municipal services. The recession has made these pressures more severe, and the nation's cities are hurting like a festering sore that resists healing.

Achievement lags in virtually all urban school districts in comparison with suburban, more affluent school systems. Students in Syracuse have fared especially poorly. Their scores on New York State's math exams are the lowest of the Big 5 in terms of the percentage reaching the state's standards and second-lowest in language arts.

Presiding over an urban school district may be the toughest job in education. The turnover rate for big-city superintendents—chewed up and spit out like sunflower seeds in a major league dugout—is high, interfering with the continuity of leadership in these places. In 1999, the tenure of an urban school superintendent was 2.33 years. Time in the job has risen slightly every year since, and in 2010, it was 3.64 years,[1] still a frightfully short time to put programs in place that make a difference for students. Syracuse and Yonkers are not members of the national Council of the Great City Schools, but the other three districts in the Big 5 are. Michael Casserly, executive director of the Great City group, said in 2012 that the districts in his group were probably under more pressure than any institutions, public or private, in the country. Casserly stated,

> Urban public schools are being told to produce results or get out of the way. We are being told to improve or see the public go somewhere else. We are being told to be accountable for what we do or let someone else do it . . . But our job in urban education is not to reflect, affirm, and perpetuate the injustices under which too many of our children suffer or to let them define us or hold our kids back. Our job is to overcome these barriers and teach all our children to the highest standards.[2]

The City's Reaction to Say Yes

The subject of Say Yes came up at the Common Council for the first time in spring 2007 during a caucus meeting. There was little information available to council members at the time except for the idea that the organization wanted to offer a program allowing graduates of Syracuse's high schools to attend college tuition free. Stephanie A. Miner, then chair of the education committee and now the city's mayor, was as interested in talking to representatives of Say Yes as they were in speaking with her. "What really engaged me," she recalled, "was the power of the idea; I saw the merit of it."

Miner and William M. Ryan, another council member, met with Schmitt-Carey over a meal to gather more information. For a while, Miner and Ryan kept much of what they learned largely to themselves as they considered how to involve the rest of the city government. They met with colleagues on the council individually and in small groups, seeking their support before publicly advocating for Say Yes.

Schmitt-Carey and her Say Yes colleagues not only had to understand the workings of education in Syracuse, but they had to sort out the even more arcane dynamics of the city's politics and the rivalries that can lead to stillbirth for a project seeking the blessing of government without giving power its due. That power is symbolized in Syracuse by the Romanesque, fortress-like limestone pile with its turrets and a bell tower that houses city government. The blossoming relationship between Say Yes and local government could not be divorced from the fact that some council members were jockeying for position to enter the race to succeed Mayor Matt Driscoll, who would leave the post in 2009. There was a perception that either Miner or Ryan hoped to use backing for Say Yes as a stepping stone in a mayoral campaign.

Miner, Ryan, and other sympathetic council members quietly considered ways in which the city could provide financial backing to Say Yes. They decided to propose that the city allocate $1 million from its reserve fund, a monumental commitment in a town scrounging for revenues. They put few restrictions on how Say Yes could spend the money, Schmitt-Carey having won their confidence as a reliable partner. Miner and Ryan invited Mayor Driscoll, a lame duck who had not played a major role in the discussions with Say Yes, to join them in signaling the endorsement of the program. He was agreeable. The three held a news conference to indicate the city's backing for Say Yes. That announcement helped raise the visibility of Say Yes and demonstrated that powerful elected officials were willing to stamp their imprimaturs on the program.

The city, like an indigent trying to be charitable, reached into its dwindling fund balances to aid Say Yes. This remarkable act of generosity, which continued through the years, came during a period when the city of Syracuse's revenues often trailed behind its budgetary needs. The support has been a testament not only to the fine job that Say Yes did in making its case but also to a deep desire to fuel the school system as an engine for economic development.

"It was unprecedented for city leadership to take $1 million from our reserves to give to Say Yes, a still fledgling program," Miner said of the commitment. "We had to horse trade with other members of council to do it." Miner explained that the possibilities that she saw in Say Yes persuaded her of how essential it was for the program to "find one or two go-to people and to romance them." She continued: "There have been other promises in the past, and the people ask why this is any different . . . There is a lot of credibility to Say Yes. The foundations are involved, and the chancellor [of Syracuse University] says it's one of her priorities. She's the eight-hundred-pound gorilla in this. Any mayor of any city has to talk about schools because they are at the root of everything."

Mayor Driscoll firmed up support for Say Yes throughout the remaining months of his term. The aviation department built awareness by hanging a massive Say Yes banner to greet travelers at the airport and putting other signs advertising the program in the terminal. The parks and recreation department worked with Say Yes to offer a program using city staff during summer afternoons to extend the hours for summer camp with sports and arts activities. The director of the mayor's office of grants joined the development task force of Say Yes to aid fundraising. The police and fire departments developed outreach, training, and recruitment opportunities for inner-city students.

In Stephanie Miner, Say Yes found the ideal governmental partner—an up-and-coming politician with the hardheaded practicality of the former labor lawyer that she was and the heart of a do-gooder. Miner had wanted to act in behalf of Syracuse's troubled public schools for a long time, but she had seen ideas for educational improvement come and go in the city. "I could list ten education issues that have been the flavor of the month, and then nothing happened with them," she said. Apparently, she tasted something different in Say Yes. "For my first six years on council," she said, "the only answer I heard for education's problems was 'more money.' This was the first time that I saw a solution. My colleagues and I helped champion it."

Miner's support and enthusiasm did not slacken after she became mayor in 2010. The city's annual allocations for Say Yes continued. Her director of mayoral initiatives represented her at the bimonthly meetings of the Say Yes operating group. Moreover, if anything, the Common Council grew even more supportive of Say Yes and its efforts to alter the course of public education in Syracuse. This zeal can be attributed, in part, to the arrival of Sharon Contreras, who was viewed more favorably by the council than the superintendent she replaced, a person with whom the council had rocky relations.

The Challenges in Getting County Support

Generally, county governments and school districts, like strangers in an elevator, keep to their own corners. Most counties in the United States have multiple school districts, and while there may occasionally be programs on which the county cooperates with them, this usually does not occur. Robert B. Suver, an official in Clark County, Ohio, said that education is low among the priorities of most of the country's three thousand counties. Suver viewed the situation from his position as chair of the Human Services and Education Steering's subcommittee on education and families of the National Association of Counties (NACo).

Suver, director of the jobs and family services department in Clark County, recognizes that many county functions—jobs, family services, criminal justice, public assistance, child protection, and workforce development, for example—have relevance to public education. His county put social workers in six of the schools of Springfield, the county's largest city. "Partnering with schools varies among the counties, and most of them don't get involved," he said, pointing out that competition for resources is one of the impediments. But as the Syracuse City School District and Onondaga County have shown, especially since the arrival of Say Yes, this separation between school systems and counties need not be the norm. The two entities can collaborate to the benefit of schoolchildren and families.

The National Association of Counties recognizes the role that its members might play in school districts. The statement of basic philosophy of its subcommittee on human services and education says that NACo supports a comprehensive continuum of services that facilitate coordination of parent education, early childhood development, social services, and preventive services to children. The statement also endorses after-school programs. Now NACo should explore how its member counties could do more to leverage these supports for local school systems.

The state of Maryland offers a model for such partnerships. The fact that Maryland has countywide school systems—which are found in about 20 percent of the states—undoubtedly makes it easier for county governments to collaborate with the one school system in the county. Furthermore, the state government in Maryland promotes this kind of cooperation. Since 1990, the state has required each of Maryland's 24 counties to have a local management board. Representatives of the health department, the office of juvenile services, the core mental health service agency, the county public school district, and the social services department all have seats on the board. Officials integrate funding streams to support the various projects they pursue together. Typical of such projects is an early childhood center in one locale that offers preschool classes for children and social services and job placement for families.

There are also the so-called Judy Centers in Montgomery County for young children and their parents. The centers are situated adjacent to or in Title I elementary schools that have large numbers of needy students, and the centers serve youngsters and their families from birth to kindergarten. These centers collaborate with other agencies to make children ready for school.

While the state has made it clear that it encourages such efforts, many of the partnerships in Maryland result from personal relationships among people eager to work together. In one county, for example, collaboration benefited from the fact that the school superintendent, the chair of the school board, and the chair of the county council grew up together. This is not unlike some of the relationships that Say Yes has leveraged in Syracuse based on personal ties. The pattern of cooperation established in Maryland has benefited public school systems and other entities in various ways. In some places, for instance, senior citizen centers have been constructed near and even attached to school buildings. Officials developed programs to bring together the children and the seniors.

It was not always this way in Maryland. Nancy S. Grasmick, the state superintendent of education until 2012, recalled that in the 1990s trying to get "people who never spoke to each other to come together was like herding cats." Now with the progress that has been made, she says, "It has been a tremendous benefit to our children and to our families."

The County's Reaction to Say Yes

Say Yes discovered a friend in Joanne (Joanie) M. Mahoney, the Onondaga County executive since January 2008 and a member of the Syracuse Common Council before that. She backed Say Yes when she was still a candidate for the executive position and before the program's launch. "I've been a supporter since first I heard about it," said Mahoney. "I saw the potential for education and, secondly, for economic development." Say Yes, in effect, gave Mahoney the opportunity to do what she wanted to do anyway: help the Syracuse public schools. "The county should be more supportive of the city's school kids," she said. "If we don't support them when they are young, they will be on the rolls forever. If you sell it right, people will recognize the need for it now, while children are young."

Mahoney presents her backing for Say Yes as a way to save money in the long run for the taxpayers of the county, which is more white and more affluent than Syracuse. A better school system in the city, according to this reasoning, will produce adults less likely to need public assistance, who can participate in and contribute to the local economy. Furthermore, if Syracuse becomes a more attractive place to live because of its public schools, then the county will not have to spend large sums of money to support an infrastructure of sewers, roads, and services for people fleeing the city for the far reaches of the county. "It is in our interest to bring people back to the core," Mahoney said of the county legislature, which her party, the Republicans, dominates by an 11–8 margin.

The county's first funds for Say Yes, $550,000, came from $7 million received in the settlement of a lawsuit under the federal Clean Water Act over the pollution of Onondaga Lake and its tributaries. Based on societal considerations that figured in the suit, residents of the affected Harbor Brook neighborhood were able to ask that a portion of the money be invested in the endowment of the college scholarship program of Say Yes. Onondaga County was also able to redirect two state grants, one for $1.3 million and the other for $700,000, to Say Yes.

The county, not the city, is the main social service provider for children in the Syracuse public schools. Say Yes's emphasis on families and the social-emotional development of children fits comfortably with the county's approach to social services. "The school district has the kids and the county has the resources," said Ann Rooney, the deputy county executive for human services and a former city budget director. "The largest percentage of kids in the school district receive services."

The county's role in social services for students, which existed on a more limited scale before the arrival of Say Yes, is demonstrated in such programs as one to help enroll eligible youngsters in subsidized health insurance programs. When it became clear during Say Yes's second year in Syracuse that many students eligible for free health insurance coverage did not receive it, Say Yes organized the school district and the county to work together to guide families through the application process. That collaborative action led to 91 percent of eligible students at 16 schools getting services through either school-based or community-based health clinics: an illustration of Say Yes's ability to overcome boundaries between agencies.

Another program provides referrals for mental health counseling to students in the city's high schools. The counselors, formerly county employees, were eventually replaced by contract counselors from community-based organizations. The county picked up almost $700,000 of the cost, and Say Yes paid a smaller share. This change meant that school principals could then supervise the counselors. Moreover, the work schedules of the counselors could be aligned with school schedules, which wasn't possible with county employees. Other programs operating with county support included one to train Say Yes representatives in the schools to assess the quality of their efforts and another to use a grant from the state in behalf of the summer offerings that Say Yes established for schoolchildren.

The partnership Say Yes facilitated between the county government and the school district is a model for using mental health, physical health, and social services in ways that bridge divisions of the sort that exist in many communities. Typically, county governments carry out activities separately from anything the school system might do. Say Yes, with its emphasis on the well-being of children so that they have the wherewithal for success, blurred such distinctions. The county's commissioners of public health and mental health, for instance, cochair the Say Yes health and wellness task force.

The Challenges in Getting State Support

While state support for Say Yes's work in Syracuse ultimately did not materialize to the extent that Say Yes had hoped, the fact that New York State is more generous to its elementary and secondary schools than many other states bodes favorably in the long run. Only California exceeds New York State in the amount that it bestows on its schools. The state's taxpayers provide the largest portion of the revenues for the Syracuse City School District.

Yet New York, like other states, has seen many of its educational initiatives fail to produce uniformly favorable results throughout the state. Places like Syracuse, which have the most to gain from such initiatives, frequently have little to show from actions taken by the state to enhance education. Early literacy, the most important factor in raising student achievement, has a sorry history in such school districts as Syracuse. "Forty years of well-meaning state and national reading initiatives have not produced significantly higher student mastery," the Education Commission of the States (ECS) stated in a 2012 report. "States have developed systematic plans to improve early reading proficiency, but translating plans into actionable strategies has proven to be the real challenge."[3]

In sponsoring its program of whole-district reform, first in Syracuse and next in Buffalo, Say Yes chose a state that *Education Week* in its *Quality Counts* publication gave the letter grade of "B," a grade well above many other states. New York State also received a "B" in the chance for success that students in the state have; an "A" for its standards, assessment, and accountability; and a "B+" for its school finance.[4]

Syracuse, like the other more than seven hundred school districts in New York, was affected by the Race to the Top Fund grant that the state got from Washington. To receive the funds, the New York State Legislature passed a law in 2010 directing the state's school systems to develop teacher evaluation plans that were subject to approval by local teachers' unions. Student performance on tests had to figure in the evaluation of their teachers, though the largest factor would be classroom observations of the teachers' work. The manner in which Syracuse carries out teacher evaluations will influence the degree to which Say Yes's push toward better education bears fruit.

Certainly, student outcomes should matter. While Syracuse may trail many other districts in its test results, New York State at large has considerable room for improvement. The National Assessment of Educational Progress shows that the state falls in the middle third of all states in the percentage of public school eighth graders proficient in math. Moreover, New York State is also in the middle when compared with other states in student performance on international examinations.[5] The point is that students in Syracuse rank low in a state that has outcomes around the middle of all states. There were good reasons for state officials to be enthusiastic about Say Yes.

New York State's Reaction to Say Yes

Any organization that wants to enlist the backing of elected officials faces the challenge, like a door-to-door salesperson, of getting doors open to make the pitch. Schmitt-Carey, daughter-in-law of a former New York governor, had family connections that eased the way to the state's political decision makers. Once she presented the case for Say Yes to then Governor Spitzer's aides, they helped her gain access to legislative leaders. Schmitt-Carey told them of the workings of Say Yes, what Say Yes had done in several locales, and the model that it would create in Syracuse. Her words proved prophetic when in 2012 Say Yes began to replicate in Buffalo what it had done in Syracuse.

Say Yes took two routes into the New York State Legislature, using contacts made through the governor's staff and cultivating members of the assembly and the senate from the Syracuse area. William B. Magnarelli, one such assemblyman, was not one of the figures to whom Say Yes initially reached out, although it perhaps should have sought to involve him earlier. He learned about Say Yes through the media when he heard of a program to enlist private colleges and universities in a scholarship program for graduates of the city's high schools. He considered the news "stunning." By coincidence, he soon thereafter got a phone call from Syracuse University asking him to meet Mary Anne Schmitt-Carey.

Magnarelli, a practicing lawyer, went to the meeting with some degree of skepticism. He had encountered various ill-fated programs over the years that claimed to be able to improve the city's schools. He came out of this meeting, though, thinking that Say Yes would bring in resources and that the organization would carefully examine what worked and what didn't. "It was clear to me," he recalled, "that this was a very responsible program that would document and answer for what it was doing. This was a major difference with previous programs—people from the outside would tell us if it was working." The idea of making the program research based and using outside experts to hold it accountable helped sell it to Magnarelli.

Say Yes asked him to become a point person in establishing free-tuition programs at the State University of New York and the City University of New York for Syracuse high school graduates. Magnarelli and other supporters rounded up a dozen and a half sponsors for a bill to do just that. He found resistance, though, from colleagues—including the assembly speaker—who wondered why the body should support such a plan for Syracuse when a similar idea was not advanced for other constituents. It wasn't just legislators who voiced such reservations. Magnarelli's own brother, who lives just outside the city, had asked him, "What about North Syracuse?"

Say Yes's backers emphasized the economic development aspects of the bill to lawmakers. They maintained that young people who received the benefits of subsidized higher education would use their learning to contribute to the city's business and industry. The legislature agreed on a demonstration model to support Say Yes's operations in Syracuse but not the scholarship program, which was too controversial.

The legislature first gave Say Yes a grant of $1 million and then a grant of $350,000, indicating that success in Syracuse could lead to the creation of similar programs elsewhere in New York State. It was gratifying to Say Yes when Governor Andrew Cuomo made the organization's work part of his economic development plan for western New York State, a step likely to provide more funds eventually for the efforts in Syracuse and Buffalo.

The Challenges in Getting Federal Support

The federal government's No Child Left Behind (NCLB) law's major impact on Syracuse and other urban schools systems was to bring attention to the disparities in outcomes for subgroups of students who were more easily overlooked before the legislation took effect in 2002. Every subgroup but one failed to make adequate yearly progress on tests in Syracuse in the 2010–11 school year. The lone exceptions were multiracial students. Thus adequate yearly progress for elementary- and middle-school-level students in language arts, for instance, was not attained by Syracuse's American Indians, blacks, Hispanics, Asians, whites, students with disabilities, the limited English proficient, and the economically disadvantaged.

The margins by which some subgroups in Syracuse did not make adequate yearly progress—like arrows falling far from a bull's-eye—were particularly wide of the mark. The district's annual measurable objectives for language arts were set at 120 for black students and 119 for Hispanics. They achieved performance index scores, respectively, of 82 and 78. White students came closer to their objective of 120 with a performance index score of 112 but still fell short.

These figures underscore the need in Syracuse for the extra funds that Washington allots based on a school system's needs. The shortfalls in scholastic achievement, more often than not, are accompanied by economic disadvantage. Syracuse's case for infusions of Title I dollars showed up in the portion of students qualifying for federally subsidized meals. The percentage of students eligible for free and reduced-price lunch, based on self-reported family income, rose from 75 percent of the enrollment in 2008–9 to 79 percent in 2010–11, and has now passed 80 percent.

Say Yes hoped that such demonstrated need would also lead to funding from some other federal programs. Two such programs, both under the aegis of the U.S. Department of Education, are the Promise Neighborhoods that support cradle-to-college solutions for needy districts and an initiative from the Investing in Innovation Fund (i3), which aims to improve student achievement.

The Federal Government's Reaction to Say Yes

In fall 2008, as soon as there was an operating program to talk about, Say Yes contacted members of the congressional delegation from central New York, the state's two U.S. senators, and officials in the federal government. Arne Duncan, the U.S. secretary of education, and Vice President Biden, as mentioned earlier, were prepped to praise Say Yes during visits to Syracuse. U.S. Senator Kirsten E. Gillibrand presided at a Say Yes event. Say Yes also met with federal specialists in urban affairs, once again emphasizing that the venture in Syracuse was in essence an attempt to trigger economic revitalization. Washington can learn from what Say Yes has achieved in Syracuse by leveraging interagency cooperation. The Department of Education is not the only agency that could help the school system and the city. Various programs in the Department of Health and Human and Services, including Head Start, have roles to play. The Department of Defense supports programs in elementary and secondary education. The National Science Foundation has years of experience in professional development for teachers. The commerce department could seek creative ways of tying business development to the reform of the school district. But so far these pieces have not been assembled in Syracuse.

Say Yes continues to hope that Washington will recognize the organization's work as a model for demonstration projects in America's small- and medium-sized, postindustrial cities. "We have a foot in the door," said Schmitt-Carey, who wants eventually to secure a federal grant in the $15-million range as an incentive to the city to commit itself to the goal of postsecondary education for all its students. She identified the Promise Neighborhoods program as one such potential source of funds. A grant, as she sees it, would be used in part to facilitate governmental work in behalf of children and families. In the meantime, the program received $400,000 from Congress through an earmark grant.

But the recession mostly thwarted hopes that Say Yes had for further earmarks and for other funding from the federal government.

The Levels of Government Operating on Behalf of the Public Schools

The various levels of government simply have passed up opportunity after opportunity to collaborate in behalf of the public schools. The fact that the United States has almost 14,000 separate school systems has undoubtedly impeded possibilities of forging separate agreements with Washington. School districts have made more progress when it comes to collaborating with each other. They join forces in some locales, for instance, under joint agreements involving student transportation, provisions for disabled students, and the purchase of some items. States sometimes create regional authorities to coordinate and oversee such activities, as New York State has done through its Boards of Cooperative Educational Services.

Even good intentions do not necessarily move government entities. Massachusetts established a Child and Youth Readiness Cabinet in 2008 to bring together government agencies to deal with problems that impinge on student achievement. Yet two and a half years later, a member of the group wrote that despite everyone wanting to do the right thing, they retreated to "bureaucratic silos where that energy gets rechanneled, distracted, or otherwise tamped down."[6]

The sturdy walls of the silos in which the parts of government operate often prove impregnable. Municipal agencies resist pursuing shared interests even in cities where mayors assume control of schools. The unprecedented advantage afforded by mayoral takeovers is a missed opportunity, like passing up a chance to purchase a winning lottery ticket after the drawing has occurred.

Boston, Chicago, Detroit, Cleveland, and New York are among the cities where mayors took over the schools. These are the very same mayors under whose aegis social services, juvenile justice, trash collection, purchasing, and other city programs exist. In too few instances have city governments linked their work to the needs of school systems. The problem is what Michael D. Usdan calls "the culture of separation . . . with public schools statutorily separated from general-purpose government."[7] Much the same is true when it comes to takeovers by the states of school systems, which have happened in 49 districts in 19 states since 1988.[8] Just like cities, state governments could mobilize an array of services for school districts, but they generally do not exploit this opportunity.

The Role of Syracuse University

Syracuse University is literally and figuratively the school on the hill so far as the rest of the city is concerned. It is the city's intellectual and economic hub. The university, with a combined full-time and part-time enrollment of 20,407 degree-seeking students, operates on an annual budget of just over $1 billion. It employs a faculty of 955 full-time and 552 part-time and adjunct members as well as a staff of 3,306 full-time and 370 part-time employees. It is the second largest job provider in the city, behind the Upstate University Health System. The university has long-standing ties to the city's public schools, but Say Yes linked the fortunes of the two as never before.

"We view ourselves as an anchor institution in Syracuse," Chancellor Cantor said. "We are a place-based institution and our history and our future are wrapped up with where we are." The university has pursued what it considers its responsibility to the city through projects in four major areas: (1) environmental sustainability, (2) the urban ecological system, (3) inclusive urban education, and (4) neighborhood entrepreneurship. The university involves itself in such enterprises as one in which its architecture school joined forces with a center founded by the state and a local nonprofit developer to nurture green technology in the city.

Syracuse University's latest, most tangible tie to the city is a physical link called the Connective Corridor running several miles from the campus into the heart of downtown. Buses ply the route down University Avenue and along East Genesee Street to whisk people back and forth. But there is much more—bike lanes, spruced up parks along the way, benches for strollers to rest, decorative lighting, new facades for businesses facing the corridor, and easier access to museums and the city's convention center. The free buses pass the university's warehouse building, abutting Armory Square, to which hundreds of students travel every day for some of their classes.

The corridor was conceived in the early 2000s as a way to unite town and gown. A tacit attraction for the city is the potential for pulling free-spending students away from their campus sanctuary so that they may more readily frequent retailers and restaurants in Syracuse. City, county, and federal sources designated almost $50 million for the project, for which construction began in 2012 with a 2014 completion date. The university is so sensitive to being perceived as trying to dominate the city that the color of signs and places to be painted along the corridor is red, not the orange by which the university is known.

From the start of her chancellorship in 2004, Cantor put a high priority on the university's relations with local public schools. In so doing, she followed a pattern established by several other major universities—the University of Pennsylvania in Philadelphia, Yale University in New Haven, Connecticut, and Boston University in Chelsea, Massachusetts, for example. Cantor created the Partnership for Better Education in collaboration with other higher education institutions in the region to support improvement in the city's public schools.

University students and faculty members of Syracuse University have long played roles in the city schools. The education school concentrated 60 percent of its teacher preparation placements in Syracuse. The university's Center for Public and Community Service sent volunteers to schools and other local agencies. The arrival of Say Yes gave Cantor a wrench for tightening the connections. In taking a lead role in establishing Say Yes in Syracuse, the university drew on its strengths and traditions, according to Eric F. Spina, the vice chancellor and provost. "It advances us as a university," he said. Syracuse University saw in Say Yes an opportunity to make its work in the public schools even more coherent and more effective.

One project in which Say Yes plays a role is the Near Westside Initiative, the revival of an impoverished neighborhood of 8,400 residents on the edge of downtown that the university began five years ago. Already sixty homes have been renovated or built, and two large warehouses, one housing the headquarters of Say Yes, have been converted to provide office facilities downstairs and combination residence-studios for artists upstairs. The area is called the SALT District to recognize the cultivation of Syracuse art, life, and technology. The historic significance of the name derives from the fact that the area, with its briny underground streams, was once a prime producer of salt.

Say Yes is striving to find ways to link the development of the neighborhood to the educational attainment of children living there. The idea, mostly inchoate at this point, involves the notion that Say Yes can use place-based strategies to promote the achievement of students and engage their families to support of their education. An assistance center for residents, funded by the Annie Casey Foundation, operates out of a local independent supermarket, Nojaim Brothers, to link people to health clinics, legal clinics, and other resources. The area roughly forms a horseshoe around a middle school and is the home of the city's largest concentration of Latinos, who make up a quarter of the neighborhood's population, the rest of which is about equally divided between whites and blacks.

Cantor's willingness to yoke the university to the public schools and to the well-being of the city at large did not please her critics. A controversial article in the *Chronicle of Higher Education* in fall 2011[9] questioned this approach. The issue was whether these activities, along with the university's dedication to promoting diversity on campus, diverted money and energy from research and scholarship. In a follow-up to the reprinting of the article in the *Post-Standard*, the city's local newspaper, Cantor was defended in letters to the editor by some of the university's deans and administrators of other institutions.[10]

"Say Yes gives us a leadership model," said Douglas Biklen, the education dean. "For the first time, there is a program in the schools into which everything can flow." As one might expect, the education school was the lead entity for the university's involvement with Say Yes, but other schools and colleges within the university also joined the mix at the urging of Cantor and Biklen. One contribution by the university was to put some Say Yes workers on its payroll.

At one point, 28 full-time employees and one part-time employee of Say Yes were salaried through Syracuse University. The university also paid for 251 Say Yes tutors. Then there was a multitude of volunteers from the university: 168 from Literacy Corps; 75 unpaid tutors; 135 volunteers from the public affairs courses; seven students from the law school to supplement instruction in the school system's courses in social studies and related areas; and a pool of 218 others who signed up for various roles.

Another assist came through the development office, where Sara Wason, executive director of foundation relations for the university, added fundraising for Say Yes to her regular duties. "I grew up in this community," Wason said, "and I believe this is the game changer for the city. Say Yes is one of the most galvanizing forces in our community, something everyone can get behind." In addition, the university assigned another development specialist to work exclusively on raising money for Say Yes. For at least one donor prospect that the university had cultivated unsuccessfully for years, the development specialist said that Say Yes and its mission finally resonated as the best opportunity to secure a donation.

What began as a love fest between the university and Say Yes, though, inevitably took on tension at some levels. Like married partners long after the honeymoon, some representatives of either side came to feel that the sharing was not equal. In sum, the university wanted a larger role in the operations of the school system than Say Yes and the school system deemed appropriate. Nonetheless, mostly good relations continued to prevail, and the university's involvement proved invaluable to Say Yes's program.

4

Getting Started in Syracuse

Say Yes and its potential partners recognized that the program's success would rest on building a coalition, for the most part locally based, to endorse and advance efforts for systemic school reform. This meant enlisting the support of key figures in government, the school system, higher education, and the business community. Some of these individuals would ultimately join the Say Yes advisory committee and/or the Say Yes operating committee, keeping them engaged for the long run.

Command headquarters for coalition building was Syracuse University. A series of meetings, mostly in either the chancellor's conference room or the conference room of the education school, brought together potential partners to hear presentations and discuss the future of the project with representatives of Say Yes. These gatherings throughout 2007 and into 2008 produced agreements and pledges to assure Say Yes of a coalition striving for successful outcomes.

Looking back on this period, Schmitt-Carey observed that, once Syracuse was identified as the laboratory for Say Yes's experiment, 9 months would have been sufficient for laying the groundwork but 12 months was even better. She wanted time to build local buy-in. "There had to be elaborate collaboration across sectors," said Chancellor Cantor of Syracuse University, a social psychologist. "You can have great cooperation at the leadership level, but if the troops don't roll up their sleeves and work together, this won't work. The pieces started falling into place."

Syracuse University, the most influential institution in the city, is a key partner that Say Yes engaged early in creating Say Yes to Education in Syracuse. When Nancy Cantor, chancellor of the university, and Mary Anne Schmitt-Carey, former president of New American Schools, fell into conversation at one of those Manhattan events attended by everyone who is anyone, Cantor asked Schmitt-Carey what she was doing as her latest project. As soon as Cantor heard that Schmitt-Carey, who had become the head of Say Yes, was seeking a place in which to launch a district-wide school reform project, Cantor said, in effect: Have I got a city for you.

Reflecting on the challenges facing Say Yes, leaders in Syracuse described the separateness of the various entities that Say Yes had to bring together. It was not simply that the layers of government, the school system, the university, and the business community resisted alignment but that long-standing habits kept them apart. Each sector, in other words, operated mostly vertically—in its own silo—without connections to other sectors. The county's budget for child services, for example, was twice as large as the school system's, and they did not combine forces for the benefit of youngsters.

Coalition Building

As word of Say Yes's intentions spread, a city-wide conversation developed, and excitement grew. Syracuse is small enough that news of the contemplated venture, like a juicy rumor, rapidly permeated the community. The beauty of Say Yes was its role as a reliable outsider, independent of parochial interests. It could facilitate cooperation among stakeholders who might otherwise not play in the same sandbox. Various factions had to perceive Say Yes as an honest broker, acting on behalf of the community and its children. Say Yes couldn't be seen as a captive of any single entity. "We are the conveners and bring people to the table," said Gene S. Chasin, chief operating officer of Say Yes. "It is part of the capacity building, the kind of coordination that doesn't normally go on."

Say Yes, like Superman, seemed to descend on the city at the opportune moment. Syracuse and other upstate cities were due to receive increased school funding from the state under a court settlement, and Say Yes proposed to help the city build its capacity for putting the money to good use. No one realized that the sledgehammer of a recession was about to batter Syracuse. "All we were saying to them," Schmitt-Carey related in retrospect years later, "was 'You're getting new money, and we'll help you make strategic investments.'" Schmitt-Carey felt the rug being pulled out from under her during the program's first year. Say Yes, without the soft footing that it had expected, had to regroup. Its consultants ran the numbers again on spending and staffing. New analyses would be applied to every allocation. Suddenly, there was no fat for Jack Sprat's wife.

Daniel G. Lowengard, the then school superintendent who retired in 2011, was among the most crucial of the original partners. The program could not realistically operate without his firm commitment, which required putting the fate of his superintendency on the line. Much would depend on him, and he, perhaps, had the most to lose personally if he stumbled with his new dance partner.

Coalition building sometimes must overcome previous divisions having nothing to do with the program at hand. In Syracuse, for instance, this meant getting past long-standing tensions between the school system and the Common Council, the body on which the public schools are financially dependent. The board of education has no tax-levying powers of its own. Some members of the Common Council did not condone the manner in which the school district had over the years spent the funds the city provided for education.

The political leadership questioned the ability of Lowengard and the school board to keep within their budget, maintaining that there was not enough accountability. The state comptroller had criticized the financial practices of the school system. He said at one point that because of shoddy bookkeeping the city would not get a $1.7 million allocation it was due to receive from New York State for its public schools. Relations were so stressed between the parties that council members at first contacted the deputy superintendent instead of the superintendent to deliver the news that they were going to include funding for Say Yes in the city's budget.

Strains between the school system and the city government were nothing new. Lionel "Skip" Meno, Syracuse's school superintendent in the 1980s, recalled that "the mayor had all the power through the board of estimate." He said that the mayor really set the school budget and that the Common Council was supportive "but kind of a sideshow with little real power." What was different in those days was that once the budget was set, the fiscally conservative school district lived within it.

As summer 2008 approached, Rachael Gazdick, whom Say Yes had appointed director of its Syracuse operation, was still the lone local employee. In Gazdick, Say Yes had a person with connections to a network and who knew the players. Looking back, she says, "I can't imagine someone not part of the university and part of the community structure being able to do this quickly. That was critical. I know what it's like to be a teacher, to run an after-school program, and I have the nonprofit perspective." She had an appointment at the university, where she was pursuing a doctorate in social sciences.

Ultimately, though, Say Yes determined that the director ought not be linked to the university and should be perceived as a more neutral arbiter, someone not burdened by the weight of institutional baggage. Gazdick continued her involvement with the program from her post at the university, but Say Yes tapped Patrick Driscoll to succeed her as director.

In Driscoll, a referee in big-time college basketball on the side, Say Yes got someone with strong ties to the larger community. He went through the city's parochial schools and earned a degree in sociology in 1989 from St. Bonaventure University, south of Buffalo. He held jobs under three city governments in Syracuse, serving as parks commissioner for nine and a half years—including time under a mayor who was his cousin—before joining Say Yes. His three children attended the city's public schools. "After I lost my dad at a very young age," Driscoll recalled, "my mother showed a will and determination to keep us on track and to ensure that we got to college. I am sure there are parents within SCSD [Syracuse City School District] that have lived a similar experience. My hope is that Say Yes continues to open a door of hope to the future."

A Coterie of Powerful Women

A remarkable aspect of Say Yes's buildup in Syracuse was the fact that it was led by women. Seldom has an enterprise of this magnitude been so dominated by women. It was just a matter of timing that females occupied key positions when Say Yes undertook its attempt to transform the city and its school system. On the other hand, one must wonder whether the degree of collaboration and selflessness would have been the same if men were in the same positions.

Mary Anne Schmitt-Carey, of course, was the president of Say Yes to Education who offered the opportunity to Syracuse and orchestrated Say Yes's entry into the city. She found a kindred spirit in Nancy Cantor of Syracuse University, without whose support the idea would have withered for lack of a lead partner with the clout to breathe life into Say Yes's intentions.

Two key office holders were, above all, the ones who won favor for the idea in the political community and among civic leaders. Joanne Mahoney, a Republican, was the Onondaga County executive. Stephanie Miner, a Democrat, was a member of the Common Council who later became the city's mayor. They both readily put themselves forward because they believed in what Say Yes proposed and saw it as, perhaps, the last best chance for Syracuse.

The fifth and final member of the quintet, Sharon Contreras (more on her in Chapter 5), arrived in 2011 when she became superintendent of the Syracuse City School District. She was to be the change agent who would prod and lead a moribund system that wallowed in the status quo even though almost everyone knew it was not working. She was tough and willing to take a stand.

When Syracuse was considering Contreras for the job, Miner telephoned the previous mayor of Providence, Rhode Island, David Cicilline, to get his take on Contreras. Miner said he told her that Contreras was smart, creative, and collaborative, but he paused and then said, "But she's aggressive. So if you're somebody who doesn't like that characteristic, you should be aware of that." The mayor of Syracuse—herself a bulldog when necessary—told the former mayor of Providence that she didn't see a problem with that.

Mary Anne Schmitt-Carey

Mary Anne Schmitt-Carey, the president of Say Yes, committed the organization to remain involved in Syracuse for years to come, recognizing that there would be no quick fix. She consistently sought to portray the connection between Say Yes and the Syracuse City School District as a partnership. Though her office is in New York City and she resides in Westchester County, Schmitt-Carey demonstrated her dedication to school reform in upstate New York by spending day after day in Syracuse. A hotel room in the Genesee Grande Hotel, located midway between Syracuse University and downtown, became her home away from home.

Schmitt-Carey's career has been largely in activities associated with school reform. At first, though, it appeared that she would pursue a role in politics. After earning a bachelor's degree in political science and English at the University at Albany–SUNY in 1987, Mary Anne Schmitt-Carey worked in political campaigns and then went to the U.S. Department of Education as director of the Goals 2000 community project. She created and managed a support network for localities striving to improve education.

Gradually, she gained a passion for having an impact on social policies that can change outcomes for people and felt that education would be the arena in which she could make the greatest difference. Along the way, she earned an MBA from the Wharton School at the University of Pennsylvania. It wasn't long until she became vice president and director of communications and public policy for New American Schools (NAS). The first Bush administration launched NAS in 1991 with the support of major corporations to foster the design and deployment of a revolution in education that would supposedly break the mold with a business-savvy approach to school improvement.

Schmitt-Carey capped off her 11-year tenure at NAS as president and chief executive officer, a position she held for six years during which the organization grew from a pilot initiative to a model for comprehensive school reform. New American Schools selected 11 designs from among seven hundred proposals. Schools in 19 states tested the designs, subject to ongoing evaluations by Rand Corporation.

Critics maintained that the reforms were too mild and too close to the mainstream. Schmitt-Carey's approach to reform, as exhibited in Syracuse, has been cautious and not radical, which is too practical to please some observers. When New American Schools merged with the American Institutes for Research (AIR), Schmitt-Carey became AIR's vice president for public policy and external relations. She moved from that role to Say Yes, taking with her a belief that improving student performance depends on linking policies and practices to research findings.

In 2000, she married Donald Carey, a financier and businessman whose father had been governor of New York. Mary Anne Schmitt-Carey is a self-professed workaholic who has built her limited free time around family and, especially, their eight-year-old daughter, Hannah. They try to break away from her punishing schedule to make a couple short trips abroad each year that include Hannah. Family is a priority for her, and it was the pull of family, shortly after her mother's death, that caused Schmitt-Carey to drop out of a social sciences doctoral program at Syracuse University that she had tried to combine with her duties at Say Yes. "The PhD is a life goal for me that I know I'll get done at some point," she said.

Nancy E. Cantor

Nancy E. Cantor, though diminutive in stature, looms large in Syracuse. Chancellor and president of Syracuse University since 2004, she made it part of her mission to advance the institution as a major player in the city. She viewed the university not as an ivory tower but as a public good meant to serve the needs of society. So it was only fitting for Say Yes to tether its fortunes to Cantor and the university as one of its first steps in Syracuse. A social psychologist by training, Cantor ranges wide in her interests and activities on behalf of both the university and the civic life of Syracuse. If anything, she has to act prudently to keep people from thinking that the university is trying to dominate the city.

Cantor, who has conducted research and written extensively on personality and cognition, earned her PhD from Stanford University and spent the first 18 years of her career shuttling between academic appointments at Princeton University and the University of Michigan. Her scholarly work in psychology contributed to an understanding of how people perceive and think about their social worlds, pursue personal goals, and regulate their behavior. Finally, she took on administrative duties at the University of Michigan, eventually serving as provost and executive vice president for academic affairs. Then Cantor was chancellor at the University of Illinois at Urbana-Champaign from 2001 to 2004 before moving to her position at Syracuse University.

In her lectures and writings, Cantor became a national commentator on the place and role of universities in America. Her views in this regard as the chief executive of a major research university put her in a very public role in which observers judged her on whether she practiced what she preached.

Cantor endured her annus horribilis during the 2011–12 academic year when the *Chronicle of Higher Education* reported criticisms of her stewardship by some disgruntled faculty members. On top of this, the university suffered through a months-long scandal involving an assistant coach of its nationally ranked basketball team who allegedly overstepped sexual boundaries, charges that were later repudiated. Whatever the pressures and the occasional controversies, Cantor never wavered in her staunch support for Say Yes. Nevertheless, she ended up announcing toward the end of 2012 that she would step down from her position and soon afterward accepted the post of chancellor at Rutgers University–Newark, to start in 2014.

Joanne M. Mahoney

Joanne M. Mahoney, known to one and all as Joanie, was the first woman elected to serve as Onondaga County executive in 2007. Her roots were in Syracuse, and although she represented the entire surrounding county, she always remembered her origins. Her parents continued to live in the house in which she was raised in Syracuse, where she graduated from Corcoran High School.

Mahoney went on to Syracuse University for a bachelor's degree from the school of management and a degree from the university's law school. After a time in private practice, she joined the county district attorney's office as a criminal prosecutor and remained in public service thereafter. Her volunteer work in political campaigns over the years piqued her interest in elective office. In 1999, she was elected to the Common Council as a member at large in Syracuse, where she served a four-year term.

Early in her county position, Mahoney showed a green streak. She launched Save the Rain, a storm water management plan to reduce pollution in Onondaga Lake and its tributaries. In 2011, the county was recognized by the federal Environmental Protection Agency as a green infrastructure partner.

Though she, her husband, and their four sons made their home in the suburbs, where a large portion of her constituents live, Mahoney was never reluctant to promote the interests of her beloved city of Syracuse. "It's simply the right thing to do," she said. "I can make a pretty compelling argument to the people who live in affluent suburbs about why they should care about what happens in the city. I collect taxes that pay for the social services for people who weren't given the resources to make it on their own." Mahoney believes that the right kind of investments in the city, like those contemplated by Say Yes, would eventually lessen the need for some of the social services that the county provided.

She did not hesitate to become a champion for Say Yes. "It is unlike anything we've ever seen," she said of Say Yes. "When you think of any problem that a city in the United States faces, you can't find one that can't be solved by creating a more educated workforce."

As a Republican presiding over a county in which the largest city leans heavily Democratic, Mahoney embraced bipartisanship. She and Syracuse mayor Miner worked closely on many issues, a kind of Joanie and Stephanie political tandem. "Historically," said Mahoney, "the city and the county had more of a battle for resources." She said that Say Yes served as a vehicle to bring together the levels of government, Syracuse University, and other entities to strive for the greater good. Mahoney's popularity was such that in 2011 she ran unopposed for her second term as county executive.

Stephanie A. Miner

Stephanie A. Miner enjoyed an upbringing in a nearby, small town that provided experiences rather different from those of many of the youngsters benefiting from Say Yes. She was the daughter of a physician and a college dean in a home in which the family discussed books and current events, and she was asked her opinion on the many topics that were broached. She also considered herself blessed to have had teachers who paid attention to her and guided her. Miner extols those teachers for finding merit in her and inspiring her.

She got her bachelor's degree magna cum laude in political science and journalism from Syracuse University and a law degree from the University at Buffalo, State University of New York. She became a labor lawyer in private practice, all the while fascinated by politics and aiding such candidates as Mario Cuomo and Geraldine Ferraro, a pursuit she began as a child—stuffing envelopes for local candidates at her grandmother's kitchen table. She was tapped by Governor Andrew Cuomo as cochair of the New York State Democratic Party in 2012, an appointment he may have rued after she charged in 2013 that his support for the upstate cities was insufficient.

Miner served two terms on the Syracuse Common Council, first elected at the age of 31. Then the voters made her the city's first female mayor in 2009, a fulfillment of her recognition as senior class president at her high school in tiny Homer, New York, where her classmates also chose her most likely to succeed. The city's *Post-Standard* newspaper called her "principled," "intelligent," and "energetic" when she ran successfully in a three-person race for mayor of Syracuse.

In an article that appeared during the mayoral campaign listing a few of her "favorite things," the paper cited football (she can throw a spiral), listening to music on headphones (the Beatles, Ella Fitzgerald, and such), President John F. Kennedy (her grandparents, Irish on both sides, were great fans), the baby grand piano she gave to her husband for his birthday (he plays by ear), and *The New Yorker* magazine (she and her husband-to-be each had their own subscription until after they married, and now each thinks that the other dominates the lone copy they continue to receive).

Miner's reasons for her early support of Say Yes are straightforward and prag-matic. She said,

> I was one of the first people to recognize the promise that Say Yes had for Syracuse. Fundamentally, the most important mission of the city and of the country is making sure that, as a democracy, we have an informed citizenry to go into the job market and that we have an economy where they can put those skills to work. We had a graduation rate that was unacceptable and test scores that were unacceptable. When you have a system that fails, people lose hope, and that is pernicious. It was easy to see that we would not make the progress that we needed to make. Educational achieve-ment and opportunity are fundamental tenets of our American democracy. When you give people a chance, they will not be a drag on the community.

Establishing a Presence

Say Yes did not enter an entirely virgin land when it came to Syracuse. The city and the school system already were trying to address concentrated poverty in the most severely impacted neighborhoods. The Westside Community School Strat-egy had established a process in certain schools to identify and link students and families to services so as to bolster achievement. The process included monitoring student progress, as Say Yes advocates. Say Yes absorbed the Westside Strategy, and Monique R. Fletcher, the social worker who headed the program, became an asso-ciate director of Say Yes in Syracuse.

The committees on which community leaders sit are meant to bolster local commitment to Say Yes's efforts and to tap into expertise. The advisory group sets overarching goals and identifies agencies' policies that impede collaborative fund-ing. The group also supports the development of sustainable solutions for making Say Yes a lasting program.

The operating group meets every other week to oversee ongoing tasks and to guide the program to full implementation. It draws its members mostly from the five partner organizations behind the school reform—the school district, the uni-versity, the city government, the county government, and Say Yes itself. The group has fewer than a dozen members, though other people attend meetings as their input is needed. The members include the school system's superintendent, dep-uty superintendent, and Say Yes coordinator; the university's education dean; Say Yes's president, chief operating officer, and executive director of the Syracuse pro-gram; the president of the teachers' union; the administrator for human resources in the county executive's office; and the director of special mayoral initiatives. Some members send surrogates to represent them at the meetings, which may not be what Say Yes had in mind in establishing the operating group.

Missing Pieces

One challenge was to enlist the support of faith-based groups and leaders of Afri-can American and Latino organizations. At the beginning, Say Yes tended, not surprisingly, to cultivate backing mainly among the power elite who could most immediately act to raise local money and provide access to influence. Gradually, Say Yes reached out to churches and minorities to give them a greater stake in the work being done to transform Syracuse.

In retrospect, Say Yes seems not to have done enough at the outset to explain its intentions to the minority community and to enlist its members as supporters. "They dug themselves into a hole," said Vincent B. Love, president of 100 Black Men of Syracuse Inc., a national civic group with a local chapter. "A lot was not explained at the beginning, and it put a sour taste in some mouths. It's hard to do damage control, but they've now done a great job in overcoming those problems."

Say Yes provided funding in 2011 so that the "first ladies," wives of the pastors at the city's black churches, could hold a series of four meetings to discuss how their congregations could best support education in Syracuse. For the most part, the churches already had youth programs, but as a result of the first lady meetings, they were able to give more direction to their work. "Just by saying we needed such a vehicle, Say Yes helped us come together and not do things only on our own," said Sandra Reid, whose husband, Kenneth, is pastor of Greater Evangelical Church of God in Christ. She heads the first ladies group.

For its part, Say Yes generated goodwill in underwriting the meetings of the first ladies group. "There had been some hesitation among people in terms of understanding Say Yes's overall purpose," Ms. Reid said. "The faith-based initiative offers a body of people who probably would have been overlooked if Say Yes didn't work through the churches. A lot of people put a lot of trust in the church, and without the churches, Say Yes would have missed a lot of them."

There was also a notable lack of attention at the beginning to parents and students. Neither of these groups is easily engaged by school reformers anywhere, though parents and students have the greatest stake in the outcome. "[C]ontrary to much of the rhetoric, urban school districts are not full of parent activists aching for an opportunity to get politically involved in school reform," write the authors of a study on parent power.[1] In many places, if parents get involved at all in education reform it is to help their children escape from the schools they are compelled to attend. Thus some of what happens in the name of school reform on behalf of parents around the country aims to provide choice, especially through vouchers and charter schools. There is also the nascent movement, beginning in California, for "parent triggers" to mandate the reorganization of a school if more than half the parents vote for it.

Eventually, Say Yes and the school district launched an initiative called Parent University, an ambitious undertaking to help parents and other caregivers learn to support their children's education, pursue their own growth, and deepen their knowledge of the school system. The program, underwritten by Say Yes, offers an array of free courses during the day and in the evenings—open as well to non-public school families and those without children of school age—at Say Yes headquarters and other locations. Participants receive vouchers for transportation, and child care is available. Among the courses offered in spring 2013 were "Parenting for Student Success," "Eat Better for Less," "Mathematics in the Common Core," "Wonderful Websites," and "Promoting Learning over the Summer." Parent

University also sponsored a conference that spring aimed specifically at men to interest them in education.

Like their parents, students in the Syracuse schools were not at first drawn into the reform activities by Say Yes in any major way. They were the chief bystanders, affected by the reforms but given little say in the process although in line to get tuition scholarships—no small reward. Some students across the United States would like to have more input in the details of their schooling. Such organizations as Youth on Board, which began in Massachusetts and started operating nationally in 2002, promote student involvement in school reform. The Annenberg Institute for School Reform gives a cogent rationale for involving students. Keith Catone and Alexa LeBoeuf of Brown University note, "[They] have the firsthand knowledge to identify systemic problems, are capable of partnering with adults to assess the validity of their assumptions, and can work on developing reform efforts where they are needed most."[2]

Say Yes, like many reformers, funneled its efforts through establishment structures and tried to be as expeditious as possible. But Say Yes was not demure about selling itself. Like a bank opening new branches, Say Yes sought attention for its program. Vice President Joseph R. Biden Jr., a graduate of Syracuse University law school, and other distinguished visitors to the city were encouraged during their visits to publicize Say Yes. There was a city-wide marketing campaign to heighten awareness of Say Yes. Quadrant by quadrant, Say Yes tried to brand itself, even resorting to billboards. Say Yes banners encircled the backboard posts in the arena at Syracuse University. Seldom did a school initiative anywhere fill a city so rapidly with its image and its promise.

Getting into the Schools

Say Yes aimed to get into its first group of schools in fall 2008 and devised a way to do so in rapid fashion. The school district naturally divides itself into four geographic quadrants, a tidy arrangement that lent a rationale to Say Yes's approach. Each quadrant has a high school with a feeder system of elementary and middle schools. A fifth high school provides technical education for students throughout the city. Say Yes rolled out the program quadrant by quadrant, starting with all the students in kindergarten through third grade in six schools in one quadrant and bringing in another quadrant annually. Adding a grade every year in each quadrant meant that in September 2011 the fourth and final quadrant joined the program. In moving up a grade each year, Say Yes intended eventually to fully bring in the middle schools and high schools.

Say Yes had to overcome the skeptics who felt that the organization couldn't possibly fulfill its promises. Implementing the program in one quadrant of the city each fall meant, of course, that it was not until the beginning of the fourth year that it operated in all the district's elementary schools. Confusion swirled around the program's intentions when Say Yes was still new, viewed as a rich uncle who had breezed in from the big city with bags of money. Thus some people in the first quadrant resisted almost anything Say Yes wanted to do, thinking that the organization had come to town solely to dispense largesse in the form of college scholarships. But once Say Yes started promoting after-school and summer programs, helped insert social workers in schools, and added other enhancements, those in the quadrants awaiting implementation grew antsy, eager to see the program arrive in their bailiwicks.

"We had to show them that this is real, that it is really happening," explained Rachael Gazdick, the original director. Some people in Syracuse saw the impact of Say Yes even if it had not yet reached the quadrant in which they lived. The spread of Say Yes's various innovations enhanced credibility and engendered goodwill. This strategy paid dividends. After three years, three-fourths of the residents of Syracuse knew of the existence of Say Yes, though only one-third knew someone who had benefited directly from the program.[3]

There was a second rollout of sorts after Sharon Contreras's arrival. She planned to hold meetings in each quadrant to get input for a strategic plan she was developing. But she revised her approach after discovering that the same small groups of people showed up for her meetings as came to school board meetings. Contreras wanted to reach residents who seldom gave their opinions to school officials. So she started going to church services and to a mosque, asking religious officials to hold forums afterward at which congregants could identify the educational issues they found most pressing.

As the quadrants took form, Say Yes inserted a site director into each elementary school to represent the organization. Say Yes provided funds to put the site directors on the university payroll, thereby holding down the number of direct employees that Say Yes had. A virtue of the arrangement was that Say Yes received a steady flow of inside information from the site directors, making the organization less reliant on the school district to keep track of developments. This gave Say Yes a degree of autonomy from the beginning.

Each site director, besides overseeing day-to-day Say Yes activities in the building, assumed responsibility for outreach to students' families and for assessing the social-emotional, health, and academic needs of children and families in order to plan and implement supports.

At first, Say Yes also placed a program coordinator in each school to report to the site director and the principal. This person collaborated with the site director to monitor students' health assessments, grades, permissions slips, medial release forms, and to oversee the after-school and summer programs for students. Eventually, Say Yes retained community-based organizations (CBOs) to run the after-school programs and got rid of program coordinators. Say Yes set high standards to identify the CBOs, requesting proposals and using a meticulous vetting process. Sustainability, from the perspective of Say Yes, called for leaving every aspect of the program in capable hands when its work was done.

In contracting with these organizations, Say Yes not only found reliable partners to help run programs but also cemented its connection to the city. When Say Yes launched the after-school program, such organizations as Boys and Girls Clubs of America and the YMCA—which had long offered similar programs of their own—worried about losing out. But Say Yes gave them a role and even modified its vetting process at the suggestion of the groups.

A task force of CBOs that formed in conjunction with their work for Say Yes gave the groups a forum and a place to exchange ideas. "What's different about Say Yes is that it is much more systematic and requires a more systematic response," said Mike Melara of Catholic Charities, one of the CBOs. "I think the task force will be institutionalized with a focus on making sure that youngsters of greatest need graduate high school and get to college."

Keeping the Secondary Schools in Mind

While Say Yes first focused on the elementary schools, grants from the Ford Foundation and the Woodrow Wilson National Fellowship Foundation allowed officials to start thinking about how the program would look at the secondary level. Say Yes and the school system sought to develop an approach that integrated planning and preparation for college and career into the secondary school curriculum so that students would have more time to get ready for their post–high school future.

Say Yes also wanted Syracuse to strengthen its middle schools so as to ensure a sufficient level of rigor and to set a foundation for multiple pathways through high school and on to postsecondary education and employment. Middle schools, which usually run from sixth through eighth grade, tend to be the forgotten element in pre-K–12 education everywhere. They replaced junior highs around the country by offering a more integrated, child-centered approach, but their workings have been largely taken for granted in recent years. Inadequate preparation in middle school may leave youngsters floundering in high school.

American Institutes for Research examined the academic, social-emotional, and health services in schools in Syracuse to determine how the available offerings comported with the Say Yes theory of action. Say Yes bases its theory of action, which culminates in postsecondary completion, on academic and personal readiness. Academic readiness rests on traditional in-school attributes—rigorous curriculum, high-quality instruction, and strong conditions for teaching and learning—and such out-of-school supports as tutoring, summer programs, and talent development. Personal readiness involves supports for social, emotional, and healthful well-being. Another side of personal readiness has to do with assistance in planning for and applying to college. Efforts to engage and support the student's family underpin the theory of action.

Say Yes formulates its approach on the premise that students will end up graduating from high school fully prepared for postsecondary education or for careers, if that were their choice. Say Yes hopes that such a change will mean that the district's enrollment will grow as the public schools become more attractive and parent engagement will increase. In keeping with its goals for the city itself, the collateral effect will mean that housing in Syracuse will become more desirable because of a better school system, employment will increase with better-prepared job candidates, and the crime rate will drop. Utopias begin with dreams. For the most part, this vision depicts a future that will take years to realize.

5

Teaching and Learning

Say Yes's greatest challenge in Syracuse was the district's need to improve teaching and learning. Say Yes could put site directors in buildings, help the school system hire more social workers, provide wraparound programs to extend learning time, make legal aid available to families, and hold students' hands through the college application process. But the organization's ability to bring about changes in the classroom was limited. Ultimately, it fell to the school system, not Say Yes, to address the fundamental issues of teaching and learning. The school district continued to have its own staff of educators, and the school board continued to hold sway over the system.

"Say Yes is a program, and it's not the district," said Nader Maroun, education committee chairman of the Common Council, which must approve the system's overall budget. "The district needs to take the leadership role." He cited the number of homeless students, 426, and English language learners, 2,634, and added, "There is a lack of a curriculum to address their needs, and the new superintendent gets this. All the economic development in the city will go for naught if we don't fix this."

Three out of four elementary pupils in Syracuse scored at the two lowest of four possible levels in English language arts in 2010–11. The numbers were slightly worse in mathematics. Experience shows that students are unlikely to achieve on grade level in secondary school if they trail badly in elementary school.

When the doors to Syracuse's schools opened in fall 2011 with Sharon Contreras as the new superintendent, she saw that the district still needed a rigorous curriculum, better professional development, appropriate instructional technology, and a comprehensive system of assessment and intervention. "Teachers are doing the best job that they can, but they don't have the tools," she said. "We are fully committed to putting the elements in place. In time, we will see whole-system transformation but not until the academic piece is better designed and implemented." By the time the school year ended in June 2012, all the features advocated by Say Yes still had not been put in place to foster higher academic achievement.

Kevin Ahern of the teachers' union acknowledged that "entrenched structures" in Syracuse were obstacles to reform. "This is not a nimble system, and it is not set up for quick change," he said. "Some things have not changed as a result of Say Yes.

We find ourselves year after year with inadequate funding from the state [the bulk of the school district's revenues originate from New York State]. Every year, we struggle mightily. We don't have a systematic goal for utilizing resources. We have built a system around grant money."

Wrinkles that weren't apparent when plans lay dormant had to be ironed out once those plans became part of the school fabric. What Say Yes can't readily control is the fact that teachers in Syracuse—like their colleagues across the country—remember innovations introduced over the years to great fanfare only to fail or be abandoned. So like other reformers seeking the support of teachers, Say Yes encountered some degree of cynicism. "We will have these kids even if the program leaves," said one elementary-level teacher, invoking the permanence of the faculty, which—like the sturdy, venerable buildings in which they work—had endured many efforts to "save" the city's public school system.

Improvement at schools everywhere often depends on teachers receiving the staff development required to carry out certain tasks. In Syracuse, the school system had a history of not providing educators with adequate in-service training. The need for staff development was illustrated by the fact that some teachers with electronic white boards in their classrooms did not take advantage of the technology the white boards provided because the teachers had not received the preparation to do so. No coherent strategy existed to help educators grow to full potential as teachers and instructional leaders until Contreras moved to put one in place. Interviews by Say Yes consultant Cross & Joftus found that district educators perceived that staff development was not aligned to any larger strategy of teaching and learning.[1]

Facing Reality

Time will tell whether a greater awareness of the role of staff development will lead to either putting a new roof on the district's structure of learning or merely placing a few buckets in strategic spots to catch the leaks. Harvard's Richard Elmore maintains that increasing the knowledge and skills of teachers is one of the three basics of school reform. The other two basics, according to him, are changing the content of learning and altering the relationship of students to the content and to the teachers.[2]

Contreras reported the dismal student achievement statistics to the community at one of her first school board meetings as superintendent, calling the numbers "unacceptable." She said that the district had to own up to its responsibility for producing better outcomes. A reporter approached her after the meeting, telling Contreras that she had never before heard anything like this in Syracuse—a declaration from a leading school official that the district was supposed to ensure that students learned. The new superintendent willingly painted a target on her back, taking responsibility for student achievement. She said that poverty would no longer be an excuse for low scores and that Syracuse's students could learn on the level of peers in surrounding suburbs. She went on a local radio program to respond to critics who took offense when Contreras said poverty and family dysfunction could not be excuses for low achievement.

Say Yes had constantly to reassure people inside and outside the school system that its program and the improvements that it fostered in Syracuse would be in place for the long run. Some parents worried that the college scholarships would dry up and that their children would not reap the benefits of the program. It is this very concern that Say Yes addressed in building an endowment for the scholarships. Sharon Contreras spoke of Say Yes being around for at least a generation.

The release of state assessment results in fall 2011 underscored the weakness of the academic program and led some people to pronounce Say Yes a failure. This attitude reflected an unrealistic feeling in some sectors that the mere presence of Say Yes in the Syracuse City School District would improve test scores, a belief that did not acknowledge that much of Say Yes's role did not penetrate the core of teaching and learning.

Special Education

Special education is a key but sometimes overlooked area that Syracuse must address if it hopes to become "the most improved urban school district in America," as Contreras described her vision. With one out of every five students classified for special education—a level that the superintendent called "excessive"—Syracuse cannot make the sort of progress that it desires without improvement in this area. Problems with the program involved not only the high number of youngsters classified as disabled but the questionable quality of the instruction they received. The question was whether special education students in Syracuse had the opportunity to reach their full potential.

An audit report paid for by Say Yes identified shortcomings specific to special education, helping Contreras set her priorities. The program was afflicted by a lack of effectiveness and sustained implementation strategies, limited professional development opportunities, inadequate staffing levels, and poor student attendance. Most significantly, there were high rates of referral to special education.

On the positive side, the same report identified some existing initiatives and practices that Contreras could build on. Among these were a strong leadership team for early childhood programs, an emergent consultant teacher model to help with inclusion, strides for controlling special education costs, and fiscal and personnel support for implementing a federal program known as Positive Behavior Intervention and Support.[3] Syracuse also did more than many districts to include its disabled students in regular classes, where they often had the support of teaching assistants.

The Syracuse public schools made slow but steady progress in reducing the numbers identified for special education. The district's 22.2 percent of students enrolled in special education in the 2009–10 school year dipped to 20.4 percent by 2012–13. The actual number of disabled students declined from 4,464 to 4,051.

The struggle that the school system faced in remedying shortcomings in the education of the disabled could be seen in the fact that some parents asserted that they would resist efforts to reduce referrals into the program. These parents apparently thought that any such move represented an attempt to deny their children needed services. On the other hand, those familiar with the situation contended that expectations were so low for pupils in special education that the children covered only a portion of the required curriculum, depriving them of the requisite background to succeed on state tests.

A Mixed Record of Achievement

It is not as if there was no progress during the early years of Say Yes's involvement, however uneven it may have been. Scores on New York State assessments rose in grades three through eight on English language arts from 2010–11 to 2011–12. Nonetheless, fewer than 30 percent of Syracuse's students reached proficiency in any of the grades. Math scores on the same state examination increased in all grades but the seventh among the same students. But only fourth graders reached the point that more than 30 percent were proficient in math.

Scores in algebra illustrated the ups and downs of the progress. Ninth-grade passing rates, which stood at 39.6 percent in 2008–9, dropped to 37.5 percent in 2009–10, rose to 47.7 percent in 2010–11, and fell back to 42.4 percent in 2011–12. The short-term effect of such initiatives as talent development, International Baccalaureate, increased Advanced Placement offerings, the high school planning toolkit, more counselors, after-school tutoring, and extended learning time added to the progress.

The number of high school students dropping out, being incarcerated, or transferring decreased from 505 in 2009 to 281 in 2010. Graduation rates inched up from 45.2 percent in 2009, to 45.9 percent in 2010, to 48.4 percent in 2011. The 2011 rate represented those who entered ninth grade in 2007 and received diplomas with their class in June four years later.[4] Ultimately, a higher graduation rate has to be achieved if Say Yes and the school district expect to show progress. Say Yes, after all, proposes to see all high school graduates in Syracuse ready for college and/or careers.

Say Yes officials said at times that what counted most in Syracuse was having more graduates of the school system attend postsecondary institutions, complete their programs, and gain employment, regardless of their test scores in the public schools. Granted that the nation has put entirely too much emphasis on testing, but to a certain extent those examinations serve as proxies for achievement, and the goal of postsecondary completion may be jeopardized if scores fail to rise markedly.

There is no disputing the desperate need for invigoration in a school system that—like a person deprived of sleep—was long bereft of pep and energy. Syracuse rests near the bottom of New York State's Big 5 cities in some education statistics. The comparable graduation rate percentages are 66.2 for Yonkers, 60.9 for New York City, 54 for Buffalo, and 45.5 for Rochester. A significant number of seniors in each district who do not graduate with their class use the summer to retake examinations they failed and to pursue credit recovery, a kind of shortcut to accumulate credits in a hurry, possibly online. Thus by August, the percentage of diploma recipients increases. In Syracuse, almost one hundred seniors completed requirements over the summer, and the graduation rate rose to 53 percent.[5]

As if the school system did not have enough challenges, another arose during the first decade of the 2000s as Syracuse became a resettlement center for refugee families directed to the city by the U.S. State Department. These newcomers—about two-thirds from Bhutan and Burma alone and most of the remainder from Somalia, Sudan, and Iraq—added hundreds of students with no background in English to the school system. They arrived on top of a growing enrollment of youngsters whose parents emigrated from countries in Latin America. The local chapters of two national organizations—Catholic Charities and Interfaith Works—took the lead in resettlement efforts in Syracuse.

Syracuse recognized that it had to shore up the tottering foundation for learning if students were to increase their chances for success. The district stepped up its focus on early learning. Of the 1,600 pupils who entered kindergarten one recent fall, 1,200 had attended either half-day or full-day prekindergarten. Say Yes and the school district not only aimed to see all four-year-olds in prekindergarten but wanted those classes to be of a full day's duration. Say Yes got the city to contribute $250,000 toward the expansion of prekindergarten, which already served children with disabilities, as federal law mandates. The number who attended full-day prekindergarten rose from three hundred to four hundred in a single year, and the district sought to have one thousand children in full-day classes within three years.

Glimmers of Progress

Paul G. Tremont, president of Scientific Research Corporation (SRC), a major company in the city and one of the most important financial supporters for Say Yes in Syracuse, was willing to wait for results in the classroom. "I'm not yet concerned," he said midway through the 2011–12 school year. "It takes time. In SRC, when we start a strategic plan, the results are three, four, five, six years out. Math and English scores can't be impacted in a year or two."

Say Yes envisioned six primary roles for the school system so far as the classroom was concerned:

1. Monitoring individual student progress
2. Fostering teacher/staff ownership of the school improvement process
3. Customizing support systems for individual students
4. Extending learning time
5. Conducting evidence-based academic planning and improvement
6. Setting expected outcomes

The principal of Bellevue Elementary School, Joanne Harlow, said that even four years into Say Yes, "academic impact remains to be seen." But if the school system continued its new focus on academic interventions, she thought there would be a more significant impact on the learning of students. She already saw changes in the social, emotional, and behavioral areas and lauded Say Yes for the increased support it provided for children and families in the form of social workers and mental health therapists. She said that Say Yes had removed some of the barriers to learning.

Sharon L. Contreras

Sharon Contreras had a front-row seat as she learned how a school district should not function. From 2004 to 2007, she was chief academic officer (not superintendent) for Clayton County Public Schools in Georgia, where the school board micromanaged the system, taking over decisions and making appointments that properly were the superintendent's prerogatives. It got so bad that the district lost its accreditation. Contreras escaped with her reputation intact and became chief academic officer in Providence, Rhode Island, from where she moved on to Syracuse, all the wiser about the ins and outs of running a school system.

As a superintendent, for the first time, she is the key person in determining whether Say Yes's venture will improve the city's public schools. "No matter how well the other elements work," she said referring to such features promoted by Say Yes as social-emotional supports and the extended school day, "if we don't strengthen the academic pillar, we can't say Say Yes was successful."

Contreras was born and raised on New York's Long Island and was so impatient that she bunched up her high school courses, attended summer school after the eleventh grade, skipped her senior year, and walked away with an early diploma. After getting a bachelor's degree in English literature at Binghamton University, State University of New York, she earned three separate master's degrees and by 2013 was just a dissertation away from a doctorate from the University of Wisconsin, Madison. The dissertation deals with high-performing, high-poverty, high-minority schools.

In Rockford, Illinois, where Contreras launched her teaching career and started her quick ascent up the administrative ladder, she ran a magnet school and played a key role in implementing a federal order to desegregate the schools. In Providence, she was responsible for an approach to instruction that improved the graduation rate and for an initiative to provide high school students with more career preparation.

Contreras's biography identifies her as the first woman of color appointed to a permanent superintendent's position at any of New York State's five largest school districts. Her father was an immigrant from Venezuela, and her mother, of African descent, was from Puerto Rico. She can get by conversing in Spanish, but she doesn't consider herself fluent.

She is divorced and has no children of her own, but she raised two of her nieces and is now raising a grand-nephew who enters kindergarten in Syracuse in September 2013. Given the responsibilities of looking after children and keeping up the backbreaking routine of running a school system, she doesn't get away as often as she would like for international travel. A highlight was a trip to Senegal, and she hopes before long to make a trip to Mount Kilimanjaro, which she would like to climb. In the meantime, Contreras has to satisfy herself with scaling the demands of her grueling job.

Instilling Momentum

To instill instant momentum and foster a can-do culture right from the start, Contreras, assisted by Schaffer Consulting, a group retained by Say Yes, began her tenure by requesting that teams at individual schools and district-wide teams carry out Rapid Results projects over her first one hundred days. These projects, mostly aimed at boosting educational outcomes, were designed to generate insights into long-term goals.

And so it was that a team at Van Duyn Elementary sought to increase listening comprehension scores of forty fourth and fifth graders as measured on assessments. The team enlisted a librarian to provide small-group instruction and used after-school programming, as well. After one hundred days, fourth graders increased their correct short-answer responses by 161 percent and fifth graders by 15 percent.

At Henninger High School, a team set out to provide support for a targeted group of seniors to pass a practice exam in math by the end of the hundred-day period. The team designed a system that allowed teachers in an entire department to aid students. The team also placed an extra math teacher in the target group's classes. As a result, communication was enhanced among the math teachers, guidance counselors, and administrators involved in the project, and 44 percent of the students who sat for the exam passed.

Contreras announced at the outset of her superintendency that she would report to the community after one hundred days in the post. She held back little when December 2011 came around. Based on many meetings, visits to more than two hundred classrooms, and the findings of consultants retained by Say Yes, she announced that the school system was unclear in its priorities, lacked curricular alignment from grade to grade, gave too little attention to planning, and was inconsistent in programming for its growing population of English language learners. It all added up, she said, to a district in which spending and organization did not regard the needs of students as paramount.

A paucity of rigor and the absence of a uniformly high-quality academic program almost certainly contributed to low achievement in Syracuse. Study after study across the country attests to the need for such elements if a school system intends to improve. Research that looks at what students "bring to" school as contrasted with "what happens to" them when they get there concludes that quality education and access to demanding and invigorating curricula are more important than their social capital, cultural capital, or even academic engagement in overcoming the black-white performance gap. The report says that tracking students into lower-level courses based on race or on social-economic standing is an obstacle to achievement.[6]

Like a general assuming leadership of an army already in the field, the superintendent wasted no time in launching major offensives to address deficiencies. The district began to align the curriculum with the state's core standards in English and mathematics, started to create a professional development plan for its educators, launched a yearlong study of academic rigor, implemented summer reading academies for elementary teachers to equip them with literacy strategies, and started to design a compensation system to take cognizance of student outcomes and professional growth.

By 2013, Contreras had obtained grants totaling $31.5 million from the state to create an Innovation Zone to infuse seven of the district's lowest-performing elementary and middle schools with more teacher support and to lend the schools flexibility in working around constraints that otherwise handcuff administrators and teachers. The grants include money to extend the day by ninety additional minutes for students and teachers and to add 14 days of professional development for teachers in the zone. The district engaged the National Center on Time and Learning and the Rochester Institute of Technology to provide technical assistance to enable the seven schools to use the extra time to greatest advantage.

The funds, derived from the federal School Improvement Grant program, call for making the participating schools either turnaround models or transformational models. The turnaround schools must replace the principal and half the staff. The two transformational schools must replace only the principal but have to mandate performance reviews for the faculty that will lead to rewards for effective teachers and the removal of ineffective teachers after giving them ample professional development opportunities. The Syracuse Teachers Association signed on as cosponsor of what the district called the iZone.

Watching one of the system's better teachers in action in his regular daily classroom activities gives a glimpse of the possibilities for the entire system.

Comprehending the Third Grade

The teacher, a thirtyish man bubbling with enthusiasm, sought to engage his third graders at Syracuse's McKinley-Brighton Elementary School before they ever opened their books to begin the reading lesson. "This is a classic story," he told them. "It is so good that they made a movie out of it," he added, apparently figuring that would grab their attention. He reviewed the skills that he wanted them to use. "First, let's talk about our comprehension skills," he said. "We have also called it drawing conclusions or inferences."

Typically, this year would be the last point in their primary education in which the emphasis would be on learning to read. It was the end of May, and fourth grade lay ahead in just a few months. The accent would shift to reading to learn. And those children not ready to make the transition, like hatchlings too weak to leave the nest, would fall increasingly behind their peers. This is the way it works in most schools across the country.

The teacher spoke to the youngsters about "taking information from the text" and "adding it to what you already know." He asked no one in particular what they were supposed to call the information they already knew. A girl piped up: "Schema," a surprising definition from a third grader. The teacher repeated, "You take the information from the text, add it to your background knowledge, and use it to draw conclusions."

The goal of the lesson, like so many previous ones, was to help the students increase their ability to comprehend what they read. Reading is much more than simply sounding out letters and parts of words. Without the ability to understand text and draw conclusions, students will find opportunities in the academic world closing around them. This particular teacher, who was recognized during the year as one of the district's most outstanding teachers, was dynamic in the classroom, almost boyish in his youthful appearance and clearly devoted to leading his students—like a Sherpa guide on Everest—to the next plateau.

Yet, despite his vigor, at least 3 of the 22 pupils (two others had been pulled out to meet in another room for special tutoring) would fall asleep during the lesson: two of them with their heads down on their desks, one sitting up with his eyes closed and his head drooping to one side. It was not as if the liveliness of the classroom induced a state of slumber. Furthermore, sunlight, an enemy of sleep, poured in through windows that lined one wall. Outside, directly across the street from the school, were the frame houses with high sloping roofs that typify this almost entirely African American neighborhood on the city's south side. The teacher periodically did what he could to rouse the drowsy students and draw them into the lesson.

Still not ready to ask the students to open the books that rested on their desks in front of them, the teacher spoke of using clues in the story, titled "Wilbur's Boast," so as to understand the characters better. He stopped to discuss the meaning of the word "boast." Most pupils seemed to know that it was synonymous with "brag." They opened their books.

This was third grade, and illustrations were sprinkled liberally through the pages. The teacher spoke to his students about drawing hints from pictures to help them understand the story. They talked about the kinds of animals in the pictures, and he guided them to the conclusion that this story took place on a farm (there were cows and goats and chickens) and not in a jungle (no monkeys, lions, or elephants). He had them read the first sentence of the story aloud, in unison: "A spider's web is stronger than it looks . . ."

The teacher encouraged students to determine the identities of two characters introduced into the story. To a child who surmised that one of the characters was a spider, the teacher said, "That's a great example of drawing a conclusion." This, it turned out, was a story extracted from *Charlotte's Web*. The story described Charlotte's leg, and the teacher, pacing the aisles, got the students talking about "femur" and "tibia." He taught in a way that emphasized not only comprehension but also vocabulary, the building blocks of understanding. The students, many of whom probably did not encounter rich language out of school, had to construct their vocabularies in classrooms such as this one. This is a key to expanding their learning.

The teacher directed the students to take out their "graphic organizers" to use as they read the story. The graphic organizer was a single work sheet with four horizontal boxes. The first three boxes were labeled "Detail," and the fourth was "Conclusion." At the bottom was the question "How does the information you wrote in this Draw Conclusions Chart help you understand plot development in *Wilbur's Boast*?" It was clear there would be no respite from the unremitting effort in this classroom to promote comprehension and to put as many students as possible on track for success in the fourth-grade classroom in which they would soon be seated.

A Strategic Plan

By summer 2012, preceding her second full year as superintendent, Contreras unveiled a five-year strategic plan, "Great Expectations," that she developed around five goals:

1. To provide all students with equitable access to rigorous curriculum with aligned instructional materials and assessments in all subjects at all grade levels
2. To recruit, develop, support, and retain effective teachers and school leaders
3. To develop infrastructure to support student success
4. To build a district culture based on high expectations, respect, and accountability for performance that recognizes and rewards excellence at all levels of the organization
5. To communicate effectively with all district stakeholders

The report set a timeline for implementing features meant to achieve each goal. It also identified ways to measure progress and promised an annual report on student outcomes. By way of illustration, the initiatives accompanying the first goal called for aligning instruction in Syracuse with New York's Common Core State Standards Initiative, building the capacity of the schools and the central office to implement the standards, abandoning instructional programs that did not support the new curriculum and the new goals, supporting emergent literacy and numeracy in the primary grades, and creating a plan for strong career education and science, technology, engineering, and math (STEM) programs.[7]

The state education department boosted Contreras's efforts by awarding the system $2 million to help it implement the strategic plan, calling for the district to put particular emphasis on building a culture based on high expectations. The district announced that it would engage a consulting group, Mass Insight Education, to provide technical assistance.

The 2012–13 school year was a tough one for teachers in Syracuse, not simply because the district began implementing the new strategic plan but because the administration wanted to infuse the Common Core curriculum into all instruction. The Common Core, at various stages of adoption in most states across the country, calls for teachers to change both the curriculum and the way they present it. The teachers' union thought the transition could have been made more effective by providing staff with more resources and more training—both of which cost money and take time, which the district did not have. Teachers complained privately about principals whom they thought were under pressure from the central office to move "full speed ahead" without consideration of the burden put on teachers by the curriculum changes.

An Emphasis on Literacy

The emphasis on literacy was apparent in all three of the fifth-grade classes I visited during the two-hour block devoted to language arts first thing every morning at Roberts School. It was midway through the 2012–13 school year, and most of these children entered first grade when Say Yes came into Syracuse in 2008. The after-school program started that school year, and the summer program began in 2009.

At this point, four years later, the pre-K–8 school of 745 students had one of the most balanced enrollments in the city: 46 percent black, 34 percent white, 9 percent Hispanic, and a smattering of others. Its 19 percent of children with disabilities was slightly less than the district at large. The school had a policy of inclusion for special education students and mainstreamed them in regular classes for the entire instructional day. The school identified only forty youngsters as having limited proficiency in English.

Achievement at Roberts, one of the city's highest-performing schools, was anchored by students from the Strathmore neighborhood, with its Tudor and colonial revival homes and some of the most affluent residents of Syracuse. The school's 57 percent rate of economically disadvantaged students was well below the city-wide rate. The school abutted Corcoran High School, which Roberts students would attend after completing eighth grade.

In a fifth-grade classroom the morning I visited, the teacher encouraged students to think about the author's purpose in writing a particular article; they had read the piece for the first time the previous day. The desks were bunched together in groups of four or six, almost as if the students were gathered around small tables. They read aloud about a scientific investigation of cockroaches, not the least bit repelled by a topic that might have disgusted their parents. "Why do you think the author wrote this piece?" asked the teacher, explaining that the author's purpose might have been to inform or to persuade or to entertain. The class agreed that the purpose was to inform the reader. It is through such lessons that students learn to focus their own writing by giving it a purpose.

Next, the teacher passed out the blue-covered journals in which she periodically asked the youngsters to record reactions to what they read. She stressed that—unlike most tests they took—there were no right or wrong answers in this exercise. They were to speculate on the author's purpose and offer opinions to back up what they wrote. "I'm going to give you a challenge," the teacher said as she walked among the groups of desks distributing the journals. "I'd like you to use quotes from the reading to support your opinion."

In another fifth-grade class during the language arts block, material from the students' textbook was projected a few paragraphs at a time on a screen pulled down at the front of the room. Narration that arrived over a speaker accompanied the projected paragraphs. The students read about cannon fire in

Charleston Harbor in South Carolina, apparently never before having heard of a place called Fort Sumter. "The defenders of the United States fort were the Northerners," the teacher told them. "The Southerners were the ones who started the attack." She had to explain several times the difference between the Northerners and the Southerners. Most of her questions went unanswered, and she ended up providing the responses. "We're going to identify the text structure of this article," she told the children.

The voice of the narrator on the speaker continued as new text appeared on the screen: "Just 82 soldiers, including members of the military band, were in the fort."

"You're reading nonfiction," explained the teacher. "You're getting pounded with information." The students were told that the soldiers in the fort surrendered. "What war will follow as a result?" the teacher asked. No one answered until one child timidly started to say, "World War . . . ," and his voice trailed off.

The teacher spoke some more about the organizing text structure, adding facts as she went along. She told them that the South seceded and elected Jefferson Davis as its president. "The bombardment of Fort Sumter was the first battle of the Civil War," she revealed to them, as some children squirmed in their seats, not terribly attentive to the start of the onslaught that would take the lives of more than six hundred thousand soldiers from both sides.

The teacher asked about clues in the writing that indicated the kind of text they were reading. She tried to get them to think about the differences in writing that focused on problems and solutions and writing that focused on causes and effects. The text went on to discuss what happened in the country after the bombardment. "This was the result of what?" asked the teacher. The students were unresponsive, not engaged by the text and seemingly bored. The teacher described events that occurred as a result of the attack on Fort Sumter. "You have to remember," she said, "when you are reading nonfiction to put the pieces together. When you understand how an author organizes his writing, then you can read it. This text structure is cause-and-effect." This revelation drew not a single comment.

In the third of the school's three fifth-grade classrooms, students sought main ideas from the text, an exercise they had pursued as a whole class the previous day. Now they were in small groups learning to approach information text differently from the way they approached fiction. This was a prelude to writing a persuasive essay.

A large poster on one wall of the room carried the title "Which University Will You Attend?" There were illustrations from such institutions as Marist, Sarah Lawrence, SUNY Institute of Technology, Syracuse University, and the University of Rochester. The poster attested to the influence of Say Yes, as did a sign at the entrance to the classroom that read "Class of 2020."

All in all, the scene in the fifth-grade classrooms—undoubtedly replicated throughout the district—underscored the devotion to literacy that has come to pervade elementary schools throughout Syracuse and the challenges of engaging the students. Many of them must make up lots of ground, having entered this race some distance behind the starting line. They must narrow the gap if they are, indeed, to be properly prepared for higher education in 2020.

Rigor at the High School Level

Dean Biklen of the education school at Syracuse University worried three and a half years into Say Yes's efforts—just months after Contreras took up her duties—whether the district focused sufficiently on academic matters. He said the system needed more rigor and better leadership at the school-building level. "One of the survey findings is that teachers buy into Say Yes but are not sure of the implementation at the building level," he said. Biklen conceded that a sense of promise remained and said that "the next four or five years will be very critical in making this happen." Say Yes, for its part, recognized that academics in Syracuse had to be more rigorous throughout the grades in order to produce more graduates prepared for postsecondary education. Say Yes promoted initiatives to help attain this goal, linking them to strengthening the curriculum, improving pedagogy, assessing students more carefully, and promoting staff development.

It is worth noting that rigor alone—in the absence of various initiatives that Say Yes and Contreras support—may not guarantee higher achievement. At least this is what the College Readiness Indicator System (CRIS) developed by the Consortium on Chicago School Research found. Higher graduation requirements and more college prep coursework led to lower pass rates, no improvements in test scores, and lower college entrance rates among students in the Chicago high schools in a research study. Measures to engage students and better professional development for teachers must accompany boosts in rigor, according to CRIS.[8]

The International Baccalaureate (IB) program that Corcoran High introduced in 2005 is a device for ratcheting up expectations in Syracuse. IB enrolls 976,000 students in 141 countries and offers courses in six subject areas that lead to final examinations and an extended written essay. Juniors and seniors at Corcoran High may pursue the full array of courses to complete an IB diploma along with their regular diploma, or they may enroll in just some of the courses without seeking the IB diploma. Many institutions of higher education award credit and advanced standing to students for IB courses, much as they do for the College Board's Advanced Placement program.

Corcoran High also began a pre-IB program for ninth and tenth graders to prepare them for the demands of the diploma program. In 2011, a total of 685 of the high school's students took at least one of the courses associated with the International Baccalaureate. Some three or four dozen juniors and seniors actively pursue the IB diploma, which about a dozen attain each year. The school's pass rate on the final exams for the IB is more than 50 percent. IB bolstered the academic culture in the school. Brian Nolan, the former principal who introduced the program to Corcoran High and later became the director of high schools for the district, said that teachers told him the staff development to provide IB instruction was the best they had ever had. It imbued them with a sense of collegiality. The program also raised expectations for teachers, who "knew that they had to deliver," according to Nolan, and for students, who wanted to rise to the challenge of the courses.

Another possible route to rigor was the Early College program at Nottingham High School and at Institute of Technology of Syracuse Central (ITC), the district-wide, technology-oriented high school. Early College, a nationwide approach that provides a combination of courses at the high school and college level, exposes students to higher education and tries to lift their aspirations by situating them on a college campus part of the day. New York State's Smart Scholar initiative funded the program at ITC as well as one of the two programs at Nottingham High. Students in both programs took some of the courses at Onondaga Community College while they were still high school juniors and seniors.

The school system installed a second Early College program at Nottingham High as a result of a grant to Syracuse University by the Woodrow Wilson National Fellowship Foundation. Controversy swirled around this program, and, to add to its woes, the funding grew uncertain. The program began in 2009 with a select group of ninth graders. In part, the dispute stemmed from the question of whether to involve juniors and seniors at the outset or whether to scale up the program as the original group of freshmen and sophomores reached the last two years of high school. The disagreements, coming in the midst of efforts to redesign the academic character of the entire school, affected relationships between teachers at the high school and certain faculty members at the university, a partner in the redesign effort.

The pursuit of better preparation took many forms in Syracuse. Corcoran and Henninger high schools implemented study tables for student athletes that met for forty minutes daily at the end of the regular school day. The coaching staff hoped that Say Yes would provide tutors, but when this assistance did not materialize, the coaches themselves took on the tutoring and delayed the start of practice for athletes whose sports were in season.

Student Monitoring

Getting students on track and keeping them there meant the equivalent of painstakingly building a proper railbed, ensuring that the trains remain in good repair, and maintaining the right speed. Say Yes wanted to leave as little to chance as possible. Therefore the organization, collaborating with the American Institutes for Research (AIR), developed a system to monitor students and provide interventions as needed.

Much of the plan, some of which is described in Chapter 2, does not rely on the sort of tests that first come to mind when one thinks of student assessment. Rather, AIR assembled indicators and benchmarks in a host of areas against which to measure youngsters as they move through the school year and through the grades. AIR grouped the benchmarks under three principal domains: (1) academic, (2) health, and (3) social-emotional. The monitoring plan gives separate consideration to such background factors as family and community interaction with the student. The three main indicators in each area are (1) test scores, grades, and attendance for academic; (2) medical/vision, dental/hearing, and other physical determinants for health; and (3) school behavior, social behavior, and social capital for social-emotional.

Depending on the category, the benchmarks might remain the same as a student advances through the grades or might differ at various grade levels. A measure of social capital, for example, is whether the student, at any age, has at least five people to turn to for support and remains involved in activities and organizations. On the other hand, a benchmark for cognitive progress in the elementary grades includes sustained attention and good memory but at the secondary level, includes being a good notetaker and organizing materials effectively.

The value of monitoring to an urban school system could be seen in the Long Beach Unified School District in California, which has a student enrollment more than four times the size of Syracuse's. In faithfully gathering and analyzing student performance data, Long Beach won commendation as a district that greatly improved itself during the 2000s. The consulting firm McKinsey & Company recognized Long Beach in a report about school systems around the world that bolstered their student outcomes.[9]

The indicators and benchmarks that Say Yes proposed for monitoring student progress in Syracuse were research based. AIR formulated them from a careful reading of the literature pertaining to what it takes for students to thrive. The indicators and benchmarks appear in a 72-page report in which one-third of the pages list the articles and books that formed the basis for the monitoring system.[10]

But educational innovations are of little value without implementation. Furthermore, not just any implementation will do. There must be fidelity to the carefully written recipe book, otherwise, the stew will lack flavor. Somehow, during the first four years that Say Yes partnered with the Syracuse City School District, the book remained on the shelf, largely serving no greater purpose than a dictionary no one consulted.

School officials were either too busy or not sufficiently committed to the idea of monitoring students. Say Yes officials did not yet have a system of monitoring ready when it moved into Syracuse and then did not do enough to prod the district to incorporate this pivotal part of the Say Yes mission into the instructional program. The bottom line was that Syracuse students probably didn't make as much academic progress as they should have during this period. Say Yes officials learned a big-time lesson here. They were not likely to make the same mistake in Buffalo or anyplace else they took their program.

Say Yes's work in Syracuse is a learning experience for the organization as well as for the school system. School reform is an activity replete with imponderables. The fluidity of instruction, more art than science, means that plans must be adjusted as circumstances change. What is certain as a result of Say Yes's intervention is that educators in Syracuse have gained insights into why classroom outcomes languished. Now they also have more awareness about what needs to be done. It is too soon to write the rest of the classroom story.

6

Outside Influences on
the Classroom

Some of the most extensive influences on the classroom come from the outside, especially from school boards and teachers' unions. The positions and policies of both of these groups go far in affecting teaching and learning. This is as true in Syracuse as anywhere else. The board of education represents the interests of the public, and the union represents the interests of the school district's most important employees: the teachers. Sometimes the two groups are in conflict as when they negotiate a contract.

School systems operate most effectively when boards and unions are not at loggerheads. This does not mean that either side has to subjugate its interests to the other but that they both acknowledge that ultimately the quality of education depends on the board and the union cooperating. Together they must strive to ensure instruction is as strong as possible and that the interests of children are no less important than those of adults. Given the recent history of low student performance in Syracuse it seems there is room for the school system's board and its teachers' union to do more to consider how their actions affect students.

The good news is that since about 2008, the Syracuse board of education and the Syracuse Teachers Association have shown that they want to act more assertively in behalf of educational improvement. For its part, the board has made headway in moving past the dysfunction that afflicted it earlier. The union has been receptive to making it easier for the central administration and principals to adopt measures promising the improvement of teaching and learning.

One could hardly attribute these changes to the mere presence of Say Yes. But Say Yes's influence has extended to the school board and the teachers' union in helping encourage greater understanding of the need for common goals. After five years, during which Say Yes became an accepted partner in the Syracuse City School District, there was reason in 2013 to think that promising days lay ahead.

Governance

Two wild cards complicated and impeded how Say Yes could play its hand in Syracuse. As an external group intervening in the school system, Say Yes had limited control over the way the deck was dealt once the players sat down at the table. The law gives school boards control over governance. This is the nature of American education, and it comes with the territory for reformers. On top this, the superintendent holds several aces and works only for the school board, not for the outside organization that wants to get things done. The students may be left holding the jokers. Thus plans for reform usually depend on the school board and the administration conceding that efforts up to that point have not been sufficient to deal with the challenges.

Say Yes or any other outside reform group with influence but no direct control over teaching and learning has limits on its role. Say Yes, like an invited guest in someone else's home, must defer to others and hope that its recommendations fall on compliant ears.

All Say Yes could do when its cohort of students in Philadelphia ended up in a school that turned chaotic was transfer them en masse to another school. In Hartford, the organization gracefully bowed out of its role when the superintendent had ideas not in sync with the goals that Say Yes had for its cohort of students. And even in Syracuse—with a superintendent it helped get hired—Say Yes representatives sometimes found themselves with less than the degree of influence they expected. Ideally, school reform arises from the inside, but frequently, outside groups like Say Yes must prompt insiders who are comfortable in their familiar garments to try on new outfits.

A local school board, as the district's governing body, sets policies and approves or disapproves the superintendent's recommendations. These functions go a long way toward determining possibilities for creating better schools. In the eyes of many, including some of its members, the school board in Syracuse was dysfunctional. It tended to immerse itself in a sea of minutia. It tried to micromanage, with the members sometimes behaving like children who dipped their fingers into places they didn't belong. School board members in Syracuse sometimes interfered in personnel decisions, seeking the reinstatement of individual staff members whose jobs were to be eliminated for budgetary reasons. Too often, some board members, all of whom are elected on an at-large basis, looked out for parochial interests in their neighborhoods rather than global issues affecting the entire school system.

Moreover, the school board, as already pointed out, did not have the confidence of the Common Council, the body that controls the allocation of funds to the schools. The difficulties with the council can be appreciated in the situational context in which the public schools consume about two-thirds of the revenues from the city's property tax levy. "How do you justify the portion spent on the schools without knowing what you are getting for your money?" asked Ryan McMahon, a member of the council whose wife was a fifth-grade teacher in the system. Like most others on the ten-member body, he felt the budget the school board expected the council to fund was sometimes opaque. McMahon favored possible mayoral control of the school system, a prospect raised in the new mayor's transitional report in 2010 but never pursued.

The Board Comes Around

Members of the school board were not among the leaders whose support Say Yes first solicited. Say Yes treated the board as a kind of junior partner, a tacit commentary on its perceived lack of clout. "To not have us at the table made it lopsided," said Kim Rohadfox-Ceaser, a former school board member who was president at the time. But the school board didn't balk and adopted a resolution accepting Say Yes's role when the organization finally came calling. By 2009, with Say Yes firmly ensconced as a partner in the system, almost all school board candidates ran on platforms supportive of Say Yes.

Say Yes's role in the district became a topic in school board elections. Most board candidates praised the organization and promised to back its efforts. Bill Bullen, elected to the board in 2011, for example, said, "Say Yes shows us that it is smarter to work closer with juvenile justice, public health organizations, and family services . . . I agree with Sharon Contreras with her assessment that Say Yes is a partnership, and irrespective of the support that Say Yes provides, if the school system is not providing the very best educational program, the results or benefits of Say Yes won't be realized."

When Dan Lowengard announced his retirement as superintendent in 2011, the school board commissioned Say Yes and Cascade Consulting Group to conduct a national search for his successor. The search produced a list of 16 semifinalists, mostly recruited by Say Yes through its extensive network and then vetted by Cascade. The board was involved each step of the way and made the final selection.

Contreras impressed council members, and they entered 2012 with confidence in her ability and her willingness to engage them as partners. Richard Strong, a lawyer and a former school board president, thought Contreras was prepared to deal with the school system's most pressing issues. "Part of the reason the superintendent was hired was to address teaching and learning," he said. "I had three children go through the system recently. I know the struggles. This superintendent has identified the needs. As a board and a community, we have to help put her plan in place and provide opportunities for her to be successful."

The superintendent and the board cemented their relationship by participating jointly in training by the Houston-based Center for Reform of School Systems designed to make governance a more collaborative enterprise. Board members and the superintendent attended a series of sessions in Santa Fe, Atlanta, and New Orleans. Though a $300,000 grant from Say Yes—not public funds—underwrote the training, some critics in Syracuse nonetheless denounced the effort as a waste of money that could have been better spent.

Calvin Corriders

Calvin Corriders, the board's vice president, was its longest-serving member, having first been elected in 2000. During the intervening years, he went on and off the board and then was appointed to fill out someone else's term. He witnessed firsthand some of the board's most egregious behavior and watched in recent years as the board came together to conduct itself more responsibly. "I am cautiously optimistic," said Corriders. Looking back on past problems, he continued, "We make excuses for why kids aren't learning. A lot of those excuses have to do with social-economic issues. And I was one of those children. The lesson is that there is no excuse—whether poor, black, white, green, or yellow—all kids can learn."

One would not readily have predicted that Corriders would become one of his community's leading lights. He was one of six children raised in a Syracuse public housing project by a single parent. "My upbringing was fantastic, or so I thought," he said looking back. "I didn't know what I didn't know. For example, I didn't know that the level of violence, the gunfire, was unusual. And I didn't know that seeing people shot was not normal. But I also grew up where there was a true sense of community. People watched out for you, and you had great friends."

He got his degree at SUNY Brockport under the Educational Opportunity Program, the state's program for economically disadvantaged students. It was working in a store and seeing a business operate that persuaded Corriders to major in business administration. He chose to make his career in banking and worked at HSBC, Chase Manhattan, and Beacon Federal before landing with Pathfinder Bank. Corriders, a vice president of the bank, is responsible for sales efforts in commercial, residential, and investment services.

Corriders's community service includes his role as a member of the advisory board of Excellus BlueCross BlueShield and his 100 Black Men of Syracuse membership. In his leisure time, he plays basketball at the downtown YMCA and enjoys traveling and reading. Among the books he most enjoyed recently was a biography of baseball great Satchel Paige. His wife, Sandra, is a business manager at Anheuser-Busch. They have two children, both at Syracuse University on Say Yes tuition scholarships.

The Unions

Any school system that has a collective bargaining contract with its staff and embarks on a mission of educational improvement flirts with failure if it does not bring the union into the discussion early on. The plan should not only involve the union but make it a full partner. Scholars who have looked closely at school reforms maintain that reform has the best chance of taking hold when it is pursued from the inside out, in other words, by taking account of the crucial role of teachers and others within the system.[1]

Say Yes's recognition of the vital role of the teachers' union was critical to the reform effort. Teachers in Syracuse realized, by and large, that it was in their interest to get better at what they did in order to improve instruction. Their leaders were largely sympathetic to what Say Yes sought to accomplish.

The Urban Teacher Contract

An early promising sign in this regard was the contract the school system entered into with the Syracuse Teachers Association in 2008, just as Say Yes came on the scene. The stars were in alignment, illuminating the first steps along the path toward much-needed change and helping the then superintendent, Dan Lowengard, meld his goals with those of Say Yes. The agreement broke new ground with an appendix to the contract creating what was called an Urban Teacher Calendar, an unofficial extension of the school year into the summer.

Extra days would be added in the summer to give students more instructional time and teachers more time for professional development. A team of teacher leaders in each elementary school was to tailor a summer program to meet the needs of both students and teachers. Veteran teachers would observe younger teachers and give them feedback. Everyone was to get a bonus for the summer work. But what looked good on paper turned out to be an urban mirage. Most of it did not happen, though the spirit remained, and the funds that were supposed to pay for it never materialized.

The new superintendent had other ideas for bolstering the staff's knowledge. As one of her first acts, Contreras swiftly reallocated $1 million in the budget for staff development and identified four Saturdays during which teachers would start getting at least some of the kind of training lacking in the past. The next year, she added two coaches to each elementary school—one in language arts and one in math—to help teachers improve their skills. By fall 2013, teachers were scheduled to receive fifty hours of staff development. The emphasis would be on implementing the Common Core curriculum, honing instructional strategies, putting more science and technology into elementary education, and adapting to a new teacher evaluation system.

"She recognized early in the game that we had to improve staff development," said Kevin R. Ahern, president of the Syracuse Teachers Association. Refusing to be handcuffed by a contract shaped by her predecessor, Contreras chose a different way to deliver professional development.

Cooperation by the Union

In another agreement, the union consented in a memorandum to add thirty minutes to the workday of elementary teachers during the regular school year to free up time for collaboration and joint planning. Various innovations in the contract, while not explicitly dictated by Say Yes, were inspired by the group's aspirations for Syracuse. "A culture of self-improvement is hard to create but essential," Lowengard said while he was still superintendent. "Teachers have to start to meet the needs that they feel they are not equipped to do. We've built the structure but have yet to build the climate. Effective practice can't be optional. It has to exist in every single classroom."

Even with concessions calling for teachers to put in more time, school hours in the high schools run from 7:50 a.m. to 2:05 p.m., a total of six hours and 15 minutes per day, while the school day consists of six hours in elementary schools. These are short days in comparison with some other systems where school days typically run seven or more hours. It is fine for Syracuse to seek to extend learning time into the summer, but it appeared that the district would do well to contract with the unions for yet a longer basic school day.

Recognizing the fiscal pressures on the school district at a time when it was struggling to make unprecedented progress, the union agreed to reopen its contract in 2011 and let the school board reduce a scheduled 4 percent pay increase for 2011–12 to 2.25 percent. In return, the board extended the contract through June 2014 with 2 percent increases in the final two years.

Thus upon assuming her duties, Contreras inherited a more manageable fiscal situation to carry her through her first three years as superintendent, and the teachers got the security of guaranteed growth in their salaries no matter how much the economy continued to flounder. In the 2013–14 school year, the starting salary was scheduled to be $42,052 for a teacher with a bachelor's degree and no advanced credits and to range from $71,430 to $76,830 for teachers with at least 25 years of experience and varying amounts of advanced credits.

Collective Bargaining as a Tool for Improvement

The Syracuse Teachers Association has joint affiliation with both national unions, the National Education Association (NEA) and the American Federation of Teachers (AFT), and both national unions bought into the promise of Say Yes, welcoming an infusion of outside aid and advice. Dennis Van Roekel, the NEA president, visited during Say Yes's first year in the district. "I believe you will get results because the plan will change the system for every child in Syracuse," he declared. "I want this to work because I want there to be a model for every child."

Various representatives of the AFT and New York State United Teachers, the statewide organization, bestowed similar blessings on Say Yes. Randi Weingarten, the AFT president, visited two Say Yes schools in Syracuse to see the program up close. She said, "By working with the district, unions, higher education, and local and state governments, Say Yes serves as a model for rethinking our approach to education and ensuring that every child has an opportunity for success. If we had more good programs like Say Yes, we'd have more children prepared to succeed in school, work, and life." Weingarten used her appearance to try to rally opposition to the annual layoffs of personnel that plagued the school system, warning that "you can't expect great reform programs like Say Yes to succeed with these budget cuts."

The Experience in Columbus

In using its collective bargaining agreement with the teachers' union as a tool to improve instruction, Syracuse adopted an approach that is finding favor in some other districts across the country. In Ohio, for instance, the Columbus City Schools and the Columbus Education Association forged a contract providing for a reform panel cochaired by the union president and the superintendent or their designees. The panel can facilitate implementation of initiatives to bolster teaching and learning and can give variances to the contract for school-based decisions.[2]

A major outcome of the agreement in Columbus, which the National Education Association Foundation supported with a grant of $1.25 million, is a system of classroom observations known as rounds, a name for an approach borrowed from the manner in which the medical field trains physicians. Columbus, unlike many other school districts, has a history of collaboration between the union and the school system that goes back to the 1990s.

Members of a group of administrators and teachers, who work in schools in the same feeder pattern, visit classrooms during the rounds, focusing their observations on instructional issues or problems that the school's improvement plan has identified. Teams of five or six members conduct four visits of 25 minutes each. The individual teams hold separate debriefings and then gather with the other teams to generate a set of guiding questions the school uses to reflect on specific practices. Richard F. Elmore of Harvard University pioneered this approach, which is detailed in *Instructional Rounds in Education*, a 2009 book by Elmore and his colleagues.

An agreement in Columbus between the union and the district prohibits using these observations in conjunction with a teacher's formal evaluation or making them part of a personnel file. Furthermore, the observation documents from professional rounds may not refer to specific teachers or classrooms.

The project in Columbus includes peer assistance, especially for second-year teachers on the tenure track. A mentor works with each new teacher. The NEA sees the program as an effort to confront the achievement gap by encouraging local unions to confer with district officials to increase teacher effectiveness and quality and to encourage community engagement. The community part of the arrangement called for involving a third party. In this case, the United Way of Columbus became a signatory to the agreement and the fiscal agent for the project. Such bargaining agreements in Columbus, Syracuse, and elsewhere serve to remind those who seek school improvement that these pursuits can benefit from collaboration between teachers' unions and school systems. This less adversarial approach may yield results that satisfy both sides and, most importantly, benefit children.

Reaching an Agreement on Teacher Evaluation

One test of the ability of the Syracuse City School District and its teachers' union to work together came as a result of an infusion of federal Race to the Top funds into New York State. In order to get a portion of the money, each of the state's seven hundred school systems had to forge agreements with their teachers on evaluation procedures. For the teachers, it meant buying into an approach they had long opposed, and for the school system in Syracuse, it meant a federal grant of $3.9 million over four years and another of $2 million over two years.

After a period of intense bargaining, the Syracuse Teachers Association agreed in a memorandum signed on June 29, 2012, to permit the district to develop and implement new evaluation procedures for promotion, retention, tenure, and termination. Interestingly, teachers in New York City were among the state's last holdouts in reaching an agreement on evaluation. The conflict between the union and the city grew so contentious that in 2013 Governor Andrew M. Cuomo threatened to impose an agreement.

In a major concession, teachers in Syracuse consented to allow student test scores to figure in up to 20 percent of the decision-making process. Judgments would be based mostly on classroom observations, which could occur three separate times during the school year. Evaluations of teachers would lead to four possible ratings:

1. Ineffective
2. Developing
3. Effective
4. Highly Effective

An improvement plan would be developed for teachers rated ineffective or developing. All in all, teachers in Syracuse recognized that improving the district would depend on them. Collective bargaining contracts have often confounded school reformers. Change has not come easily, and it is highly questionable whether an evaluation system of the sort implemented in Syracuse would have been approved by the union without government pressure. What counts, though, is that it happened, and the hard work that produced it should be harnessed by both sides on behalf of better student performance.

***

The principals served as the workhorses upon whose compliant shoulders reform initiatives were introduced in Syracuse. They received no commensurate pay increase at the outset for the extra time they spent in their schools. They had to be instructional leaders; they had to ensure that staff members did the jobs expected of them. Possible staff development for principals and the extra demands placed on their time did not merit sufficient attention from the district as Say Yes's plans unfolded.

Some principals routinely found themselves working from 7 a.m. to 7 p.m. under a more demanding regimen. The principals' union said it did not request added compensation for the extra effort. Members would have been satisfied simply with being included in the planning process; however, they did not feel they were adequately consulted. The teachers' union, on the other hand, was less willing than the principals' union to let its members provide extra work without additional compensation. "We have a little thing called 'the contract' that needs to be negotiated," said teachers' union president Ahern.

A Framework for Learning

Contreras took the crucial step early in her second year as superintendent of promulgating a framework for teaching and learning in the Syracuse public schools. This document was a step toward bringing order and organization out of a system that allowed too many teachers to do their own thing, creating a patchwork curriculum that varied from school to school in both scope and sequence. Furthermore, implementing a framework meant that teachers could be observed, coached, and evaluated in a fairer, more predictable manner.

The rubrics that accompany the framework allow for teachers to be rated in accordance with the agreement reached with the union. There will be less guesswork about what a teacher who proves less than highly effective must do to improve. Professional development may be planned accordingly. Syracuse, in other words, put itself on the path to academic improvement by making the details of academic rigor clearer. The characteristics of rigor, as defined by the 23-page framework, are the following:

- clear understanding of and focus on the core knowledge of each discipline
- challenging mental effort appropriate to master the core knowledge
- active use of the knowledge in meaningful ways

The framework calls on teachers to plan, teach, analyze, and adjust their teaching, thereby establishing a learning environment for their students. Planning has four parts in the framework: (1) using data to set goals, (2) aligning lesson plans to district curriculum and standards, (3) selecting a balance of resources that facilitate student growth and mastery, and (4) investing students and their families in the learning process.

The teaching portion calls on teachers to communicate standards-based learning goals and their relevance, to demonstrate a clear and comprehensive understanding of content and curriculum, to incorporate multiple strategies to facilitate student interaction with and mastery of the content, to facilitate evidence-dependent questioning and thinking, to provide opportunities for students to solve complex problems and tasks, and to monitor student progress and to adjust strategically.

In order to analyze and adjust their teaching, teachers must collect student data to inform instruction in the short term and to adjust long-range planning, This analysis and adjustment also involves engaging in reflective conversations with other teachers about student progress. All the steps should produce a better learning environment for students. The framework in Syracuse examines the learning environment in terms of the extent to which it is positive and respectful, the use it makes of learning routines and space, and the degree to which teachers have established an atmosphere in which students become accountable for their own learning.

The rubric for evaluating a teacher's planning, for instance, deals with the rigor of classroom materials. The framework, as applied to this category, identifies a highly effective teacher as one who involves students in selecting rigorous texts and tasks appropriate for their individual levels of achievement. The effective teacher acts on his or her own to select rigorous texts and tasks and shares the rationale. A developing teacher selects texts and tasks at the appropriate level of rigor for some students but not necessarily for all students. An ineffective teacher selects texts and tasks at an inappropriate level of rigor.

In evaluating a teacher's quality of instruction, a rubric under teaching that applies to making the instruction clear and comprehensive looks at the manner in which the teacher connects the work to students' prior knowledge and other subject areas. It identifies the highly effective teacher as one in whose classroom students—without prompting—show understanding of these connections. The effective teacher has to engage most students in discussion about the connections to get the students to make the connections. The developing teacher occasionally connects current learning to prior knowledge and/or other subjects; only some students in these classrooms discuss the connections. The ineffective teacher does not connect current learning to prior knowledge and/or other subject areas.

***

Clearly, everything that affects teaching and learning will not originate in the classroom. What happens outside the classroom by way of planning and through policies of various bodies affects instructional practices. Whatever the origin of policies and procedures, though, they should be considered in the context of what they will mean for student growth. Moreover, implementation will usually depend on the knowledge and skill of teachers and their acceptance of what others are asking or expecting of them.

7

Extended Time for Learning

Given the high rate of poverty in Syracuse and the fact that so many children enter school lagging behind their more advantaged peers, Say Yes—at its heart—sought a commitment from the school system to extend the school day and the school year. The goal is to widen and deepen the experiences youngsters have beyond the normal school calendar. Both the after-school and summer programs seek to inculcate cognitive enrichment and to yoke the extra time to the curriculum. A grant in 2011 from the Wallace Foundation was designed to assist Say Yes in these efforts.

For the last twenty years, some of the nation's educators have urged schools to find more time for learning. They view the traditional school calendar as an anachronism and say that more learning time during the hours and days when children aren't normally in school is crucial to overcoming gaps between advantaged and disadvantaged students. The Charles Stewart Mott Foundation recognized this need as far back as 1935 when it began supporting the community school concept to keep buildings open beyond the usual school hours.

Extended learning time and after-school programs in particular have become the pet project of major foundations in the years since 2000. They back these efforts with relish. Ford Foundation, Wallace Foundation, George Soros's Open Society Foundation, the William T. Grant Foundation, and others have poured money into programs that seek to make better use of time, including weekends and summer.

In May 2012, more than one hundred individuals and organizations banded together to form the Time to Succeed Coalition, running a full-page advertisement in *The New York Times* advocating that "our kids need more time in the classroom." Then near the end of 2012, the Ford Foundation announced a collaboration with the National Center on Time & Learning to create a partnership that would take its first step by working with 35 schools in ten districts in five states to develop high-quality and sustainable expanded learning time. The pilot project scheduled the program to start in fall 2013. The Say Yes foundation is in tune with this movement.

There were precedents for this trend. The federal government sponsored the National Education Commission on Time and Learning that in 1994 issued an early pivotal report on the topic *Prisoners of Time*. The Charles Stewart Mott

Foundation and the George Lucas Educational Foundation supported *A New Day for Learning*, a 2007 report. Other groups released reports in subsequent years, culminating in two important documents in 2011: *Making Summer Count*, from Rand Corporation, and *Reimagining the School Day: Making More Time for Learning*, from the Wallace Foundation. Despite the flurry of interest, though, by 2011 not many more than two thousand of the nation's schools had added or were experimenting with school days at least 10 to 60 percent longer and school years of up to thirty days longer.[1] For the most part, the 180-day school year remained as fixed in practice as breakfast in the morning and dinner in the evening.

Individual stories attest to the importance that an after-school program can have in some lives, especially for youngsters in the inner city, where idle hours after the end of the school day can prove deadly. Shavar Jeffries looks back thankfully: "When I was ten, my mother was killed. Shortly thereafter, my father abandoned my family. My grandmother took me in and put me in after-school programs run by the Boys & Girls Club of Newark, where I received academic, social, and emotional support that she could not provide by herself. These programs helped change my life."[2] Indeed, Jeffries went on to attend Duke University and Columbia Law School, serve as a senior executive in the New Jersey attorney general's office, and become an associate professor of law at Seton Hall University. In 2013, he was running for mayor of Newark.

The nation's largest school system, New York City, probably has the most after-school activity. But it is a hodgepodge, comprising many separate pieces that fit together like a jigsaw puzzle with some of the pieces missing. Some schools rely mostly on local funds, others on state funds, and still others on federal funds. In addition, foundations and parent groups sponsor some of the programs. Some principals work directly with individual nonprofit groups to support particular after-school activities, like chess or robotic clubs. There is not even an official count of how many of the city's 1,700 schools offer after-school programs. Some parents must pay for the services, while others get them free.

To further confuse the issue, one of the most highly regarded offerings, operating in 55 of the city's public schools on a $16-million budget, is known by more than one name. Originally called The After-School Corporation and sometimes recognized by the initials TASC, it has transitioned toward the name ExpandED Schools. Most distinctive and most important about this organization is its effort to integrate regular school hours with those that normally follow the regular school day.

The largest part of the enterprise in New York is the city-operated Out-of-School Time (OST) Program, overseen by the city's Department of Youth and Community Development. The most recent study of this program led to conclusions that could help Syracuse and other locales bolster their programs. It pointed to the need to establish an explicit structure to promote a learning environment, enforce an attendance policy that emphasizes engagement, use outcome measures to evaluate the program, recruit capable staff, and train and monitor that staff.[3]

The tide of opinion is running strongly in favor of extended learning time, but one hopes the zeal does not blind advocates to the need to ensure that extra time adds up to a significant benefit for children. "[S]ome worry that it may be gaining steam too rapidly as a fix for schools that lack the know-how, resources, or research to implement it effectively," stated an article in *Education Week*.[4]

After-School Programs in Syracuse

Say Yes began an after-school program in six elementary schools for pupils in kindergarten through third grade in the first quadrant in December 2008, just months after it began operating in Syracuse. A summer program for the same target group started in 2009. The program expanded as Say Yes reached into the other quadrants. Whatever the outcome of Say Yes's efforts in Syracuse, it could be that the after-school and summer programs will be the most enduring as they pose the least threat to the status quo. Research has shown that structural add-ons that do not disturb the standard operating procedures of schools have the best chance of lasting.[5]

Say Yes provided transportation for students both after school and during the summer, a mundane but vital feature to encourage families to let children participate. Otherwise, participation in extended learning time programs can languish. Some families in Syracuse, for example, could not attend a celebratory barbeque one year for lack of transportation. "The transportation piece is critical," said Debra Schoening, supervising director of school improvement for the district. Say Yes appealed unsuccessfully to a foundation for a contribution of $25,000 to pay for families to attend open houses at school and for busing for summer field trips.

How It Is Organized

The after-school program in Syracuse operates for two hours every afternoon, Monday through Thursday in the elementary schools for all grade levels. Starting just after 3 p.m., most schools devote the first hour to academics, extending the content subjects of the school day. By and large, regular classroom teachers lead these sessions. Sometimes the teachers tutor children, and other times they help with homework. The district pays teachers for this extra time commitment but does not require them to take on the assignment. This is one difference between a formal extension of the school day by contract and doing it as an add-on, as happens in Syracuse and most other school systems with late-afternoon programs.

During the second hour, beginning by 4 p.m. and ending by 5 p.m., the program focuses on enrichment—a potpourri of cultural offerings ranging from dance to art to music to creative writing. Students produce work about which they can feel a sense of growth and achievement by, say, exhibiting it, performing it, or making presentations of it. This part of the program tries to follow a widely used model of enrichment, originally employed for gifted students, that seeks to develop children's talents and creativity. Some regular teachers stay for the second hour, but most of those who lead students during this time are not regular teachers.

Some schools apportion the time differently. Syracuse's Frazer K–8 School, for instance, uses the two additional hours entirely for academics on Mondays and Wednesdays and then has only enrichment on Tuesdays and Thursdays. With teachers and teachers' assistants constituting most of the after-school staff on Mondays and Wednesdays, the school uses the time to integrate intervention practices for students who struggle with concepts covered during the regular school day in math and English language arts. Staff members who provide social-emotional support are available to students during the first hour of the program all four days.

A representative of a community-based organization retained by Say Yes provides oversight for the after-school program at each school in conjunction with a lead teacher. Say Yes awarded contracts to the community-based organizations (CBOs) to operate the second hour of the program. Children remain in their own schools for the after-school program; they no longer have to be transported to other sites as happened before Say Yes arrived, when CBOs like the YMCA and Boys and Girls Clubs provided the facilities.

The role of the CBOs in the after-school program raises several questions about the best way to take advantage of this added time, issues that school districts everywhere must address as they, too, extend the school day. Say Yes's approach in Syracuse puts some of the control of the time in the hands of noneducators. Also, in eliminating the role of the Say Yes site directors, who formerly oversaw after-school activities, Say Yes diminished its direct influence on the program. The partnership that Say Yes established with the CBOs had the effect of placating groups that might otherwise have resented Say Yes for usurping a portion of the day that was an important revenue source for them.

The question remains, though, of whether the after-school program provides the academic substance that so many youngsters in Syracuse require in order to wipe out learning deficits. Some schools in the city clearly have more effective after-school programs than others, and the degree to which the academic portion should tie itself to the school day remains unresolved by Say Yes and the school administration.

The after-school program is voluntary for students, who pay nothing to enroll. A little more than half of elementary school youngsters join. There is concern that some children who have the most to gain do not enroll. Moreover, behavior problems on the buses, where there were no aides to supervise youngsters, led to the exclusion of some students whose parents were sometimes told by after-school officials simply that their children could not attend the session because the transportation run no longer made it possible to include them.

Up Close at Meachem School

Mike Spring, a social worker who doesn't "profess to be a teacher," represented Catholic Charities at the Meachem School, a pre-K–5 school. Regular teachers presided over 13 of the 17 classrooms, and teachers' assistants ran the other after-school classes. Many children remained in the rooms in which they had sat during the school day and had their regular teachers, lending some continuity to this portion of the day that is not always found in such programs. In visiting a number of classrooms, I discovered that during the first hour, the so-called academic part of the afternoon, students spent most of the time doing the homework assigned to them during the regular school day. Some teachers walked around their rooms assisting children, and others sat at the front, available to youngsters who requested help.

Students in a classroom of mixed third and fourth graders did multiplication problems on a worksheet. Multiplication homework on worksheets was also the order of the day in a room that had only fourth graders. Some observers might wonder whether filling the hour with homework is the best use of time, but this was how the classroom teachers wanted it done. It was apparently the only way to ensure that the participating children would do their homework and not show up the next day with worksheets as blank as a freshly erased chalkboard. There was also more opportunity for teachers to provide individual help with homework as after-school classes were smaller than regular school day classes since not all students took advantage of the free program.

The homework a classroom of fifth graders was doing involved a review of the scientific method about which the children had been learning for about two weeks. The unit taught them to follow a procedure that involved stating a problem, gathering information, giving a possible solution called a hypothesis, testing the hypothesis, and then recording and analyzing the test data.

The busily engaged students were preparing for a lab scheduled for the next day. The teacher wanted to hone their powers of observation so that they could draw inferences, make predictions, and classify what they learned in the lesson. The next day they would wear goggles as they mixed borax, corn starch, and glue to create "flubbers"—polymers formed from a chemical reaction. The assignment: See how high the flubbers will bounce so as to discover whether changing the mix of ingredients alters the outcome of the experiment.

In yet another after-school class of fifth graders, the teacher led a rather traditional lesson on mathematical place value. She asked students to identify the place of various numbers in the figure 634,298,502.78, which she projected onto a screen. "What is the place of the 9? What is the place of the .7?" she asked, continuing in this fashion. Students came to the front of the room, next to the screen, to give their answers. Gradually, she shifted into subtraction problems involving decimals. The students eventually turned to their homework, several pages of problems such as rounding to the nearest tenth or nearest one hundredth and working with the order properties and the grouping properties of addition. And so it went during the first hour of the program.

Gears shifted smoothly as children segued into the second hour of the program. At Meachem, this might mean going to an art room to string beads into jewelry, beating drums in the music room, playing soccer in the gym, doing step dancing with a touch of hip-hop on the stage in the auditorium, or any number of other possibilities that stirred the juices and broke the focus on academics.

An evaluation of Say Yes's after-school program praised the qualifications of staff and credited program directors for their attention to the ability of the staff to facilitate positive interactions and maintain student engagement and enjoyment. Yet this document, the Afterschool Implementation Report of 2012, raised questions about the informality of program monitoring and the wide variations in staff development. Sessions to orient staff members varied from two hours to two days. The report challenged Say Yes to give more support to recruitment, hiring, and training of staff. There were also questions in the report about the universal use of a project-based approach to programming.[6] It is probably safe to conclude that Say Yes's after-school implementation is as good as most offerings of this kind and better than many.

As for the impact of such programs in the long run, one may turn to a meta-analysis of many programs by the Afterschool Alliance, an advocacy organization supported by foundations, corporations, and the U.S. Department of Education. Pulling together the findings of many studies, it offers the following findings:

- improved school attendance and engagement in learning
- improved test scores and grades
- increased benefits with more frequent and more regular attendance
- the largest gains for students at greatest risk
- positive impact on self-concept and decision making
- a view that programs keep children safe
- reduced truancy and improved behavior[7]

The Summer Program in Syracuse

The summer program for elementary pupils in Syracuse operated all day for four weeks with academics in the morning and recreation and enrichment—featuring experiential learning—in the afternoon. The program sought to prepare children for the classroom work they would face in the fall. Undergraduate and graduate students from Syracuse University received stipends to serve as counselors. School officials wanted families to regard summer attendance as merely an extension of the school year, not a kind of punishment, which is often the case with summer school. Attendance during the summer rose each year.

The program ran for six weeks when Say Yes started it in 2009 and was trimmed in length mostly for financial reasons. The shorter duration concerned some people given that youngsters probably would have benefited from a longer program. The average student loses about one month of academic knowledge and content between the end of one school year and the start of the next. The losses are worse for low-income students.[8] Teachers must devote weeks in the fall to getting them back to where they were when vacation started. The right kind of summer program can help compensate for what experts call summer-learning loss.[9]

The extension of the school year into summer in Syracuse had the feel, during the morning academic portion, of the regular school year. No-nonsense teachers from the regular faculty met with students in classrooms in which until a few weeks earlier the students had sat for their regular classes. There were few concessions to the season. Teachers wore the attire of serious workers and upheld classroom decorum in this season of sandals and shorts, when youngsters would otherwise be playing, swimming, and lolling about.

Up Close at Huntington School

Elementary-age children from three separate schools assembled in Huntington K–8 School, a formidable brick structure from the 1920s with walls so thick that cell phones can't readily receive a signal in some areas. This classic, two-story building has the wide corridors and spacious stairwells seldom seen in newer schools, which are designed as if children shrank over the years so as to conserve space and save construction costs. Many of the classrooms at Huntington display American flags and wall clocks, though the times on them varied.

One morning in one of the classrooms, 14 children scheduled to enter fifth grade in the fall practiced their reading. The teacher, in a black, sleeveless summer dress and with an authoritative voice that projected to the far reaches of the room, asked the children to read aloud to each other. The students were preparing for a reading test. A cacophony of voices filled the room as she had each student see how many words he or she could read in one minute. She warned them in advance: "Don't just focus on how fast you read. I'll be looking for comprehension."

As in many of the nation's elementary classrooms, there was a word wall on which the teacher had inscribed new words as students first encountered them in their books. The latest words included *Sahara, Mediterranean, prospered, Ghana,* and *hieroglyphs.* The topic at hand was ancient Africa. The teacher reminded the children that reading was not meant to be an activity they pursued only at school. She told them they had to read at home, as well, if they wanted to reach reading levels they ought to attain. If any of the children wanted to differ with her opinion, they didn't say so. This veteran had complete command of her classroom.

Down the hall, 13 students who had just completed the fourth grade were also studying Africa. The teacher assigned different groups of students to prepare oral reports on the specifics of the people about whom they had read—their food, festivals, homes, and clothing. As he or she got ready to speak, each youngster took the seat in the middle of a horseshoe-shaped arrangement of desks, where the teacher had previously sat. Now the student, holding the attention of peers, as the teacher had done, could be the center of attention. The students were to emphasize the main ideas about each topic in their reports. Among the main ideas that most impressed the children were that the people traded slaves for gold, their clothes differed from group to group, children used shells and seeds to play games, and slaves were allowed to own property.

In yet another classroom, where music played softly in the background, children about to enter third grade played a kind of Jeopardy! quiz to promote their math skills. A homemade game board had pockets from which questions could be pulled depending on the sort of category each table of four students chose. The possible selections dealt, for instance, with subtraction, addition, and shapes of objects. The students could pick the number of points the right response would be worth. Each group went for broke and picked 25, the maximum amount of points for answering the toughest question.

The first group of students selected "Shapes," clearly a venture into geometry. The teacher held up a shape that had been assembled from pieces. She asked how many blocks made up the shape, which was quickly identified as a square.

The students got the right answer: eight. Then it was on to "Subtraction Action" and a question about Bobby, who bought a dozen doughnuts, ate two of them, and gave two to both of his friends, Joe and Mario. How many doughnuts remained?

"It All Adds Up" category yielded a question that gave students four sets of numbers—3 + 6, 5 + 6, 8 + 2, and 9 + 2—and asked them which set totaled 10. Then another question, designed to test their skills of estimation, involved looking at various numbers quickly and deciding which numbers represented the sum of 25 and 34. The teacher used the occasion to discuss "rounding up" and "rounding down," skills that would help the students in their estimates.

All in all, the summer academic curriculum was scripted, and the teachers had limited leeway to vary from it, except in terms of their methods of presentation. "What I try to do," said one of the summer school teachers, "is bring in as much literacy as possible. I reinforce vocabulary and clarify students' misconceptions. I try to give them questions that cause higher-level thinking. I want them to respond in full sentences. How they speak is how they write." Some teachers set pedagogical goals that may not have been spelled out in the curriculum but that the teachers nonetheless considered to be to the students' advantage.

Summer school had its complications. The 491 students assigned to Huntington attended voluntarily. Among those who did not enroll were students who had the most to gain from the experience. Furthermore, some who signed up came only sporadically. Some who attended most regularly were among the best students, who had the least need for an extended school year. Thus, class sizes on a given day could range from a dozen to more than two dozen. Moreover, it was not necessarily clear to the teachers which students were classified for individualized educational plans during the regular school year, leaving them without information they needed to meet the special needs of youngsters with disabilities.

The Enrichment Portion

The other part of the summer program involved enrichment from 11 a.m. to 2 p.m. Mondays through Thursdays. After a morning of academics, elementary-age students, from kindergarten through fifth grade, participated in activities more typical of summer camp—often with a learning component. Youngsters could choose at the beginning of the summer session whether they wanted to concentrate on science and technology or the arts and then maintained that focus throughout the weeks of the afternoon program. Most of the counselors were college students.

In one such classroom, a counselor in a blue Say Yes t-shirt sat in an easy chair reading to a dozen children sitting on a rug and looking up at her. These were former kindergarteners who would be in first grade in the fall. She held the book wide open, sitting at an angle so that they could see the pictures. The group had gone to the zoo the previous week. Now they learned about habitats and the differences among animals that live in jungles, forests, and oceans. It was clear that the counselor, enthusiastic about her assignment, lacked the classroom management techniques of the professional teachers who met with the students earlier in the day. She had to keep pausing to get these six-year-olds to pay attention.

In another classroom, students in the upper elementary grades mixed concoctions of corn syrup and water in a study of liquids and solids. They followed directions they had obtained online from a program called Hooked on Science. The counselors prodded the youngsters to discuss what they observed in the experiment. Almost everyone agreed that the mixture was icky. They were intrigued as they watched a liquid transform itself into a soft solid. Even the color changed. The youngsters, though, were slow to mention their observations, and the counselor had to keep soliciting their input:

"The bottom is hard, and the top is soft," a child finally volunteered.

"When you touch it, it feels like something that's alive," said another.

"It's gooey, like strawberry milk," came another response.

They turned their attention to the properties of corn starch, which the students had learned can expand, explode, or solidify, and then followed it with another discussion of the states of matter. Tomorrow, the instructor told the students, they would spray glue on sand and see what happens.

Youngsters who elected to spend their enrichment time on the arts had an entirely different experience. They were in the school library rehearsing for a performance of *The Jungle Book*. The children sang one of the show's songs, "The Bare Necessities," as a counselor accompanied them on a portable keyboard. Then they assumed their choreographed positions to dance to the music. These arts students—including children from all the elementary grades—spent their entire summer rehearsing for the show they would present to other students at the end of the summer. Only three boys were in the group of more than a dozen children.

Elsewhere in the building, youngsters changed into their bathing suits and took lessons as part of the YMCA's Urban Swim Program, offered in conjunction with the mayor's office. An annex with an Olympic-sized pool was added to Huntington during a 1984 modernization. Swimming lessons are in short supply in many inner-city areas, and so the children tended to be beginners. The YMCA distributed swimsuits and towels so that those who wanted to participate could do so.

"We test them for their skills and give them a lesson each day," said the instructor, a sports and aquatics coordinator for the downtown YMCA. "Many of the kids are apprehensive about being around the water." Swimming is an optional part of the summer school, and parents have to sign up the students to participate. Interest was so high that the program had a waiting list. For nonswimmers, lessons began with learning to jump into the water, putting one's face in the water, and opening one's eyes underwater. Then the children learned how to float on their bellies and on their backs, until, finally, they were ready to swim for 15 seconds, first on their stomachs and then on their backs.

***

Any large-scale, national solution for extending learning must await a school calendar redesign. For their part, teachers say that adding hours and days to the schedule will depend on districts paying them more money. Citizens, on the other hand, especially in these difficult economic times, are not eager to increase the burden of school taxes.

In the meantime, officials of after-school programs would do well to examine their practices. A study in Philadelphia of school-based community centers found that program management is key and chances are that not all summer programs are well managed. "When youth of all ages rated an activity as well managed, they reported getting more out of the activity at each step in the learning process," said the report. It also found that students felt more engaged when they had input in shaping activities and that adult support was crucial in engaging youngsters in activities.[10]

8

Making Time More Productive

As a long-range objective, Syracuse wants to stretch the regular calendar to run through much of the summer so that parents and students will regard it as a seamless extension of the school year. In the meantime, Syracuse's new superintendent hoped to see the summer program restored to at least the six weeks that it originally ran. An element of the $4.2-million grant from the Wallace Foundation included money to pilot, evaluate, and refine extended learning time. These efforts could, presumably, set the stage for Syracuse to give its students more time for learning.

Money is an issue in Syracuse and elsewhere when it comes to summer and after-school learning and other ways to extend the traditional school day and year. When revenues are insufficient for the task, school systems look for outside funds. This was the case in New York City in 2012, when private donors provided $1.7 million for an Early Literacy Skills Camp for first through third graders and for a Twenty-First Century Skills Camp for sixth through eighth graders. But such ventures, aimed at youngsters who need extra help, served only 720 students in a district with an enrollment of more than one million.

In fiscally stretched California, some districts mounted summer programs in 2012 only by tapping into foundations and outside funders. In Sacramento City Unified School District, for example, half the money for summer programs came from donations by such organizations as the David and Lucile Packard Foundation, the Magic Johnson Foundation, and Best Buy. Similarly, other northern California unified school districts such as Elk Grove and Twin Rivers also relied on outside funders to support summer school. As it is, the regular school year lasts just 36 weeks a year and often amounts to less than it appears. Testing consumes a growing number of hours and days of the school year. Moreover, when schools dismiss students early due to staff development meetings or weather emergencies, those partial days still count as full days toward meeting the 180-day requirement.

Longer School Days, Longer School Years

Massachusetts, a national leader in seeking to lengthen the school day, funded pilot programs to give students about an added two hours a day. The Expanded

Learning Time (ELT) Initiative began in 2006 and by 2012 had spread to 19 schools in nine of the state's districts, encompassing 10,500 students. The districts used state funds to redesign the school day, adding time for core subjects, enrichment, and teacher planning and professional development.

The program's guiding principles involve three hundred extra hours of learning for each student; an emphasis on improving academic outcomes; a separate redesign approach for each school to take cognizance of such factors as labor agreements, compensation, and work schedules; and partnerships with colleges, community-based organizations, health centers, and businesses. The program started with eight schools in the first cohort and added schools in subsequent years. Altogether, 78 percent of participating students were from low-income families.

Advocates of longer school days who contend that such initiatives are a panacea for low student achievement would be disappointed by the results in Massachusetts. The impact on performance is inconsistent, lacking any clear pattern of improvement in achievement scores. On average, extended learning time produced no statistically significant effects after one, two, three, or four years of implementation on state tests for third-, fourth-, or seventh-grade English language arts or on math or science in the eighth grade.[1] Moreover, both students and teachers complained of feeling fatigued by the extra hours. Nonetheless, researchers found that extended time led to a more sustained focus on literacy instruction and separate enrichment classes in which almost all students participated. Sixty-five percent of teachers in the affected schools joined in collaborative planning time weekly or more often.

Outcomes of the Massachusetts initiative underscore the need to monitor the implementation of extended time programs to ensure fidelity to some sort of plan for using the extra time wisely. Schools in Massachusetts had great flexibility in deciding how to expand their schedules. Maximizing the value of such programs may mean more closely watching how schools use the time.

In Chicago, the teachers' strike at the opening of the 2012–13 school year focused national attention on the issue of extending learning time. Rahm Emanuel adopted the idea of a longer school day almost as soon as he became mayor. The city's school day of five hours and 45 minutes was one of the shortest of any big city in the country. At first, Emanuel called for a seven-and-a-half-hour day for students in elementary school. Eventually, the mayor shortened his demand, and elementary students ended up gaining 75 minutes while those in high schools got thirty more minutes each day. The Chicago Teachers Union objected vociferously to any possibility of working longer for the same pay, even filing an unfair labor complaint. The school system ultimately agreed to a salary increase and promised to hire more teachers to relieve class loads.

The battle over the length of their working day helped lead to the strike, but the teachers' action revolved around more than that issue. The form that teacher evaluations would take also figured in the dispute. Amid the controversy, some critics sided with neither the teachers' union nor the city, calling the longer school day simply a matter of babysitting. Joseph Epstein, a Chicago-based essayist, wrote that a longer school day in the city "can only mean more torture for kids not really receiving a good education to begin with."[2]

Even in France, with its national education system, the president's call for adding a fifth day to what was a four-day school week elicited cries of outrage from teachers. He proposed to open schools for a half-day on the fifth day and to shorten school hours on the other four days to compensate educators for the longer week. They still objected, though, saying they already had a heavy work load and should be paid more if the weekly schedule grew by a half day.[3]

In the United States, it was parents as well as teachers who objected to a longer school day in North Carolina's Charlotte-Mecklenburg district. The school board added 45 minutes to the elementary and middle school day in 2011. The action helped save money by reducing bus runs. But there was a push in 2013 to eliminate the extra time by those who said it burdened children to attend school from 9:15 a.m. to 4:15 p.m.

Other Ways to Extend Learning Time

A longer school day and a longer school year are the most obvious extensions of learning time, but they are not the only possibilities for extracting more time. Regular attendance makes it more likely that a child will have more time to learn. Time on task is way to ensure that students get more out of their lessons. Homework is so common that it is readily overlooked as one of the routes to more learning time. Saturdays remain largely unexploited as learning opportunities. Independent study is another vehicle for making time more productive. Tutoring, too, accommodates the need for more learning time. The Internet has opened a world of possibilities for students to pursue more learning from home in typical after-school hours.

A plethora of holidays throughout the year close down schools on as many as a dozen individual days, and winter and spring breaks knock weeks at a time out of the schedules of most districts. Recess, too, could be evaluated in terms of the number of cumulative days it consumes.

Attendance

The most obvious way to give students in Syracuse and elsewhere more time for learning is to make sure they come to school. Excessive absence robs some youngsters of learning time. Children of all ages are chronic absentees, and the problem is worst in high schools, where students have more control over their time. If they would only attend school regularly, they would be in a position to gain more from their education. A study of results on the National Assessment of Educational Progress, reviewing data since the mid-1990s, shows that students with high rates of absenteeism score disproportionately at the basic or below-basic levels. In fact, one-quarter of those at below-basic levels missed more than five weeks of school during the year.[4]

"By third grade," write the authors of another study, "the children who missed too much of kindergarten and first grade are falling behind in reading, research shows. By sixth grade, chronic absence becomes an early-warning sign that students will drop out of high school."[5] The researchers urged Congress to insert into any reauthorization of the federal education law a requirement that the percentage of students missing 10 percent of school days serve as a metric in grant applications and assessments.

A study of school absences in New York City found that in 298 schools, at least 20 percent of fourth graders were chronically absent—missing 10 percent of school days or more. This problem correlates with low achievement.[6] The *Boston Globe* analyzed attendance at that city's public high schools and found that more than a third of students are chronically absent. At just one school, East Boston High, half the enrolled students missed at least 19 days—amounting to 10 percent of the school year—during the 2011–12 school year.[7]

By and large, high school students in Syracuse also miss about 10 percent of their school days, according to attendance figures from the district. The only one of the city's five high schools in which more than 90 percent of the students consistently attend classes is the Institute of Technology of Syracuse Central, known as ITC, where youngsters from throughout the city enroll by choice. The four neighborhood high schools have annual attendance rates ranging from 85.1 percent to 89.1 percent. The problem manifests itself in all grades at the city's high schools. Students do not attend school more regularly as they move through the higher grades. Syracuse students in middle schools tend to have better rates of attendance than those in high school. It is not unusual for 95 percent of the Syracuse students in grades six through eight to be at school regularly.

Absenteeism is not a problem that schools alone can solve. Schools need help from the home. Adults must wake up early enough to ensure children prepare for school in a timely fashion. It is up to the family to underscore the importance of regular and punctual attendance for students. These are habits that will prepare young people for many aspects of their lives.

This is not to say that schools cannot do more to combat absenteeism. Young people want to belong; they want to be a part of something.[8] Schools that do more to connect with their students should be able to increase attendance. In addition, lessons should engage students and involve them in their learning. Schools have no obligation to entertain students, but they ought to be able to hold their attention with instruction that is compelling and well planned.

Early starting times, especially in middle and high school, adversely affect attendance and tardiness. Ringing the bell at a later hour might have a favorable effect in this regard. A study of later school starting times in the Wake County Public Schools in North Carolina found that delaying the bell by as much as an hour—changing from 7:30 a.m. to start at 8:30 a.m.—led to increases in standardized test scores of at least 2 percentage points. This impact was greatest among low-achieving students.[9]

Absenteeism exacts a price beyond the loss of learning time. Many states base financial aid to school districts on average daily attendance. Young people who are not present when teachers take attendance jeopardize the fiscal health of their schools. And the situation may be even worse than the numbers show. I have spent time at high schools that take attendance in the morning and then students proceed to cut most of their classes the remainder of the day.

School reform of the sort promoted by Say Yes should end up creating a climate that is inviting to students, one in which students want to go to class because teaching and learning is more engaging. A comparison of attendance in the Syracuse City School District from the 2010–11 school year to the 2011–12 school year does, in fact, show slight increases. At the elementary level, where Say Yes had its greatest impact, average daily attendance rose from 91.4 to 92.2 percent. There are at least a half-dozen elementary schools in Syracuse at which attendance averages between 94 and 98 percent, which compares favorably with almost any urban school. Only time will tell if attendance statistics hold and continue to improve as Say Yes grows its program into the upper grades.

Time on Task

In 1963, John Carroll, a psychology professor, wrote a seminal article that got educators talking about the link between learning and the time spent learning.[10] The topic received wide attention by the 1970s, when California's Beginning Teacher Evaluation Study examined what it referred to as academic learning time. This notion has been on and off the radar of educational researchers ever since. One researcher writes, "Many educators are now convinced that if student time on task is increased, an increase in student achievement will follow." She cautions, though, "They [teachers] need to know how to use time effectively in a variety of activities, how to vary time with different achievement groups, and how to support students to keep them on task."[11]

Researchers reporting their findings in Teachers College Record found that "minutes spent on instruction" make a difference in achievement growth for low-income students and for black students in kindergarten and first grade, the two levels the scholars examined. Time is more important than teacher quality or type of instruction, according to this study. Some educators define time in this sense as "opportunity to learn." A caveat of the researchers is their assertion that "low achievers tend to get the worst teachers," and, therefore, time in the hands of such teachers may not be used to the greatest advantage.[12]

In other words, unless teachers use time well, chances are that increasing the number of school days and the length of the school day may not deliver a payoff in terms of greater achievement. There are implications here for the initial preparation of teachers in colleges of education and for the professional development they get once they work in school systems. Teachers need the classroom management skills to deal with disruptions, the ability to hold the loss of time to a minimum during transitions from one activity to another, and the knowledge to individualize the work and engage all students.

A Blended Day

At Thurgood Marshall Academy Lower School (TMALS) in Harlem, just across the river from Yankee Stadium, they eschew the label "after-school." They regard the late afternoon hours as simply an expansion of the school day. Joshua Livingston of Abyssinian Development Corporation (ADC), the community-based organization that partners with the school, said TMALS had successfully "erased the hard line" that in most places separates the regular school day from the after-school portion.

The day runs from 8:30 a.m. to 5:30 p.m., and at least some of the classroom teachers remain the entire time, usually continuing to teach the children with whom they spent the earlier part of the day. In the late afternoon, though, they no longer feel obliged to provide a specified number of minutes to each subject in order to meet the requirements of the Common Core curriculum. They welcome the opportunity to deliver more flexible instruction so they may reinforce the lessons taught earlier and cover material to which they had to give short shrift.

The late afternoon is a time, for example, during which some pupils perform science experiments for which there was not sufficient time earlier. The school, in part, attributes increased scores in English and math to the extended day. A third-grade teacher, for example, takes advantage of the added time to review with the students the homework they handed in earlier, making the homework a basis for a learning experience she does not have time to develop earlier in the day.

Like all public elementary schools in New York City, TMALS—which 214 pupils from kindergarten through fifth grade attend by choice—ends the contractual portion of the day at 2:50 p.m. for most students. Attendance beyond this point is voluntary, but more than 90 percent of students choose to stay. Most youngsters eat snacks and do their homework for about the next 35 minutes. Then just before 3:30 p.m., the expanded day continues with a two-hour block that twice a week consists of academics and twice a week offers enrichment activities such as art, dance, and sports. On the fifth day, Friday, most children perform community service.

Ten of the 11 classroom teachers remain until 5:30 p.m. on at least some days and receive a stipend for doing so. Volunteers from the community and members of the federal government's AmeriCorps program augment the regular faculty and lead many of the enrichment activities. The school leverages the help of such organizations as the Studio Museum in Harlem. The entrepreneurial principal, Dawn Brooks DeCosta, stretches the funds she gets from the city's education department so they cover 30 percent of the cost of the expanded learning time. ADC, an arm of Abyssinian Baptist Church, pays 10 percent of the cost, and the rest of the $350,200 budget for the expanded program comes from a potpourri of grants for which the school constantly scrounges.

The approach at Thurgood Marshall Academy, housed in a former Catholic school, exemplifies the ExpandED School model that The After-School Corporation of New York City has encouraged in a group of pilot schools. Under this philosophy, TMALS strives to spread the schedule, the budget, the curriculum, the staffing, and even the professional development over a nine-hour day. Each spring, a detailed planning process puts all these pieces in place for the coming school year. When, for instance, the school purchases microscopes for the expansion of science education in the late afternoon classes, the planners consider how teachers may make use of those same microscopes before 2:50 p.m.

While Thurgood Marshall Academy and other pilot schools in the ExpandED model have not fully blended all aspects of the longer school day, these models are well ahead of what Say Yes has achieved in this regard in Syracuse and ahead of most other extended day programs around the country. These pilot programs lead the way in demonstrating what a fully integrated school day may look like.

Homework

People don't ordinarily think of homework as an extension of the school day, but that is what it is—for better or for worse. Most frequently, homework allows students to review what they have learned or prepare for what will be taught next. Homework also may provide enrichment, going beyond regular lessons to raise learning to a higher level. Homework may also be a waste of time, merely busy work that adds little to children's learning while appeasing adults concerned about idleness.

Teachers usually have less control over homework than they do over lessons they impart in person. The home environment may not support students in doing such work. Youngsters may not have a quiet place to study; there may not be a desk or even a table available. There may be no one to answer questions that arise. Students may be tired or have too many other demands on their time to do their homework. Schools, in other words, cannot count on homework to extend learning. Psychologist Kenneth Goldberg maintains that there may be good reasons why some students do not do their homework. It is not necessarily that they are lazy or unmotivated, he says, but they may have unrecognized learning problems, and their slow pace of learning may lead to endless struggles to complete the assignment.[13]

However, the most diligent students tend to complete their homework assignments, and the most dedicated parents tend to reinforce the school in encouraging their children to carry out the assignments and may help or coach their children in the work. The impact of doing homework, though, may not always have the intended effect. A study of math and science homework assigned to eighteen thousand tenth graders found that time spent on homework has little connection to better grades but has a positive effect on performance on standardized tests. The authors say teachers should give greater thought to how to use homework more effectively and to what purpose.[14]

Critics of homework abound, but many studies have found that homework—properly conceived—can promote scholastic achievement, especially at the secondary level.[15] Research also indicates that more homework—to a reasonable extent—makes a greater contribution to student achievement than too little homework.[16] Therefore, a school system trying to overcome learning gaps among its students, as in Syracuse, would do well to view homework—properly employed—as one of several vehicles for providing additional time for learning. But all homework is not equal. It is up to teachers to be sure that homework amounts to more than just busy work. Moreover, teachers should try to give students feedback on their completed homework assignments.

The Syracuse City School District recognizes a role for homework in its stated policy, but whether this policy always prevails is questionable. Policy #4730 states that teachers should ensure that homework assignments are purposeful and clear and explained in advance in class. The policy goes on to say that the work should be reviewed, corrected, and returned to students in a timely manner. The Syracuse policy also sets parameters for the amount of time students should devote to homework and the frequency with which it should be assigned—twenty minutes four times a week in the second and third grades with the time devoted to homework growing to sixty to ninety minutes daily in the eleventh and twelfth grades.

Taking Advantage of Saturdays

Saturday is a wasted day in elementary and secondary education. The five-day school week reigns, and educators presume that children require not one but two days of rest, more than God needed to create the world. The Harlem chapter of Say Yes has shown the possibilities of a new paradigm by holding classes on most Saturdays throughout the calendar year, something that has not happened in Syracuse.

Students in the Harlem Say Yes program attended 53 different middle schools, and so it was a challenge on Saturdays to provide them with classes that interlocked with their regular weekday studies. The existence of the new Common Core curriculum, though, allowed the Saturday classes to operate with some assurance that the studies would link to the children's Monday-through-Friday work. Furthermore, the Saturday teachers, all paid stipends by Say Yes, were drawn from among the faculty students saw during the week.

And so it was that I visited the Say Yes Saturday program on one particular Saturday in February 2013. Classes met in seven separate classrooms at Teachers College, Columbia University, near the Harlem homes of many of the students. They were eighth graders on the brink of entering high school.

Youngsters were studying the Greek myths in an English class where, after learning about myths and the 12 labors of Hercules during two previous sessions, they now prepared to write their own myths. Three charts taped to the wall in front of them guided their work. On one, as a sample of what they might do, the teacher had invented a mythological creature, named her Jessopia, and ascribed her attributes. On another poster, labeled Character Strengths and Faults, the teacher guided the students as they brainstormed through Jessopia's characteristics based on the attributes the teacher created for her. The third chart, still blank, was one on which the students would sequence the myth.

In another classroom, this one devoted to math, the teacher projected equations, one after another, onto a screen. The students honed their knowledge of polynomials and factoring. Mathematical terms filled the air: radicals, perfect square factoring, factor out the GCF (greatest common factor), use the FOIL (first, outer, inner, last) method to multiply two binomials, write each polynomial as the product of two binomials. Hands shot up as students volunteered to come to the front of the room to provide solutions. Correct answers won the response,

"Take one," from the teacher who had put a large box of donut holes from Dunkin' Donuts on a desk.

Lights were dimmed in a social studies classroom on this Saturday morning. Students watched a documentary about the Triangle Shirtwaist Factory fire that occurred just more than one hundred years earlier several miles south of where they now sat, killing 146 young garment workers, many of whom, like these mostly Latino students, were immigrants. Grisly photos flashed on the screen as the students learned from a slide show that the workers had to jump from ninth-floor windows because firemen's ladders didn't reach that height, and exits were locked by bosses who didn't want workers to take breaks or steal materials. The lesson required students to read a reprint of a *New York Times* article from March 26, 1911, about the conflagration, to circle words they didn't understand, and to write two- or three-sentence responses to ten questions pertaining to the documentary and the article.

Finally, in a science class, the subjects of the day were DNA and genetics. Students reviewed the manner in which charts and graphs convey information and then went on to fill out personal inventories of their own physical traits. The teacher made sure they understood the terms, asking a student to explain, for example, what "dominant" means when it comes to genetics. Eventually, the content would segue into conversations about Jurassic Park and cloning.

This is a typical Saturday for students in the Harlem chapter. The program has four sequences, each lasting six to eight weeks and corresponding to the seasons. They have more than a month of Saturdays off between sessions, freeing up weekend time for whatever use they choose. Students select classes in two subject areas each sequence. Every class runs for an hour in the morning, then following a break for lunch, students pursue nonacademic activities in the afternoon.

Attendance on Saturday is voluntary, and Say Yes finds students more prone to attend when they have to commit only to a specified sequence. Thus the long breaks between sessions. Once committed, though, Say Yes expects students to attend; program representatives phone their homes if they are absent. About 280 of the chapter's 385 students attended at least one of the Saturday sequences. Some of those who don't attend are students at charter schools, which require their own Saturday classes.

And Yet Other Possibilities

There is no end to the possibilities for capturing more time for learning. After-school tutors aid many public school students. Business has been lucrative for tutoring companies that have come to prominence in the last two decades: Sylvan, Kumon, Kaplan, and Princeton Review. During the first decade of this century, online tutoring companies grabbed some of this business; included among the major Internet tutors were Tutor.com, Growing Stars, TutorVista, and eTutorworld. In addition, thousands of current and retired schoolteachers have found a valuable source of income, perhaps undeclared, in tutoring individual students and small groups of students outside school settings. The late Stanley Kaplan, whose business became one of the biggest in the tutoring field, began by privately tutoring students in his Brooklyn basement. Now the *Washington Post* owns the company he founded.

Highly motivated students use the Internet on their own to extend their learning. Sitting in their bedrooms, they gather information online to pursue school assignments, and tens of thousands of high school students take online courses. Society has only just begun to discover the ways in which the Internet may expand time for learning.

Schools should also examine lost learning time in terms of the hours and days that schoolchildren spend with substitute teachers. On any given day, 5.3 percent of regular teachers are absent, creating the need for substitutes. The break in continuity of education is worse for some students than for others as 36 percent of teachers nationally miss more than ten days of instruction. Teacher absentee rates tend to be highest in schools with the greatest percentages of minority enrollment.[17]

Only about 42 percent of the "subs" who fill in for absent regular teachers go through an orientation by the school district, and fewer than 10 percent of them get skills training. Twenty-one states do not require substitute teachers to have more than a high school diploma.[18] Regular teachers will always have some days when they can't come to work, but school districts could do more to fill their shoes with highly qualified substitutes who keep instruction flowing. Studies show that the students who lose instruction because substitutes teach too many of their class sessions pay the price in diminished achievement.

***

So time is a valuable commodity when it comes to education, a treasure waiting to be claimed. Once lost, the gift of time cannot be recaptured. Schools should examine time as a resource—just like textbooks and technology, for example— that when used properly can promote learning. Schools that squander time rob students of a part of their education.

Weaving a Web of Social and Emotional Support

Health needs of all sorts—social, emotional, and physical—tend to get overlooked in school reform. Say Yes, though, proceeds on the assumption that children do not readily learn when they are hungry, homeless, or living in dysfunctional settings. These problems impact the classroom, allowing what occurs outside the school building to undermine the climate for learning. A place like Syracuse's Fowler High School with its more than one thousand students illustrates just what is at stake in attempts to change educational outcomes. Up to half of the school's ninth graders usually disappeared by the middle of the tenth grade, dropping out for many reasons that become obstacles to getting educated. One recent year, more than 85 students were pregnant or already mothers midway through the school year.

"Students come with needs we can't always address in the classroom," said Anne Marie Voutsinas, a former president of the Syracuse Teachers Association. Say Yes, working with the school district, supports the services of social workers, mental health workers, lawyers, and others whose intervention can clear away barriers to learning and permit educators to focus as much as possible on instruction. One may reasonably assume that students are less apt to be plagued by mental health issues and learn better when schools take cognizance of their physical, social, and emotional needs.

It is not merely because children are poor in places like Syracuse that their learning is impaired but because of the negative experiences associated with poverty. Economic and social pressures may produce an unpleasant home life. Family struggle may lead to family dysfunction. The mobility resulting from the inability to pay rent, for instance, forces frequent moves, leading to discontinuity of instruction. Most significantly, these many factors may produce stress in a child, almost certainly affecting scholastic performance.

An examination of the causes of the achievement gap for African American boys highlights the major role that risks in their lives play in reducing academic achievement. "Compared to having no risk experiences," write the researchers, "African American boys who experienced one, two, or three or more risks demonstrated significantly lower reading and mathematics achievement."[1] Some of the risks identified by the research are maltreatment, lead exposure, homelessness, low maternal education at birth, inadequate prenatal care, and low birth weight. "African American boys had higher rates for all but one of these publicly monitored risk[s] included in this study as compared to White boys and these rates surpassed all national rates," says the journal article.[2] It was with such risks in mind that Say Yes set out to help the schools in Syracuse to deliver more services.

The social-emotional and physical factors that affect school-aged children are viewed by the Centers for Disease Control and Prevention (CDC) of the U.S. Department of Health and Human Services in terms of the risks they pose. The CDC monitors these risks in its Youth Risk Behavior Surveillance System. These behaviors are the leading causes of death and disability among the young. They involve unintended injuries and violence, sexual behaviors, substance abuse, unhealthy diets, and inadequate physical activity. Seventy-two percent of all deaths among the nation's 10- to 24-year-olds result from just four causes: (1) motor vehicle crashes, (2) other unintended injuries, (3) homicide, and (4) suicide.[3]

A report on elementary and secondary schools in California sought to emphasize the links between health needs and academic achievement. "Studies confirm what we already know intuitively," the report states. "If a child misses school due to asthma, cannot focus due to a toothache, has not physically developed properly due to inadequate nutrition or is preoccupied with fears of violence or faces excess stress, even the best teacher armed with the most interesting curriculum may not be able to teach him."[4]

The Australian Scholarships Group studied the social and emotional health of ten thousand elementary and secondary students in that country. The group's report concludes that large percentages of students experience social and emotional difficulties, girls suffer more from such afflictions than boys, bullies find it difficult to think before they act, and social and emotional health decreases from primary to secondary school. The report points out the need for teachers to learn about students' resilience, learning capabilities, and social skills in order to understand their social and emotional health.[5]

One way that Say Yes sought to relieve pressure on students and their families was by easing some of their legal burdens. Families with ready access to lawyers can, like drivers with a GPS device, better navigate the system. Thus Say Yes helped establish seven legal clinics, situated mostly in schools. Volunteer lawyers steer parents of schoolchildren to nonprofit legal services and take on about 15 to 20 percent of the cases themselves on a pro bono basis when no referral is possible. The fact that many lawyers prefer to volunteer during the day and many clients want services in the evening complicates efforts. So two of the clinics have evening hours.

Someone in each of the city's larger law firms acts as a Say Yes coordinator, rounding up colleagues to volunteer for the clinics. The greatest demand for legal help by parents of schoolchildren involves tenant issues, substandard accommodations, mortgages, foreclosures, and family law—child custody, child support, child abuse, and divorce. The clinics struggle to persuade families to avail themselves of free legal services and to get parents, especially immigrants, to understand that the lawyers are their advocates and are not law enforcement officials.

Even such basics as a child's vision, which certainly affects the ability to handle schoolwork, may not be addressed in some families. Terry B. Grier, the school superintendent in Houston, came to realize that tens of thousands of his students—in the nation's seventh-largest school district—had visual impairments preventing them from reading properly or seeing the board at the front of the room. He collaborated with community businesses, public organizations, and philanthropists to provide vision screening for students.[6]

A positive school climate can comfort students, enveloping them in a healthy, safe, and reassuring environment. A setting of this sort cannot be taken for granted. Many forces intervene to create clouds that render the climate less than sunny in some places. Urban districts like Syracuse must do all they can to forestall the forces that interfere with learning. Youngsters need to gain the ability to get along with peers and react reasonably to events that occur in school. They must learn to form healthy attachments and come to regulate their behavior. If they do not, they will disrupt classes, threaten other students, and make it difficult for teachers to provide instruction.

Edvantia, a nonprofit consulting organization that seeks to link research knowledge to practice, maintains that school climate is so important that schools should have "climate coaches." Such a person would take the lead in developing schoolwide strategies to address social, emotional, and behavioral barriers to learning. He or she would serve on the school's leadership team to ensure the integration between teaching and learning and students' social and emotional well-being.[7] Say Yes moved in this direction when it replaced its site directors at each school with student support specialists and linked them to Huntington Family Centers, a social service agency, to create a position resembling the climate coach that Edvantia envisioned.

Putting Effective Resources Closer to Children

Interviews conducted on behalf of the Onondaga County mental health department, the Syracuse City School District, and Say Yes found that despite a high commitment to social-emotional enhancements, there were no uniform district-wide systems to identify and support students in dire need. Also, the school system had no behavioral-emotional crisis procedures, no integration of child-serving agencies with the schools, and often lacked policies for mental health providers to follow when working with schools.

The report went on to assert that principals in Syracuse should better understand how to deal with high-needs students and that teachers need better classroom management skills to handle disruptions, which may signify the overflow of a child's social-emotional volcano. It found that Say Yes site directors had no clear-cut priorities in this regard. Also, the report maintained that university interns in social work, psychology, and counseling required more training and coordination in conjunction with placements in public schools. Access to care for students was wanting.[8]

These findings two years after Say Yes's arrival in Syracuse represented a call to action. Say Yes set a goal of situating resources closer to children and families so as to provide easier access to services, not unlike the placement of fire extinguishers at strategic sites throughout the school building. Every elementary school had a social worker when Say Yes arrived, and the organization arranged for a second social worker in each elementary school, striving toward a ratio of 250 pupils per social worker. The ratio was threatened by financial cutbacks in 2012. But the conversion of the site director position to student support specialist provided a person who could help plug the gap.

On an afternoon when I interviewed a social worker at a school in Syracuse, she had already endured several challenging experiences just that morning. She had spoken with a sixth grader, the subject of a tug-of-war between her parents in a custody case. She then had a separate meeting with the girl's mother. Next, there was the boy who shared feelings he still had in connection with his father's suicide the previous week. Also, a girl who was the target of bullying sought advice, and the social worker gave her suggestions for maintaining her self-control. Finally, the social worker met with a parent to discuss her child's poor attendance.

Parents have expressed their appreciation for the contributions of the social workers. A parent told me how impressed she was by the ability of her son's school to give greater attention to the emotional needs of students with more social workers on the job. Her son was an academic achiever but a shy child. A student bullied him, and she spoke with a social worker who helped move her son into a different group of students where he no longer felt threatened. The school also gave the youngster a chance to build his self-esteem by letting him volunteer, carrying a walkie-talkie and helping other students get on and off the buses. Now more confident, he ran for a class office. "This is a big step for him," his mother said. "He's been made to feel comfortable. Say Yes looks at all aspects, including the social dimension."

Promoting Mental Health

If it turns out that a family needs regular home visits, the school refers the case to Huntington Family Centers, which is paid through funding from the state. Say Yes played an instrumental role in making this connection. Depending on the situation, Huntington puts families in touch with various resources in the community and assists in developing effective relationships between school and home. Hillside Children's Center is another agency that school social workers may summon as a result of Say Yes's brokering role. Representatives from Hillside meet with students in small-group settings regularly during the after-school program to provide academic advisement, monitor progress, and speak to students about completing their work in timely fashion.

School-based mental health programs, while aimed at children, cannot ignore the home settings that affect youngsters even as they sit in classrooms. It is therefore often crucial for the school to tighten its link to the family. Mental health problems of parents put at least 15 million children in the United States at risk in a given year.[9] And there is no assurance that despite these difficulties parents will get professional attention, leaving schoolchildren to cope with dysfunction at home even as they try to succeed in school.

Too many youngsters around the country need interventions that never occur. Delayed mental health services beget mental health problems that blossom fully before students complete their education and may very well severely handicap people by the time they reach adulthood. "Understanding that adverse childhood experiences can lead to a cascade of social, cognitive, and emotional problems, high-risk behavior and ultimately early death is the first step in addressing them," writes Susan F. Cole, director of both the Trauma and Learning Policy Initiative of Harvard Law School and Massachusetts Advocates for Children.[10]

It makes abundant sense to promote good mental health in those who are still of school age, as Say Yes recognized in embarking upon its work in Syracuse. "If a child's mental health needs are addressed early and treated properly, he is much less likely to require costly special education programs for social emotional reasons," states a report that estimates that five thousand children in the District of Columbia lacked access to treatment.[11]

Troubles can multiply when school systems fail to put a priority on the mental health of their students. In 2012, a joint hearing of the education and mental health committees of the New York City Council led to a declaration that there were not enough school-based mental health services to deal with students who need such interventions.

Maria Newman, a reporter for *The New York Times*, wrote in one of the newspaper's blogs of a seventh grader taken by ambulance to a hospital after she had threatened to harm herself and another student. In a different case, a teacher summoned the city's emergency medical service to deal with a student who became disruptive during a test. A legal services lawyer told *The New York Times* that a single hospital in the Bronx got 58 such emergency medical service calls from schools in just one ten-day period in February 2012.[12] Good school-based programs, as those in Syracuse, try to head off such extreme measures.

A report in New York City examining the causes of chronic absenteeism found that the problem could not be divorced from poverty and various pressures on poor families. It pointed to the need for support services. "Having just one person in their school who has a reasonable workload and is dedicated to family outreach on these kinds of issues—as opposed to school governance or academic issues—would make a real difference," the report says, summarizing the attitude of teachers.[13]

The Promise Zone

Another initiative of the Syracuse City School District, called the Promise Zone, is supported by New York State with federal funds from the Substance Abuse and Mental Health Services Administration that flow through the county and into the schools. The program put mental health clinicians in schools to provide children with psychotherapy unavailable from school social workers. Say Yes backed this approach, which placed mental health clinics in 31 schools by 2013. Previously, a youngster had to travel to some distant site for such services.

These school clinicians function as part of a student support team that includes the Say Yes student support specialist, a school social worker, a school psychologist, and a building administrator. The model for funding through the Promise Zone calls for schools to prioritize and address major problems among their students. This approach changed the conversations of school personnel about their most troubled students.

The model includes a triaged approach to intervention. Eighty-three to 86 percent of the students in a typical elementary school in Syracuse generally receive no special attention beyond targeted small-group instruction. Anywhere from 13 to 18 percent of the enrollment fit into a second group, having greater needs. They are taught social skills and encouraged to manage their conduct. The school periodically assesses their behavior and may refer some of these youngsters to outside agencies. The smallest group, fewer than 10 percent of the enrollment, receives the most support. They are subject to intensive interventions and have individually designed behavior plans. Their parents get training, and the students meet with representatives of outside agencies. Safety is paramount—the safety of the child involved and the safety of other children with whom he or she comes in contact—in determining which cases merit the greatest attention.

School teams in Syracuse meet to discuss the needs of individual youngsters. A team might decide, for instance, whether a child's issue is truly a matter of mental health or the result of some occurrence in the family. This way the district can funnel scarce mental health services to students with the most need. The team develops a plan for the family as well. Parents or guardians must agree to meet with team members in order for the school to implement a plan for the student.

A separate group of 16 family support specialists deals exclusively with parents and guardians. Like the student support specialists, they are on the Huntington Family Centers staff. They cover all the school system's elementary and middle schools. "A lot of parents," said Peter Ashworth, one of the family specialists, "have their own negative history with education. Going to these meetings can be very intimidating to them. They don't know what a behavior plan should look like. Having a person representing the school but who is not part of the school district [which the family specialist is not] can be empowering to parents."

At Syracuse's Lemoyne Elementary School, by way of example, the team meets for at least an hour, beginning at 1 p.m. Monday afternoons, to screen cases referred to it. The week that I visited the school, near the end of 2012, a discussion involved a child who periodically walked out of some of the special classes— art, music, and physical education. This wasn't happening in the child's regular classes, and the regular teacher did not even know that it occurred in the special classes. The team still had not found an explanation for the fourth grader's peripatetic behavior and could only speculate that perhaps the student did not like some of the teachers of the special classes or could not get along with seatmates in those classes.

Another case that the team considered involved a fourth grader who aroused concerns for his safety. The boy did his work while in the class but left the room periodically without permission to wander around the building, perhaps even going outside. The team had previously tried to deal with his conduct by scheduling breaks from the classroom for him throughout the day based on good behavior. But he had control issues during the breaks, acting aggressively toward other students and even toward teachers, and he sometimes could not be found during that time. Now the team talked about increasing the restrictions put on him during the breaks and setting a goal of eventually being able to diminish or eliminate the breaks.

A Range of Problems That Impact Learning

A student's mental health profoundly influences his or her learning, which can easily fall into a sinkhole of misconduct. The challenges in Syracuse's secondary schools are particularly acute. Forty-eight percent of students at this level, compared with 18 percent in elementary schools, rate their schools as in need of improvement when it comes to physical and emotional safety.[14] Disruptive behavior among children in urban low-income communities is almost three times as prevalent as the national estimates.[15] Mental health counseling has the potential to calm the environment and let teachers focus on instruction instead of dealing with disruptive youngsters.

On the topic of social-emotional peer climate, 76 percent of high school students in Syracuse—more than twice as many as in elementary and even more than in middle schools—indicated a need for improvement.[16] "Anxiety issues lead to behavior issues," said Robert C. Long, the Onondaga County health commissioner and cochair of the Say Yes health and wellness task force. Across the country—and perhaps in Syracuse as well—students may perceive school climate more harshly than those who work in schools. Asked in a survey whether the climate in their schools is conducive to teaching and learning, 23 percent of principals and 52 percent of teachers said it was not.[17]

The Syracuse City School District, spurred by the support of Say Yes, made strides in marshaling assistance for students and their families. This progress was bound to help improve the learning climate in classrooms. Huntington Family Centers served 1,038 children in the school system in 2011. The organization had 16,478 client contacts, including 3,186 home visits with youngsters attending the Syracuse public schools and their families. Each of eight elementary schools made 15 or more referrals to Huntington during the year. Families with the lowest incomes had the most referrals. Behavioral problems figured in 75 percent of the referrals in the Syracuse schools. Ninety-five percent of families said that the services helped improve school attendance, 96 percent reported improved school performance, and every family said that the services led to better relationships between home and school.[18]

"A lot of kids seen as oppositional have great emotional problems," said Monique Fletcher, the Say Yes associate director who leads the organization's health and wellness program in Syracuse. She maintained that attention to their mental health reduced students' discipline problems and made it easier for teachers to teach. The school system had previously tried various interventions without great success. After it came on the scene, Say Yes helped facilitate these services throughout the school year. Say Yes also sought to extend the services into the after-school and summer programs that the organization helped establish in the district. Say Yes student support specialists and Say Yes family support specialists work with representatives of community-based groups to enable them to assist children and families that need services.

Nevertheless, discipline problems still bubbled up five years after the arrival of Say Yes and despite increased attention to social-emotional concerns. A controversy over whether suspensions fell disproportionately on black and Latino students devolved into a tense, racially-tinged discussion among an overflow crowd at a school board meeting in May 2013. Some speakers charged that schools in Syracuse were dangerous and unruly places and others maintained that minority students were singled out for punishment. The school year ended on this ominous note.

Related to the social-emotional activities are behavioral planning and support provided through the Positive Behavioral Interventions and Support (PBIS) approach promulgated by the U.S. Department of Education. PBIS in Syracuse is a tool that schools may use to identify, adapt, and sustain productive discipline practices. School leaders set expectations for an entire school building so as to recognize and reward good conduct. Some schools distribute coupons or tokens to students who demonstrate responsibility, respect, and safe behavior on a consistent basis. Students may redeem the handouts for rewards. Ideally, schools can measure effectiveness in terms of academic outcomes. Fletcher concedes, though, "Expectations don't mean it's always happening."

Monique Fletcher

Monique Fletcher is a linchpin in Say Yes' efforts to help the school district pay more attention to the social-emotional well-being of its students. Born and raised in Quincy, Illinois, on the banks of the Mississippi, Fletcher was a member of that town's small African American population. Her mother owned a child care business, and her father was a firefighter who had a part-time janitorial and carpet-cleaning service. She speaks readily of how fortunate she was to grow up in an intact, two-parent household. She has an older sister who did not attend college and a younger brother who became a college professor in Florida.

Fletcher was widely known as a basketball star at Quincy High School, where she led the girls' team to the state tournament. She signed a letter of intent to attend the University of Missouri on an athletic scholarship even before the season ended. The scholarship was offered before she suffered a devastating injury to her anterior cruciate ligament, the infamous ACL that afflicts so many female athletes. The team didn't go far in the tournament without Fletcher.

Her injury never healed sufficiently for Fletcher to regain her former prowess. Missouri nonetheless carried her on its roster for two years and honored its commitment to a four-year scholarship. Her studies became her main focus, and she got her bachelor's degree in social work. After graduation, she worked in a group home in Atlanta for abused and neglected teenage girls.

Fletcher decided to attend graduate school in social work at Syracuse University, putting her in a new geographic orbit from which she never descended. Master's degree in hand, she ran a youth program for residents of the Syracuse Housing Authority and after that worked for the county as the family and community coordinator of Head Start. She moved on to run a small program in Syracuse, the Westside Community School initiative, which Say Yes eventually absorbed, a merger that led to Fletcher becoming an official of Say Yes.

So what drew this former basketball player to social work and, specifically, to its application in school settings? "I think every person deserves a quality educational experience," Fletcher said. "This is the only way to change outcomes. It is woven into my own experience. Until someone gets an education and is gainfully employed, they can't overcome poverty. Say Yes is a good fit for me, with my degrees and my mission as a social worker." And incidentally, Fletcher still plays recreational ball, though her moves aren't what they were back at Quincy High, before the injury.

Other Kinds of Supports

More than seven thousand students in the Syracuse public schools were not enrolled to receive insurance for health services though most were probably eligible for subsidized programs. As mentioned earlier, Say Yes coordinated efforts to identify and help students and their families with a part-time facilitated enroller provided by the Salvation Army. When a grant was about to expire, Say Yes devoted more than a half-hour at one of its operating committee meetings to a discussion of how to replace the enroller. The conversation involved officials from Say Yes, the school administration, the teachers' union, the county's social services department, and others. Seldom do most school systems have so many high-powered folks jointly focusing on such a topic, and almost certainly it wouldn't have occurred if not for Say Yes.

David Sutkowy, the county's social services commissioner, was part of the group at the meeting and remarked upon the need to get systems talking to one another to overcome the complications of having to make annual renewals of children's eligibility for health services. "Their families are not invisible to other providers," he said. "We can do a better job of sharing information about cases." That comment shifted the discussion—in a windowless room in the school system's barnlike teachers' center—to issues of privacy and confidentiality and consideration of how best to honor legal requirements while doing everything possible to deliver health services to children.

Say Yes got similarly involved—but less successfully—when teenage mothers faced a major obstacle in trying to continue in high school until graduation. It turned out that many were late to school or altogether missed classes because they spent hours each morning using public transportation to take their children to day care. "A lot of students have dropped out or are barely hanging on," said

Debra Schoening, the system's go-between with Say Yes. Say Yes and its allies began exploring ways that the district, working in conjunction with various agencies, might better serve teenage mothers and pregnant students who sought to remain enrolled. This time, Say Yes's inquiries led nowhere, and the problem persists.

Brian Nolan, director of high schools and president of the principals' union, welcomed the various added services for students as a result of Say Yes's intervention and hoped that this would lead to higher achievement. "I'm a big supporter of Say Yes," he said. "Their supports and resources are ones that we can't provide. Say Yes eliminates barriers. Then the real focus can be on classroom instruction. It's possible that we can bring all this in and still have the same results, if we still have poor instruction. This should refocus our instruction and reshape what we do."

The Responsibilities of Schools

Like parents of teenagers, schools have varying degrees of control over their students and over the factors that affect the feelings of students. Certainly, every school owes it to youngsters, as a starting point, to ensure that the setting is safe, which sometimes requires interventions to protect students from themselves and from others. Schools may also strive to ensure that staff members do not chip away at the self-esteem of students and that bullying does not occur. All this is in addition to keeping substance abuse and gang activity out of the building. Ultimately, children who feel good about themselves can have better relationships with their classmates, and the atmosphere for learning will be more favorable.

Social-emotional health and physical health are intertwined and not easily separated. While she is not a mental health expert, the school nurse typically is a first line of defense when it comes to issues surrounding a youngster's well-being. Altogether, 74.6 percent of American schools have the services of a registered nurse at least once a week, but only 41.3 percent of all schools have full-time registered nurses. Nurses are found more frequently in secondary schools than in elementary schools.

These figures are from 2007, the last time that the National Association of School Nurses published a survey. The numbers have almost certainly diminished in the difficult financial times that have befallen the country since then. As a matter of fact, several urban school systems including Los Angeles, Cleveland, and Philadelphia are known to have reduced their corps of school nurses during the years since 2007. These districts are certainly headed in the wrong direction.

The Syracuse school system, despite enormous fiscal pressures, has been able to maintain a nursing corps of 37 full timers and 2 part timers, covering each of its more than thirty buildings except for two instances in which nurses with other assignments also take responsibility for small, nearby schools. Two nurses are permanent substitutes to ensure coverage when regularly assigned nurses are absent; two are assigned to off-site prekindergarten classes; and three cover multiple private and charter schools. In addition, the district has 14 school health aides who move among the schools to help the nurses.

A Plethora of Factors Affecting Health and Safety

The idyllic vision of schools as secure citadels of learning is as antiquated as castles with moats. The massacre in 2012 at Sandy Hook Elementary School in Newtown, Connecticut, left no doubt about the ever-present dangers. Those who would have schools ignore such possibilities are probably also in a state of denial about the impact of bullying, gang activity, and substance abuse among schoolchildren. Efforts at school reform, as in Syracuse, must acknowledge the existence of such threats.

Anyone who wonders why schools should be concerned about substance abuse need only look at the statistics. The use of marijuana among students at least once during a typical month reached 21.4 percent for twelfth graders, 16.7 percent for tenth graders, and 8 percent for eighth graders during 2010. In fact, marijuana use grew more prevalent than cigarette smoking among students.[19] Without a doubt, some of those youngsters are stoned in class. The National Center on Addiction and Substance Abuse at Columbia University estimates that one out of every five American high school students who has ever used tobacco, alcohol, or illegal drugs might be addicted. Some experts maintain that substance abuse among students can be a predictor of adult addiction. That is the reason the University of Michigan's Institute for Social Research calls the survey on drug use that it carries out for the federal government "Monitoring the Future."

Gangs are an ever-present peril at inner-city schools. Just ask the police department in Syracuse about gangs in the city. Young people searching for a sense of belonging are, like fruit awaiting harvest, ripe for the kind of family unity that gang membership appears to offer them. And where there are gangs, there are threats to those who spurn membership. Violence, criminal behavior, and drugs are lethal parts of the mix. The specter of gang intrusion into at least two of the high schools in Syracuse stirred sufficient concern for Say Yes to speed up its plans at the start of 2013 for assigning personnel to help the district confront gang activity at this level.

It is hard to imagine schools without bullying. Generations of young people have had their school experiences soured by peers who intimidate them and even do them physical harm. In recent years, though, schools have increasingly taken measures to deal with this outrageous behavior. The social and emotional dimensions are important in both diminishing bullying and providing succor to students who suffer at the hands of those who would oppress them. Yet just as educators have more actively combated bullying, they face it in a new form distinctive to the twenty-first century: cyberbullying. The anonymity of the computer and social messaging lent a new dimension to bullying. One challenge in coping with this kind of behavior is that, for the most part, it occurs outside the walls of the school building. Nonetheless, regulations and laws in some states have tried to hold educators responsible for stopping cyberbullying, an expectation that can prove unreasonable.

Social-Emotional Learning

A full social-emotional program in schools includes not only supports such those Say Yes facilitated in Syracuse but an academic dimension as well. Some schools around the country devote curriculum units and entire courses to subjects that enhance students' social and emotional development. Educators can thread social-emotional learning (SEL) into almost any subject when appropriate opportunities present themselves.

A goal is to help students of all ages become better able to comprehend, manage, and express the social and emotional parts of their beings. They learn about social skills and relationships, reflect on their inner feelings and self-awareness, and dissect the meaning of responsibility. Ideally, they grow in their ability to regulate their conduct and have less of a need for interventions.

Another goal is to head off risky behavior. Despite the web of supports that Say Yes helped the Syracuse City School District put in place, social-emotional learning itself got short shrift. Say Yes encouraged school officials from the beginning to institute such courses and curriculum units at all grade levels, but little happened in this regard. Such education may yet find a place in the schools of Syracuse but apparently not until officials address more pressing needs and funds are redirected.

Second Graders Get in Touch with Feelings

The 14 second graders positioned themselves on a carpet facing their teacher, who sat on a chair next to an easel on which she had placed a white board the size of a poster. She drew a large oval in preparation for sketching in the rudimentary features of a face. She was getting the students ready to do the same on smaller papers her assistant had placed on each of their desks so that they could produce "I" messages when they returned to their seats.

The teacher encouraged them to think about the stories they had read and to select characters about whom they would write such messages as the following: "I feel ____ when ____." They rehearsed the assignment using the characters in two books they had read, *Oliver Button Is a Sissy* and *Chrysanthemum*. Oliver enjoyed activities associated most often with girls, and Chrysanthemum was a girl with an unusual name that led to her being teased.

This was Bartle Elementary School in Highland Park, New Jersey, a building that houses all the system's 415 second through fifth graders. The students learned about "I" messages in their weekly health class, and now their classroom teacher integrated that social-emotional lesson into the daily language arts instruction. She began by asking them to define an "I" message. "It describes your feelings to someone else," said one student. "It tells how you feel and what you want them to stop doing," said another.

She asked the youngsters to think about how Oliver Button felt in the book with the eponymous title. First, the children spoke of some of his feelings—scared, disappointed, and sad. "And when did he feel one of these ways?" the teacher asked. "When the boys teased him," responded a child.

"Why do they tease him?" asked the teacher, going on to answer her own question: "Because he likes to do girl things: jump rope, take long walks, dance." Thus the book's title. "Did Oliver Button use an 'I' message?" she asked.

A student responded that Oliver did not use an "I" message to tell his classmates how he felt when they teased him. Another interjected, "It probably would have helped, and he would have solved the problem earlier."

The teacher wrote Oliver Button's name at the top of the white board and drew features into the oval of a face to make him look sad. At the bottom, she wrote, on Oliver's behalf, "I feel _____ when _____." The idea was for the students to fill in the blanks with words and phrases of their own. Now they understood what they were to do when they got back to their seats: select characters from their readings and write "I" messages from the perspectives of their chosen characters. If all went according to the script, they would eventually—through a succession of such lessons—improve their abilities as incipient decision makers, making them better able to recognize certain emotions in themselves and in others. This was one tiny piece of social-emotional learning, second-grade style.

A Professional Approach to Social-Emotional Learning

Scholars who examined 213 separate studies of social-emotional learning involving 270,034 students in kindergarten through high school across the United States conclude that students who have the benefit of such teaching, compared with those who do not, exhibit improvements in social emotional skills, attitudes, behavior, and academic performance. A reason for the higher academic outcomes, researchers theorize, is that "students who are more self-aware and confident about their learning capacities try harder and persist in the face of challenges."[20]

The Collaborative for Academic, Social, and Emotional Learning (CASEL) is dedicated to embedding social and emotional learning in the core of elementary and secondary education. CASEL carried out a project with eight school systems in 2013 to provide staff development for implementing this kind of learning and to gather more research on the impact of such programs. The organization also publishes a compendium of exemplary social-emotional programs based on evidence of effectiveness.[21]

Getting Ready for College

The lure of free college tuition was the flashing neon sign that first drew attention to Say Yes to Education in Syracuse. Some people, focusing on the attraction of the tuition offer, were blinded to the essence of the program, which seeks to boost aspirations and underscore the importance of hard work in elementary and secondary school. Say Yes wants the program to lead students to prepare better for college and to persevere once they get there. When Sharon Contreras arrived in Syracuse as the new superintendent and began touring the schools to meet the children in the summer program, the first words she heard from students were that they intended to go to college, an unfamiliar mantra from elementary pupils in an urban school system.

Chancellor Cantor of Syracuse University worked the phones like a political operative to create what became known as the Higher Education Compact portion of Say Yes. Using influence and persuasion, she and others assembled a roster of colleges and universities that agreed to award financial aid to help cover tuition costs for Syracuse's high school graduates headed to higher education. The imperative for raising hopes and dreams could be seen in figures showing that almost half the students who entered the city's public high schools dropped out.

Syracuse is not the first city to develop such a program for its high school graduates. The Kalamazoo Promise and the Pittsburgh Promise are similar in purpose. Only Syracuse, though, with the carefully crafted plans of Say Yes, linked the promise to extensive reform of the entire school system and to building a new relationship between the schools and the rest of the community.

Eshan Escoffery was in that first group of students who went off to college on scholarships that Say Yes provided in 2009. A gifted musician, he knew that he wanted to pursue higher education, but he didn't know how he could afford to do so unless he first worked for several years after high school graduation to raise funds. "If I didn't get the Say Yes scholarship, it would have been very difficult for me to go," he said. "The program is a huge opportunity for the students of Syracuse to consider their future and their careers." Now Escoffery, a bass trombonist who can play virtually all brass instruments, is at Syracuse University, sitting in the symphony orchestra and studying jazz improvisation, among other subjects.

Similarly, Ruby Brown got a Say Yes tuition scholarship without which she said that it was unlikely she would have been able to attend college. She was raised by a single mother and has four older sisters. By the time she was a high school senior, she was trying to develop a backup plan for her life, assuming that she would not go to college. She confessed that the bleak outlook punched a hole in her motivation. During her senior year in high school, she recognized that the scholarship could change everything. "Then college was an option, and this forced me to motivate myself and work hard so that I could open that door," she said. "The possibility of a scholarship opened my eyes to what needed to be done and helped me mature." She went off to Clarkson University in the cold, far northern reaches of New York State to study psychology. By the time a bachelor's degree was in sight, she was thinking about a master's and what she could do with it by going back to Syracuse to help clients with mental health issues.

Eshan Escoffery and Ruby Brown typify the many students in Syracuse who have found hope and purpose as a result of the scholarship offer. "Many of our students don't have the means for college tuition but knowing that Say Yes will help them if they meet all of the criteria is a load off parents and gives students more oomph to strive for what they want to become," said Jeannie Aversa, a teacher in the city.

Say Yes's college scholarships will likely aid not only the direct recipients but the generation that follows as well. Such an outcome would promote the other part of Say Yes's objective—namely, elevating the fortunes of the city. One way to close the achievement gap and realize the attendant benefits is to ensure that more children have college-educated parents, such as the parents that Escoffery and Brown may eventually become. "Facilitating higher education attainment by blacks has the added, perhaps even more important, benefit of mitigating the black-white literacy gap in the children of those who achieved higher education attainment," conclude researchers who examined literacy trends in the United States.[1]

Say Yes's tuition scholarship program addresses the two big issues of the early twenty-first-century college-going population: affordability and accessibility. Average tuitions in the 2012–13 academic year at four-year public colleges and universities in the United States were $8,655 for in-state students and $21,706 for out-of-state students. On top of this, students residing on campus faced a $9,205 charge for room and board. The more affordable average tuition at two-year community colleges was $3,131. Average tuition at nonprofit private institutions was $29,056, and the cost was $39,518 with room and board included.[2] Most private institutions of higher education have gradually priced themselves out of reach for the majority of students.

The College Board estimates that two-thirds of all students receive grants to defray their costs. Colleges and universities themselves provide much of this aid, while some of it comes from the federal government in the form of Pell Grants and college work-study funds. Thus the sticker price for institutions of higher education, like the manufacturer's suggested retail price of a new car, is not what all students end up paying. Moreover, many students and their parents take loans.

When it comes to accessibility, especially at selective colleges and universities, the matter goes beyond cost to questions of whether the student's academic preparation and accomplishments are acceptable to the institution. Poorly prepared students, regardless of their ability to afford the cost, may find selective schools inaccessible. Say Yes recognizes this challenge and prods the Syracuse public schools to give young people a better foundation for postsecondary success. Furthermore, Say Yes provides coaching, tutoring, college visits, and other enhancements designed to make students more apt to become candidates for admission to selective schools.

In one of the most confounding of findings, researchers who analyzed scores on ACT and College Board examinations discovered that a majority of applicants with low family incomes but high academic ability never apply to a competitive college. Apparently, these students, who score among the highest 10 percent on admissions tests, tend to apply to the same less selective colleges as their equally poor but lower scoring peers.[3] One cannot help but wonder what sort of advice they receive from high school college counselors.

Free Tuition

The goal of going to college captured the imagination of people and made almost palpable the new reality that Say Yes wanted to inculcate in the community. Visitors to some kindergartens when the term began in 2009 saw banners proclaiming, "Welcome to the Class of 2022," implying that all the children would complete high school. That's the sort of message that Say Yes wanted to convey.

Shortly after he became state education commissioner, New York's highest-ranking school official, David Steiner, traveled to Syracuse to learn about Say Yes. He was intrigued by what he heard. "What are the core drivers, and can we replicate them?" inquired Steiner, who has since resigned from the post and is now the education dean at Hunter College of the City University of New York. "We have to think very hard about that. The model makes sense." Enthusiastic backers of Say Yes cited the possibilities of replication. "If this works here, taking on a whole city school district with all of its problems, it may be a blueprint for other places," said Assemblyman Magnarelli.

The free-tuition provision initially covered all the school system's graduates—regardless of financial circumstances—who spent their tenth, eleventh, and twelfth grades in the city's public high schools and graduated. Say Yes sought to build an economic development program for the city. This meant making the Syracuse City School District attractive to the middle class. What better way to draw and retain those families than through the offer of free college tuition for their children?

Public schools can be among a city's chief attributes, and this is why Say Yes originally offered the tuition-free program to all income groups. There is a reciprocal benefit to this phenomenon. If families want to live someplace because of the public schools, they may have to pay for the privilege in the form of higher property taxes. Then the public schools can count on a healthy source of revenues if the residential tax base thrives.

Free college tuition, though, was a gift horse that had cynics peering into its mouth with suspicion. Some minority members in Syracuse scoffed at the offer, figuring the program was meant primarily to benefit affluent white kids who would go to college in any event. It became clear as acceptance of the free-tuition offer grew that children from Syracuse's lower-income families would gain from it, and, eventually, the prospect of postsecondary education altered the nature of conversations in schools and at dinner tables. College attendance, once an unimaginable option, became a tangible goal.

But as the public came to regard the prospect of free tuition less warily, a crisis ensued. On a Friday night, at the beginning of a fall weekend in 2009, shortly before the mayoral election, members of the Common Council heard that eligibility for free tuition would be capped at private colleges and universities. Youngsters from families with incomes greater than $75,000 would no longer qualify for the offer at these institutions. Most private institutions in the Higher Education Compact felt they could not continue to justify awarding scholarships to students from more affluent families, especially in light of the economic squeeze and dwindling endowments. People commented sarcastically that Say Yes had become Say Maybe.

A junior partner at one of the city's law firms said that his wife, a physician, had been urging him to move to the suburbs after their child completed elementary school in Syracuse. When Say Yes with its promise of free college tuition came along, the young lawyer was able to convince his wife not to put their house on the market. His undergraduate alma mater, the University of Rochester, was among the private institutions participating in the Higher Education Compact. The couple anticipated that their child would attend the same university as part of the program and save them lots of money. When the cap was imposed, his wife again pushed to move to the suburbs.

Worst of all, Say Yes leaders had known of the looming tuition cap for at least a month without telling elected officials of the policy change, an omission that turned out to be a matter of negligence rather than deviousness. Syracuse University and Cooper Union in New York City were the only private institutions that did not impose the cap. "People said, 'I told you so,'" recalled Stephanie Miner, then a member of the Common Council and now mayor of Syracuse. "This added to the cynicism."

All was not lost. Private institutions of higher education—including such schools as Columbia, U Penn, and Tufts—continued their offers of free tuition to students from families with annual incomes below $75,000. Many such schools want to diversify their enrollments and find it difficult to recruit students from urban areas like Syracuse, where the names of these institutions are as unfamiliar as the capitals of Balkan countries.

Furthermore, Say Yes retained the free tuition offer for families at all income levels whose students entered the State University of New York (SUNY), the City University of New York (CUNY), and various community colleges; these state-supported members of Say Yes's Higher Education Compact greatly appeal to Syracuse's high school graduates. The SUNY and CUNY schools also have lower tuitions than almost all four-year private colleges and universities and Say Yes can more readily afford to provide scholarships to these institutions.

Say Yes and its allies want to build a $20-million endowment fund to underwrite the tuition scholarships in perpetuity. By 2012, donors had pledged more than $7 million to the fund. The most generous promise was $5 million from the Scientific Research Corporation (SRC), a company that deals mostly with environmental and intelligence issues principally through contracts with the federal government. SRC's president Paul Tremont deliberately made his company's pledge a matching grant to inspire another $5 million in gifts.

Paul G. Tremont

Having grown up in Syracuse, Tremont watched the start and stop of previous ventures that had been heralded as boons to the community. He viewed Say Yes differently, as a vehicle to eventually help make the public school system a supplier of future employees for his company and future leaders for the city. "An educated workforce allows businesses to grow," he said. "Having highly trained professionals on staff creates the potential for innovative solutions that can help the United States remain a world leader in technology." Tremont walks the talk. His only child, a daughter, majors in engineering at Rochester Institute of Technology.

Tremont's Syracuse roots run deep, nurtured by a strong devotion to both family and education. He proudly says that his parents taught him and his four brothers the value of hard work and education. He attended parochial schools in the city, getting his high school diploma from Bishop Ludden, where the Gaelic Knights continue to excel in basketball. His mother still lives in the city. Tremont is a graduate of the SUNY College of Environmental Science and Forestry as well as Virginia Tech, where he got an MBA. In addition to the financial backing his company provides to Say Yes, SRC participates in Say Yes's Community Leadership Council, and the company's employees volunteer in various aspects of the program.

He maintained that SRC's tagline of "redefining the possible," exemplifies the can-do attitude that all of Syracuse needs to exhibit so that the city might overcome obstacles standing in the way of improving its public school system. "Say Yes is a model that provides the supports, scholarships, and motivation to make a difference in the lives of many, both directly and indirectly," he said. Tremont worked at Synectics Corporation from 1980 to 1985, when he joined SRC. He rose through the ranks, serving successively as an analyst, program manager, director of the company's information technology center, vice president, and executive vice president before becoming president in 2011.

Tremont has a no-nonsense demeanor that segues into his avid interest in sports, including those he plays. He radiates a winning attitude. He golfs and still plays competitive softball. But there is a softer side to him, as well, especially when he is in the kitchen, where he enjoys cooking and baking.

Say Yes Scholarship Requirements

Students are eligible for the Say Yes scholarship if they reside in Syracuse, have continuous enrollment in one of the school district's five public high schools or its one charter school and remain enrolled from tenth through twelfth grade. They must apply and be admitted, meeting all admissions requirements, at an institution of higher education in the Say Yes Higher Education Compact.

Also, students must apply for financial aid at the college and meet all deadlines, completing the necessary paper work. The Say Yes award is a "last dollar" scholarship, meaning that the amount is set only after the college determines what a student will receive from other sources. Loans, though, are not part of the equation and do not count against a student in setting the scholarship amount. The Pittsburgh Promise is also a "last dollar" scholarship, whereas the Kalamazoo Promise is a "first dollar" scholarship, meaning that the student gets the full amount for which he or she is eligible and then the college builds a financial aid package on top of it.

Candidates for the Say Yes scholarship must enroll as full-time college students within one academic year after high school graduation. Satisfactory academic progress in college is required to remain eligible for the scholarship. A student who completes fewer than 12 credit hours in the fall or does not maintain a 2.0 grade point average can make up for it by taking additional credits in the spring and/or by raising the grade point average.

A student at the end of the first year in college who has not completed a minimum of 24 credit hours and does not have at least a 2.0 average loses eligibility for funding the next year. Students who do not meet the standards of academic progress at the end of an academic year may enroll in college courses over the summer to make up for deficiencies, but Say Yes will not pay the bill. A Say Yes scholarship covers four semesters at a two-year college or eight semesters at a four-year college. Students should strive to complete at least 15 credit hours a semester to earn their degrees during the time period that Say Yes will fund.

Initially, Say Yes did not include the city's only public charter school, Syracuse Academy of Science, in the tuition program, but its students became eligible for the scholarships in September 2012. No such arrangement was made, though, for Syracuse families using Catholic schools, and this was a source of contention. Christian Brothers Academy, a secondary school just over the city's eastern line that draws heavily from Syracuse, worried that the scholarships offered to graduates of the public schools would impede its ability to continue to attract students coming out of parish schools. In fact, Christian Brothers Academy mailed a letter in 2012 to families of sixth graders at the parochial schools boasting of its record in sending students on to college, a clear challenge to Say Yes and the lure of its scholarship offer.

The concern of the Catholic schools was not without merit. Such families as the Boyles transferred children from Catholic to public school so that they could qualify for the scholarship offer. "I have four kids, and my husband and I did the math," Susan Boyle said. "We will save $900,000. I can use the savings to pay for private lessons for the kids and other things I might not otherwise be able to afford. It would have been much more difficult to afford to pay for college." Susan Boyle became president of the PTA at the district's Roberts School, which her two younger children attended.

What effect would it have if Say Yes limited its college tuition scholarships even further, excluding not only students at nonpublic schools but those from middle-class families who are now eligible? This could happen if the cutoff for eligibility were a family income of less than, say, $50,000. Say Yes could divert aid to the neediest students to help pay for on-campus living expenses as well as for more than four years of studies. It is well established that the college students least likely to graduate are those from the poorest families.[4] Financial pressures drive many of them to drop out. But one can hardly ignore that these students tend to be the least prepared for higher education and may simply discover that they can't handle the work.

In any event, Say Yes certainly could stretch its funds farther by targeting assistance on the neediest students. Any such change now, though, would be a public relations nightmare given the frosty reception that Say Yes got when the city discovered the scholarships for private higher education would not be offered to students from all income groups, as people were originally led to believe. Furthermore, making the scholarships widely available was meant to help hold and attract middle-class families to Syracuse. There is some evidence that is happening, though this will be clearer over the long term.

A similar issue has been at the heart of the national debate over preschool education, which some advocates maintain should be universal. Others say that increasingly scarce money should be aimed only at the neediest children, leaving other families to pay on their own or provide experiences within the home that prepare youngsters for school. One of the arguments in behalf of universal preschool is that programs will be better protected and supported if the entire population has a stake in them. Much the same point could be made in favor of a high cutoff for the tuition scholarships in Syracuse—if the money holds out.

The Say Yes Scholarship in a World of Mounting Student Debt

The Say Yes tuition scholarships are especially valuable in light of the impact that college loans are having on the nation's students, who by the end of 2012 had accumulated almost $1 trillion in debt in federally guaranteed loans and another $150 billion in debt on private loans. Say Yes removed a major worry from the shoulders of Syracuse families and their college-going youngsters.

On average, America's college undergraduates relied on borrowed funds to pay for 27 percent of their college costs during the 2011–12 school year. Grants and scholarships covered another 29 percent of costs. This meant that 44 percent of the cost of attending college had to be absorbed by current income, savings, and gifts from relatives and friends.[5] In Syracuse with its many low-income residents, students who don't get loans, grants, or scholarships would have to struggle to afford higher education without the Say Yes scholarships.

For the two-thirds of students in the graduating class of 2011 across the country who borrowed to finance their college education, the average debt was $26,600,[6] meaning that these former students must devote a considerable portion of income from a postcollege job to paying off loans. Interestingly, the portion of debt incurred by borrowing money to get an education has been growing in recent years at the same time that Americans have been reducing their debt on credit cards and home mortgages, according to the Federal Reserve Bank of New York.

The federal government restructured the student loan program in 2010 to assume much of the responsibility that had previously been carried out by private lenders. A report to Congress in 2012 by the U.S. Department of Education and the new Consumer Protection Financial Bureau assails the practices of some private money lenders—especially the lenders to students attending for-profit trade schools. The report deems these lenders as little better than those responsible for the subprime scandal on home mortgages. "Many borrowers might not have clearly understood the differences between federal and private student loans," states the report.[7]

Adding to the unease of student borrowers has been the difficulty of declaring bankruptcy on these loans, the repayment of which has been as mandatory as death and taxes. Some relief came from the federal government, first in 2009 with the Income-Based Repayment Plan that linked repayment to discretionary income. Then in 2012, the Pay as You Earn repayment plan allowed for lower monthly repayments. Nonetheless, the pressures associated with repayment have deterred increasing numbers of college-going youth from attending the expensive, first-choice institutions that accepted them. They opt for second or third choices that are less costly.[8] The situation is exacerbated in many states by the actions of legislatures that have lowered funding levels of state-supported colleges and universities, forcing tuitions and costs at these institutions ever higher.

Guaranteed Scholarships in Other Cities

The Pittsburgh Promise, a pledge to pay up to $40,000 toward higher education for graduates of the city's public schools, shares many goals with Say Yes. The program seeks to increase high school completion rates, college readiness, and success in postsecondary education. As an outcome, the Pittsburgh Promise aims to produce a well-prepared workforce that will meet the needs of the city's employers.

The program envisions the development of the city's neighborhoods and ties itself to the reform of the school system. The promise of the scholarships is meant to mitigate and reverse declines in the city's population and in the school district's enrollment. These goals overlap with those that Say Yes has in Syracuse. While the Pittsburgh Promise has a less direct connection to reform than Say Yes does in Syracuse, the school system sees the promise as an organizing principle by which the schools, for their part, help all students prepare to benefit from the scholarships. A $100-million commitment by the University of Pittsburgh Medical Center (UPMC) underlies the Pittsburgh Promise. A grant of $10 million launched the program, and then UPMC contributed an additional $90 million as a challenge grant to spur a campaign to raise $150 million over ten years.

All graduates of Pittsburgh's public schools, including its charter schools, are eligible for the scholarships regardless of a family's financial need or income. A candidate must have at least a 2.5 grade point average and maintain a minimum attendance rate of 90 percent. Also, he or she should earn admission to an accredited public or private postsecondary institution in Pennsylvania.

Like the Say Yes scholarship, the Pittsburgh Promise aims to encourage long-term residence in its city. Children who enroll in the city's public schools as kinder-garteners and remain continuously enrolled through the twelfth grade are eligible for the full scholarship amount of $10,000 per year. The percentage of support declines depending on the grade in which a youngster enters the school system. Students who begin in the system at ninth grade get 75 percent of the maximum amount, $7,500 toward each of the four years of college.

The Pittsburgh Promise began with the city's high school graduates of 2008, and by fall 2012, some 3,800 students had entered higher education with the schol-arships. Almost half the students enrolled at just three schools—Allegheny County College, the University of Pittsburgh, and Penn State. The retention rates from the first to the second year of college have been equal to or higher than the national averages.

The Kalamazoo Promise was one of the first programs of its type, launched in 2005 by a group of anonymous donors. It pays a maximum of 100 percent of the four-year tuition for graduates of the city's public high schools who attend state colleges and universities in Michigan. Students who begin in the Kalamazoo Pub-lic Schools in kindergarten receive the maximum amount, and it tapers off from that point, dropping down to 65 percent of the tuition for students who enter the system at ninth grade.

All the school district's students are eligible for the scholarships, and they get ten years to use the financial assistance. They have the ability to start, stop, and resume the scholarship support unlike students in Syracuse. In its first five years, the Kalamazoo program led to larger enrollments in the school system and a higher rate of college attendance by high school graduates. Statistics from the Kalamazoo Promise show that anywhere between 74 percent and 82 percent of the graduates of the city's high schools use the scholarship within one year of graduation and that as many as 87 percent use it at some time. White and black students make almost equal use of the scholarship.

Unlike Say Yes, the Kalamazoo Promise involves no formal interventions into the school system, leaving that role to district officials and to the community. "We are the carrot, a catalyst," said Bob Jorth, executive administrator of the scholar-ship program.

An interesting aspect of the Kalamazoo Promise is the research conducted in conjunction with the scholarship program by the W. E. Upjohn Institute and by the college of education at Western Michigan University. Researchers study whether the program improves the progress of students through their K–12 education and whether it leads them to enter postsecondary institutions with better preparation. Research sponsored by the W. E. Upjohn Institute found that the existence of the scholarship program has significant effects in decreasing the number of days stu-dents spend on school suspension and increasing the grade point averages of black students specifically.[9]

Building an Infrastructure to Support Enrollment and Completion

Say Yes hired Christopher Walsh, a former financial aid dean at Syracuse University, as the first director of the scholarship program. He was succeeded in 2012 by Erin Corbett, who had experience in private school admissions and college financial aid. Walsh, as the original director, developed a pilot program for Say Yes that high schools throughout central New York State could use to coach and counsel students and their families through the circuitous search for financial aid. This program tacitly acknowledges that high school counselors, who ordinarily deal with scheduling, social work, and other burdens, have insufficient time remaining to guide students applying to college.

The Syracuse district and Say Yes sought additional help via a grant from the state's Higher Education Services Corporation to hire an extra counselor for each high school to coordinate activities dealing with college access, particularly scholarships through the Higher Education Compact. After the state turned down this request, Say Yes paid $80,000 to develop a comprehensive formula that shifted the key role of guidance counselors in Syracuse's middle schools and high schools to helping students with their postsecondary planning.

The situation that Say Yes wanted to remedy in Syracuse was not unusual. A study by Public Agenda found that 62 percent of young adults feel the advice they got from high school guidance counselors about higher education was poor or fair at best.[10] Furthermore, while more than 80 percent of secondary school counselors agreed that a top goal of theirs should be to ensure that all students complete twelfth grade ready to succeed in college, only 30 percent overall and only 19 percent at high-poverty schools saw this as their school's mission in reality.[11] The imperative for improving counseling and preparation for college can be seen just over the horizon, where—as soon as 2020—45 percent of the nation's public high school graduates will be nonwhite, an increase of 7 percentage points over the class of 2009.[12] What will happen if urban school systems such as Syracuse, which enroll large numbers of these students, do not improve their ability to set students on course for higher education?

A report from the College Board in 2012 said that too many school counselors are not in a position to help students get ready for college and careers. "[T]heir graduate schools fail to train them for this mission, schools pull them away from this critical work, and their administrators do not hold them accountable," the report states.[13]

The Financial Aid Counseling Network, a partnership between Syracuse city schools and Say Yes, engages financial aid personnel from such institutions as Syracuse University, SUNY Medical Center, LeMoyne College, and Onondaga Community College to serve as sponsors to postsecondary counselors at the high schools. The sponsors guide the counselors who, in turn, coach students as they deal with the dreaded Free Application for Federal Student Aid (FAFSA). The sponsors give the counselors a step-by-step process to try to ensure that they will handle every facet of the intricacies of the aid application. This effort by Say Yes is a huge boost for students and their families. Research shows that providing direct help with applications makes students more apt to enroll in college and receive needs-based aid.[14]

It fell to Walsh, as well, to establish an opportunity grant program so that Say Yes could provide $2,000 toward room and board for each of its students living on campus. He wanted to make the support more all encompassing, especially at costly private colleges and universities. This sort of assistance cushions the financial burden of college attendance for students from low-income families. "The real challenge," he said, "will be how effective we are in changing the population and choices in higher education. Right now, college choice is stratified by income. The primary goal is to improve the college-going rate and access to college."

To this end, Say Yes tries to make high school staff in Syracuse more aware of the details of the Higher Education Compact and get them to act more assertively to interest students in attending college. One discussion at an operating committee meeting of Say Yes, for example, dealt with creating information packets for high school staff, putting posters on walls, and assembling a library of video testimonials from Syracuse high school graduates enrolled in college. The point was that free tuition alone is no better for a high school student who has not the slightest idea how to get to college than a MetroCard is for someone who has never walked through a New York City subway turnstile.

Say Yes also invested in On Point for College, a nonprofit program already operating in the school district. The program provides personnel to hold the hands of students—often the first college-bound members of their families—through the entire application process and after acceptance. On Point offers personal assistance to students, even transporting them to and from campus once enrolled. The group's assistance goes so far as setting up a student's dorm room with linens and other supplies and, as its final form of help, sending someone to witness a student's commencement if no family member plans to attend.

Getting Them Ready

Ultimately, financial aid for college is not sufficient if students are academically unprepared and lack the resilience to overcome the setbacks that so frequently discourage young people from persevering. On New York's Regents Exam, a proxy for college preparation, only one of Syracuse's four neighborhood high schools, Corcoran, had scores to match high schools across the state. Henninger fell below but close to state averages, and Fowler and Nottingham trailed state averages by more considerable margins.[15]

Eshan Escoffery, the student mentioned earlier, started his higher education at Onondaga Community College, for example, and quickly discovered that his high school preparation was inadequate. He said he was weak in the core academic subjects and had to spend an extra term at the two-year institution before qualifying to transfer to Syracuse University.

Thus Say Yes said it would establish a collegiate preparatory academy to help students get ready for college. Say Yes planned to make the academy, underwritten by a grant from Verizon Foundation, a prestigious undertaking for the school system's most promising students. Students would enter the academy based on selective criteria, willingness to participate, and commitment to attend college. The academy planned to give participants access to Naviance, a web-based data management system that keeps track of grade point averages, test results, college choices, application information, and career possibilities. The plan called for tutoring sessions four afternoons a week. The academy was supposed to begin operating before the end of the 2011–12 school year.

It never happened. What looked promising on paper did not materialize because no one from Say Yes worked with the high school principals to solicit their opinions on the plan for the academy. In other words, Say Yes did not bother obtaining buy-in. It was a well-intentioned, glaring mistake. By the end of 2012, finally aware that it was dancing the fox trot without a partner, Say Yes was ready to start over. It brought the high school principals into the process and hoped that they would assume ownership and that there could still be a collegiate preparatory academy—designed and supported by the high schools.

The tutoring was the only part of the academy that Say Yes had implemented, but in abbreviated form. The paid tutors, students from Syracuse University, did not receive training for the task and were unclear about their assigned duties. Rather than using a central location as planned, where all the high school students and the tutors would assemble, the university—unaware of the original plan— dispatched the tutors to the individual high schools. They worked in classrooms to aid students as teachers taught lessons. What originated as a proposal for a prestigious academy became tutoring for anyone who needed it, and the trappings of an academy were abandoned.

What did remain was a separate plan for SAT coaching sessions, carried out in partnership with the 100 Black Men of Syracuse. The sessions convened on Saturdays. One goal of boosting scores is to make more youngsters more acceptable to highly selective colleges. SAT coaching is open not only to students in the city but to some students in suburbs and parochial schools as well. Participants receive Blackboard accounts so they may access the tutoring online when unable to attend in person.

Tutoring Syracuse's Students

The manner in which the tutoring evolved as the only remnant of Say Yes's collegiate preparatory academy could be seen one morning in a social studies course at Fowler High School. The teacher sped through a lesson that in a single class session ranged from the Roman emperor of the late third century, Diocletian, to Muhammad, some three centuries later. All the fluorescent ceiling lights except one were turned off so the dates and information projected on a screen could be seen more clearly.

The teacher spoke of Constantine, a successor to Diocletian who converted to Christianity, and said that the Romans' elaborate system of roads helped in the spread of the new religion. "You're going to read about something that is happening in Arabia at about the same time that the Roman Empire is falling," he explained in setting the stage for the reading they were about to begin. He said he would give them practice questions the next day and a test the following day.

Katie McNeil, a junior in teacher education at Syracuse University, was assigned to sit with a particular student and help guide him through the lesson. About 20 percent of the students at Fowler High are classified for special education, but McNeil's student was not one of them. He just read at a level below that expected for the class. McNeil tutored in this class twice a week. The teacher sent her the daily lessons in advance by email to prepare her for the day's work.

McNeil helped the student she tutored cope with vocabulary as the words appeared in the reading, first asking him if he knew the meaning of "harsh" and then asking about "nomadic" as the passage turned to the lives of desert people in the Arabian Peninsula. When the teacher asked how the people earned a living and the student knew that it was through trading, the student exulted over his correct answer. The teacher had distributed a list of questions that the students were to consider as they read the text so that they could seize on the main points. The students were to write the answers to the following questions on the worksheet:

- What was Muhammad's job, and why was he respected?
- What happened to Muhammad's children?
- What would Muhammad do in a cave?
- What happened in 610 CE—what was the angel telling him to do?
- What had God chosen Muhammad to do? What did he eventually become?

The tutor encouraged the student to go back and scan the reading as he considered each question. "So what did Muhammad eventually become?" she asked him. When he didn't know the answer, she pointed to the portion of the text in which he could find the answer.

"A prophet," the student exclaimed.

"Kind of like a messenger," the tutor said in response. "Remember when we talked about Paul?" she asked the student, reminding him that he learned earlier in the year about Paul's role in spreading Christianity.

In another classroom, two tutors aided a math teacher in reaching the students. Smeha Iyer, a master's degree student in information management at Syracuse University, assisted a student trying to use algebraic concepts to solve geometry problems. There were 13 problems on a two-page worksheet that contained the homework for the day.

The student had just completed a problem in which he had to use the relationship between supplementary angles to find a solution. Now he had gone on to another problem that called on him to use the relationship between consecutive angles for problem solving. "The angle is equal to what?" Iyer prompted him with a question about a diagram in which a line crossed two parallel lines, and he was given an equation that he was to solve for x. Tutor and student discussed the degrees of the angles. She encouraged him to use a graphing calculator.

"Do you divide this?" the student asked about a number that he produced on the calculator.

"You don't divide it," the tutor said. "You can subtract 80 on both sides."

"Now you divide, right?" asked the student as he proceeded toward a solution. Finally, he arrived at the correct answer.

"Perfect!" the tutor complimented him.

But that was just the start of the homework. There were still problems to solve dealing with the slopes of lines, equations relating to lines parallel to and perpendicular to a given line, and a quadratic equation.

Iyer paused to speak with me, discussing the challenge of serving as a tutor. She pointed out that it was not always clear to her as a tutor just how much knowledge of the subject the students possessed. She always had to feel her way, trying to determine how much she was required to fill in. The students needed more help than the teacher alone could provide.

Other Kinds of Support for College Success

Though Say Yes started the scholarship program during its first year in the district, the main impact at the secondary level is not likely to come until elementary children work their way up through the grades. Therefore it will take some time before the reforms initiated by the district with the support of Say Yes spread through the entire school system, like water filling a swimming pool. When that occurs, Say Yes hopes that more students will consistently emerge from high school ready for postsecondary education. The connection between the scholarships and making the most of their high school education is implicit, but sometimes it appears that Say Yes and the district have not done enough to ensure that students recognize that link.

"Now a lot of them need remedial work in college, and they are not passing the state Regents tests at the rate we would like," said Walsh. "College success is set in middle school and high school, and our goal in the long run is that every student will be ready academically."

In the meantime, more than two hundred students in Syracuse's secondary schools benefit from Advancement Via Individual Determination (AVID), a program predating the arrival of Say Yes and sharing the goal of Say Yes to make students college ready. Say Yes considers itself a good fit with AVID, which reaches seven hundred thousand students in 4,600 schools throughout the country. AVID involves a daily elective course in which students receive carefully structured tutoring and learn to record and analyze thorough class notes. In addition, subject-area teachers undergo training by AVID to enable them to introduce more rigorous material so as to get students to reflect more deeply on their lessons.

AVID operates in Syracuse's four neighborhood high schools and in all but three of the middle schools. The program, mainly directed at students whose prior achievement is in the C+ to B– range, is selective in that youngsters must volunteer to be in it. The district's budgetary constraints reduced the number of AVID courses and limited teachers' exposure to AVID's staff development.

AVID seniors at high schools in Syracuse, like their counterparts around the country, plan to go to college at higher rates than students not in AVID. The percentage planning to attend college increases with the number of years they are in

AVID. Among non-AVID seniors in Syracuse, for instance, the portion in 2012 planning on attending college was 56 percent. For seniors who had spent three years in AVID, the rate was 75.6 percent. The impact of AVID on Syracuse students in terms of test performance, though, was not significant. They scored no better than non-AVID students on the state's high school Regents exams in math, English, social studies, and science.[16] It could be that deficiencies in the district's instruction and curriculum afflicted all students equally.

Is College Worth the Cost—Even with a Scholarship?

Unfortunately for Syracuse's new high school graduates, the opportunity afforded by Say Yes to grab the golden ring comes at a time when the ring has grown somewhat tarnished. The nation's deep recession gave rise to chatter about whether a college education is worth the effort and the cost. Debate has ensued almost since the establishment of Harvard College in 1636 over whether one attends college to increase prospects for employment or simply to become more fully educated. Many advantages having to do with knowledge and wisdom remain, but the value of a degree in the job market became shaky at a time when millions of Americans were out of work and the economy barely produced new jobs.

A choice among full-time jobs with the possibility of upward mobility is no longer the sure thing that it was for previous college graduates. Only 51 percent of those who got bachelor's degrees in 2011 were employed full time nine months later. Eighteen percent worked part time or were unemployed and searching for work. Another 5 percent were unemployed and not looking for work. Most of the rest attended graduate or professional school. Moreover, those who got degrees during the recession, from 2009 to 2011, earned $3,000 less on average in their first job than those who received bachelor's degrees before the recession began.[17]

The United States has entered a new era in which even college graduates sometimes must be content with part-time jobs and low pay. Some in the current generation of graduates moved back in with mom and dad because they could not afford their own places. Exacerbating the situation is the finding that only four in ten of the jobs obtained by 2011 graduates required a four-year degree and only two in ten young degree holders saw the job as being on their career track.[18]

Yet high school graduates like those in Syracuse continue to place their faith in college. So many young people in the United States feel this way that in March 2011, for the first time in history, more than 30 percent of American adults age 25 and older had a least a bachelor's degree.[19] Even during recession, more education means a better chance for a job and higher pay than would have been available without a degree. In a report titled *How Much Protection Does a College Degree Afford?*, Pew Charitable Trusts found after examining Current Population Survey data from 2003 to 2011 that the decline in employment and wages was considerably worse for those with less education.[20]

Figures from the U.S. Bureau of Labor Statistics in early 2012 showed that unemployment ranged from 14.1 percent for those who had not finished high school to 8.7 percent for those with some college to 4.9 percent for those with bachelor's degrees, to 2.5 percent for those with doctoral degrees. Weekly pay followed a similar pattern ranging from $451 for the least educated to $1,665 for the most educated. Education is not an antidote to unemployment, though it eases the way through the worst of times. Even some post–high school education is better than none. Workers with two-year associate degrees or some formal learning beyond high school lost 1.75 million jobs during the recession and later gained 1.6 million jobs after 2009. Those with a high school diploma or less lost 5.6 million jobs and continued to bleed jobs after 2009.[21]

But degrees in some fields pay off better than degrees in other fields, and, in general, graduate and professional degrees hold higher rewards than bachelor's degrees. An analysis by the Center on Education and the Workforce at Georgetown University showed majors in various engineering fields, computer science, and math start work at the highest salaries (all above $80,000). Far behind these fields, the majors that result in the lowest starting salaries (none above $40,000) are fields such as counseling, early childhood education, religious vocations, social work, and drama.[22]

So salaries aside, the gift of a tuition scholarship for graduates of high schools in Syracuse is apt to lead to a better life even in the midst of economic uncertainty. Say Yes is on the right track in seeking to see all students prepared for college so that they may benefit from the scholarship and whatever the future may hold.

A Summer Bridge

Say Yes, in collaboration with Onondaga Community College (OCC), launched its Summer Success Academy in 2011 for a select group of tuition-scholarship Syracuse high school students scheduled to attend the college in the fall. The common denominator for the students was their failure of one or more of the college's placement tests in reading, English composition, or math. The students, in other words, were designated for noncredit remedial courses. The academy offered them an advanced opportunity not only to acclimate themselves to the campus but also to try to pass the remedial courses during the summer so they could move directly into regular, credit-bearing courses when the academic year began in the fall.

The academy program in 2012, when I visited it, ran for five weeks from 8 a.m. to 5 p.m. Members of the OCC faculty taught courses during the morning hours, and tutors met with students in the afternoon to help with homework and guide them through material with which they struggled. In addition, the students took the First-Year Seminar for one credit during the summer, a course that otherwise would have been required in the fall. Say Yes made the Summer Success Academy free to participating students and scheduled it again for 2013 for the third year in a row, extending it to six weeks instead of the previous five.

Onondaga Community College is the mother ship for Syracuse students continuing on to higher education. It enrolls the largest portion of them, accounting for more than 90 of the 540 graduates of the city's public high schools who entered colleges and universities in 2012. The sprawling, wooded OCC campus, just over the city line, is a one-hour bus trip for some Syracuse students, all of whom received free bus passes during the summer from Say Yes.

The director of the Summer Success Academy for Say Yes in 2012 was Germain Soto, a doctoral student at Syracuse University. Soto, of Puerto Rican heritage, had the background to relate to this group of students. He was raised in a New York City housing project. He got the break of a lifetime when Prep for Prep plucked him from a public school to provide him with a coveted place at the Collegiate School, one of the city's elite private institutions and the alma mater of such prominent New Yorkers as the late John F. Kennedy Jr. With that preparation, he went off to earn a degree at the Ivy League's Cornell University.

The Success Academy at OCC began summer 2012 with 34 students and became a class of 31 after 2 who did not make the adjustment withdrew and another showed up only once. The academy has room for just a small portion of the eligible students.

Colleges around the country have found that students consigned to remedial courses, especially more than one such course, are generally less likely to obtain their degrees. Such students worry about whether they have the skills to do college work and whether they will be able to keep up with assignments. The academy was formed at OCC not only to help young people bolster their skills but to give them confidence in their abilities. Altogether, about half of the graduates of Syracuse's public high schools arriving at OCC must take at least one remedial course.

One of those I interviewed at the academy had a pretty good idea why he ended up in remedial courses in reading and English composition. He attended a charter school for the middle grades and returned to a regular public school because he didn't think he was learning enough. Then at Syracuse's Henninger High School, he conceded that he didn't pay attention in his classes and didn't understand what was expected of him academically. He liked being on the varsity football team but was disappointed to spend most of his time on the bench.

After he got his diploma in 2012, he attended the Summer Success Academy at OCC aiming to get the remedial courses out of the way. He said that the scholarship he received from Say Yes aided him financially and his summer at the academy helped him get organized. And, eventually, he hoped that success in college would lead to a good job, ideally as a chef. He figured that without the scholarship he would have had to take on two jobs to afford college.

Trying to Succeed in Remediation

In partnering with Say Yes, Onondaga Community College sought to increase student retention. OCC already ran a similar summer program for some students who received New York State's educational opportunity grants. The goal of both summer programs, according to Kristine Duffy, the college's vice president for enrollment management and student development, was to teach students how to be students.

During the first summer that the academy operated, in 2011, its students lived in the college's dormitories, a group of attractive buildings with the look of an upscale condominium community. By all accounts, the students enjoyed a more complete college experience, which would make the adjustment easier when they joined the 3,200 freshmen on campus in the fall. However, Say Yes did not continue the residential aspect because of the added expense.

An evaluation of the first Say Yes Success Academy found that students in the summer residential program had better academic outcomes during the regular school year than commuting students who did not have the advantage of the summer program. Passing rates for the summer residential students were 88 percent in English composition, 88 percent in reading, and 68.4 percent in math as compared with 73.6 percent, 78.3 percent, and 56.1 percent, respectively, for the nonacademy students. Furthermore, a questionnaire administered to the summer students showed that 83 percent either agreed or strongly agreed that the academy met their expectations. Ninety-five percent agreed or strongly agreed that they would recommend the academy to others, and 92 percent agreed or strongly agreed that they were better prepared for college as a result of their summer experience.[1]

Even without using the dorms, the academy in 2012 was able to continue offering some features to ease the transition for the Say Yes students, including weekly sessions at which OCC department chairs addressed the students to familiarize them with the college's regular academic program. Also, Wendy L. Allen, the academic services director, held a half-hour meeting with each academy student to discuss the strengths he or she exhibited on tests that had been administered. She tried to relate their strengths to what they needed to succeed in their prospective academic majors. "They can achieve more by focusing on their strengths than by making comparable efforts to overcome their weaknesses," Allen said of the approach she took with the students. She made sure the students knew they could turn to her if they encountered difficulties during the school year.

Trying to Make Up Ground in Math

Given that the academy had fewer than three dozen students, it was possible to keep summer class sizes small, thereby allowing instructors to devote more attention to each student. Thus only six students sat in a remedial math class one morning as their teacher led them through the mysteries of factoring trinomial squares. They had already learned that different types of polynomials require different kinds of factoring.

Lessons earlier in the week probably did not constitute the first time that these students from Syracuse encountered math problems of this sort. Chances are they had seen such problems in the eighth grade and delved into them again in high school, in both algebra and algebra II. "A lot of this they have done before, and they might have done it successfully," Heather Liggett, the teacher, told me. "But if they didn't use it, they might have forgotten part of it. It looks confusing but not if we take it step-by-step." The students reviewed problem after problem, ever alert to the nonfactorable ones that Liggett threw into the mix to try to trick them as they factored using three different methods.

These students and others in the program were off to see tutors in the afternoon. Some spent the tutoring session practicing for a test the next day, trying at one point to solve negative five over four divided by negative three over four in parenthesis, a problem from a beginning algebra book. The tutor asked one particular student what annoyed her about the problem. "Fractions and minuses," the student responded, more or less giving up on all of it.

"The operation is what?" asked the tutor, trying to draw her back in.

"Divide," said the student.

Finally, the tutor reminded the student that she could "deal with the signs later on" and that she should divide five over four by three over four. And so it went until the student—in a eureka moment—exclaimed, "Oh, oh. I get it."

Another student from Syracuse, sitting at the same table and also seeking help in math from the tutor, said to me, "I learned this in my high school years, but I got in trouble and found it hard to learn. Now I'm trying to learn it again. In ninth grade, my math teachers kept quitting. I had three different math teachers and a sub. I failed algebra, but they put me in geometry. I went to summer school, and I failed algebra again. I failed geometry and never got to trig. I asked for help, but I didn't get it. I switched high schools, and finally they helped me pass algebra."

A student from the class I had observed in the morning, who had gone to a different tutoring session, told a somewhat similar story as he hovered over a desktop computer: "I went to Henninger, and I didn't learn anything there. Math had gotten screwed up for me around middle school. The teacher made it confusing. It's working out better this summer. I'm getting a better understanding of math. I didn't have good judgment when I was younger. Now I'm more motivated, and I see that getting a college degree will make all the difference for a job." This student ended up passing both of his remedial courses in the summer but couldn't sustain his motivation as a college freshman during the 2012–13 academic year. He dropped out, saying of higher education, "I basically gave it up because it was something I didn't want," though he conceded, "I know it is something that people need."

A lack of maturity and insufficient motivation during their high school years is a background that many remedial students seem to share and that they readily acknowledge. As a result of past inattention to academic work, they are left empty-handed—like carpenters who go to jobs without the tools they need, the missing tools in this case being those required to build the underlying structure of an education. The Summer Success Academy and the college tuition scholarships they receive give them a second chance, which some appear more resolved than others to use to their advantage.

Trying to Make Up Ground in English

Some Syracuse students had no trouble with math; it was reading and composition that troubled them. One such student, Timmy Nguyen, had been told by his school counselor that if he kept up his grade point average he could qualify for a Say Yes tuition scholarship. This sounded good to him as he wanted to become an electrical engineer. He liked math and did well in the subject. Events and competitions sponsored by the Southeastern Consortium for Minorities in Engineering (SECME), a national organization that encourages minority students to pursue math and science degrees, nurtured his proclivity for math. Nguyen, of Vietnamese heritage, was even part of a team that entered a regional robotics competition.

But Nguyen's interest in math and science did not extend to other subjects. He admitted that in high school he did just enough work to scrape by in English. He blamed only himself for his shortcomings in English classes. Nguyen thought, in looking back, that the English teachers spent too much time preparing students for tests.

So it was no great surprise to him that he did not pass the placement tests in reading and English composition at Onondaga Community College, where he ended up in the 2012 Summer Success Academy. When he took the courses at the academy he liked them because the teaching methods appealed to him and there were tutors available, as well, offering him a chance to keep up with the work. "I'll be ready for college in the fall," he said, looking ahead to becoming a full-fledged student with remedial courses behind him. He even thought of trying out for the lacrosse team, continuing with a sport that he played in high school.

Students like Nguyen met with a tutor who had them highlight the main ideas in yellow as they went through a reading assignment. The text, titled "Advantages of Small Business Ownership," was an unusual topic for this group of urban kids, but perhaps it represented the challenge of searching for meaning in unfamiliar content. "Do you see a key word here?," the tutor asked a student about a passage. The tutor pointed out that the word "additionally" might be a clue that another main idea was coming. The students took notes as they read, dividing a paper by a vertical line down the middle so they wrote questions about learning objectives on the left and answers on the right side.

These were some of the learning objectives with which they dealt as they looked for main ideas:

- Specify the advantages of business ownership.
- Summarize the disadvantages of a small business.
- Analyze why many small businesses fail.
- Describe how you go about starting a small business and what resources you need.
- Evaluate the demographic, technological, and economic trends affecting the future of small business.

And so it went in remedial reading as students learned to derive meaning from text—lessons without which they had little chance of success in college, lessons that one assumed would have been conveyed to them in elementary and secondary school. As Emmanuel Awuah, the interim vice president of academic services at OCC, explained, "In high school, the responsibility was on the teacher. In college, the responsibility is on the students." In just a few weeks, the students would have to be ready to take on the challenge of reading books in regular courses, though support services, counseling, and advisement would be available from the college.

In a remedial composition course, the instructor had assigned five separate essays to the students over the length of the summer. The tutor for this course said of the students, "Mainly, they need confidence. They are much more capable than they think they are. Confidence comes with positive reinforcement. I focus on what they *do* know."

Students in this course had the opportunity to approach the topics in a more personal way than many had done in high school. The teacher encouraged them to understand that the first words they put on paper did not represent the final product. In fact, they received no grade on the first draft. Instead they got comments they were supposed to use for redrafting their work. The tutor expected the final draft to meet grammatical standards. "I'm a stickler," he said proudly.

A draft submitted by one of the students exhibited both the quality of her writing and her growth as a writer. She titled the piece "A Change in My Life." She wrote, "Taking this course changed my whole perspective of writing. No one had ever told me that I had a potential talent in writing. No one has ever told me that I had any type of talent at all. I felt better about myself when Professor [Christopher] Altman told me in one of the comments on my essay, 'I don't know if you realize it, but you are a stunning writer' . . . He made a great impact in my life. It made me realize that there is so much more to me than knowing how to play tennis."

When she arrived with her family in the United States from Puerto Rico, as a young child, she spoke no English. She advanced sufficiently in her studies to start thinking about college when she was in middle school. Participating in Advancement Via Individual Determination (AVID) helped whet her appetite for further studies.

But to her disappointment, when she was accepted to OCC with a Say Yes scholarship, her placement tests indicated that she would have to take remedial courses in reading and composition. This followed a series of setbacks when it came to writing. "I was discouraged from writing in high school," she said. She didn't like the writing assignments in high school because they dealt mostly with marshaling facts, which bored her. She welcomed the assignments in her summer remedial composition course because they gave her an opportunity to write about herself and to offer opinions.

Both of her parents worked for the Syracuse City School District: her mother as a teacher's aide and her father in technical support. She wanted to major in fitness and nutrition. For her, college was a must and moved her toward her goal of doing things on her own. "You should not have to rely on others," she said. "And the only way to do that is with education."

Another student I interviewed knew as early as the ninth grade that she wanted to go to college. Her parents had attended college. She even knew she wanted to get a degree from Syracuse University so she could become a preschool teacher or run her own child care center. As she went through Syracuse's Corcoran High School, where she played varsity tennis, she heard from the media and from guidance counselors about Say Yes and its tuition scholarship. Along the way, the student met some Say Yes representatives and found them accessible, ready to answer questions she had about the scholarship and college. By the time she got her diploma in 2012, she was still intent on heading off to college even though her brother had dropped out and her sister chose not to pursue higher education. But she dismissed any thoughts of not attending college.

She qualified for a Say Yes scholarship but realized that she had to bolster some of her basic skills before she could gain admission to Syracuse University. So she settled for Onondaga Community College, where her placement tests showed that she must take remedial courses. She enrolled in remedial courses in reading and English composition in the Say Yes Summer Success Academy in 2012. She reveled in her achievements in the composition class. "I've definitely become a better writer," she said. "I pay a lot more attention to detail."

Why, though, did she have to reach a college campus before sharpening her composition skills? "In high school," the student explained, "the teachers were so focused on preparing us to pass the Regents tests that they did not look closely at kids' problems and how to fix them. They should say, 'This student needs something extra. Let's work on it.'" If anything, the responsibility of being the mother of a three-year-old son made her more single-minded about college as she gained her academic footing in the academy. "Now in our country," she said, "you have to go to school if you want to do anything with your life." It was clearly her hope to enhance her accomplishments.

Other Bridge Programs

Summer bridge programs for incoming freshmen in need of remediation are widespread. Kristi Eck, an education program director with Say Yes, first had the idea that her organization should get students onto the OCC campus before regular classes began in September. She assumed a major role in bringing the Say Yes Summer Success Academy into existence and keeping it running.

Across the country, summer bridge programs enroll 51.7 percent of students entering two-year colleges and 19.9 percent of students entering four-year colleges.[2] Often institutions require the courses for students who score below a specified level on placement tests. The remedial courses they must take in the summer generally last from four to six weeks and are therefore presented at an accelerated pace. It is still too soon for a substantial longitudinal evaluation of the program serving Syracuse students at Onondaga Community College, but the good news is that all the students taking remedial courses in the Say Yes Summer Success Academy in 2012 passed every course. That is a remarkable achievement.

Research literature contains hundreds of studies of bridge programs at individual colleges but a paucity of meta-analyses that pull together and assess data from a multitude of studies. Some evaluations deal with groups of colleges that are part of the same study. One such study, which received more attention than many others, tracked students at eight colleges in Texas from 2009 to 2011.[3] The research represents a collaboration of the Texas Higher Education Coordinating Board and the National Center for Postsecondary Research, part of the Community College Research Center at Teachers College, Columbia University. The results generated a number of publications and presentations.

An analysis based on this study shows that during the fall, following their participation in the bridge program, students are more likely to pass college-level courses in math and writing and to attempt higher-level courses as compared with peers who did not go through the bridge program. The bridge program does not have as much of an effect on reading ability, though, as it does on math and writing.[4]

Some other findings are not particularly encouraging. As compared with similar students who did not attend the bridge program, those who went through it did not attempt or earn more academic credits in the subsequent two years of college. Differences in achievement between the two groups in the subjects taught during the bridge programs disappeared after two years, and there was no evidence that the bridge programs had an impact on persistence toward degree completion.[5] Among the additional findings are the following:

- Recruiting students to summer bridge programs is difficult.
- Mixed ability classes and an accelerated format prove difficult for faculty.
- Some sites struggle to use tutors and mentors effectively.
- So-called outsiders who present general college knowledge to students are minimally effective. The informal sharing of college knowledge by professors and just being on the campus and becoming familiar with the college are more effective.

Whether students take remedial courses in summer bridge programs or during the regular academic year, there has long been the question of whether having to enroll in these noncredit courses slows down the pursuit of a degree or even gets students entirely off track. The common wisdom has been that remediation militates against completion of college.

In 2010, the Bill and Melinda Gates Foundation began to invest $110 million in research to transform remedial education. Nine colleges and universities got grants from the Gates Foundation in 2012 to develop massive open online courses (MOOCs) for students assigned to remedial education. In supporting this work, the Gates Foundation maintained that "[f]or most students these remedial courses do not lead to a college degree" and that "three out of every four students who take remedial courses will not graduate within eight years."[6]

Research on students who entered the City University of New York at the start of open admissions in the early 1970s presents a counterview. "Contrary to critics' contentions, our analyses suggest that remedial courses do not depress graduation rates for most students, and that remediation may reduce college dropout rates in the short term," concludes a book that examines the results over thirty years.[7] This experience may be the exception, though.

There is, in other words, still a great deal to learn about how to make bridge programs most effective. One would think that after all these years of remediation its impact would be known with some certainty and that students willing to expend the requisite effort could have some assurance about the outcome. Higher education is America's research engine, but apparently colleges and universities have not done a good enough job of studying some of their own programs.

Placement Testing

All too many students get scores on placement tests that require remediation, euphemistically called developmental education. Whatever name one uses for the courses, they usually carry no academic credits, cost students the same amount as credit-bearing courses, and slow the pursuit of a degree. In fact, the Community College Research Center found that students who are not required to take remedial courses have a 40 percent chance of completing their two-year degrees within eight years, while those who must take remedial education have only a 25 percent chance of getting degrees during the same period.[8]

Interestingly, the two organizations that dominate remedial testing are the same two that account for most college-entrance testing. The College Board calls its exam Accuplacer, and the ACT has a placement test named Compass.

One outcome of the increased emphasis on college readiness and the push to have more students complete college has been an interest in moving away from placement tests that lead to remedial courses, as if ignoring students' lack of preparation will miraculously make them successful in college. In any event, an article in *Education Week* identified a trend in which colleges are looking for alternatives to placement tests, including taking greater account of high school grades. It is a somewhat questionable move given the degree of grade inflation, the lack of uniformity in the marks, and differences in the content of courses from one high school to another.

Complete College America, a nonprofit group based in Washington, issued a report calling remediation "a bridge to nowhere" that 1.7 million students travel annually at a cost of $3 billion to them and to the states.[9] Instead of remedial courses, which the organization says only 62 percent of students at two-year colleges and 74.4 percent of students at four-year colleges complete, it proposes students with weak academic backgrounds go directly into credit-bearing courses that offer special provisions for them. For instance, tutoring would be embedded in such courses, and sometimes courses might be extended for an extra term to give students more time to complete the work.

The State University of New York (SUNY), an institution that wants to reduce the need for remedial courses, presents another approach. In part, SUNY hopes to make remedial testing less necessary by working with the state education department to develop assessments in elementary and secondary schools that signal earlier when students are not on track to handle college-level work, like gauging whether a car is traveling fast enough to reach its destination by an appointed hour. An examination near the end of the sophomore year of high school, for example, could throw down a red flag to warn some students, while they still have time to change speed, that they are not progressing at a rate that will make them ready for college by the end of senior year.

Ready for College

Presumably, remedial courses of the sort Syracuse students took at Onondaga Community College would not be necessary if students emerged from high school prepared to handle the work in higher education. This lack of preparedness received unprecedented attention during the first decade of the twenty-first century. Say Yes, in its efforts in Syracuse, made college readiness a key part of the program.

A main reason for the growth of the college readiness movement has been the inability of at least half the students admitted to institutions of higher education to earn degrees. Academic failure is not the sole reason students fall by the wayside, but it is the principal explanation. The country has made progress in enlarging the ranks of those who complete high school and apply to college. The national high

school graduation rate reached 78.2 percent according to the latest federal figures.[10] Unfortunately, a student is not necessarily ready for college just because he
or she takes the requisite courses in high school. A study of the content of courses
in algebra I and geometry found that the degree of rigor was often less than one
might expect.[11] Course titles may be misleading, and the material may be less challenging than colleges expect.

High schools, particularly in urban settings like Syracuse, have devoted far
less attention than suburban high schools to making students ready for the challenges that await them in postsecondary education and to increasing their motivation and perseverance. The next step by educators must involve ensuring success
through improved preparation. A group of college presidents drawn from all
sectors of higher education urged just such a goal on the nation in a 32-page report
with a title that said it all: *College Completion Must Be Our Priority*.[12]

A report issued jointly by the National Center for Policy and Higher Education
and the Southern Regional Education Board identified five main reasons for the
gap between college eligibility and readiness to do college-level work:

1. Pre-K–12 and postsecondary expectations are disconnected.
2. Courses and seat time do not guarantee skills and knowledge.
3. Traditional readiness assessments—the SAT and the ACT—do not measure
   college readiness.
4. Schools and teachers are not accountable for teaching to college-level
   standards.
5. Colleges are not accountable for degree completion.[13]

Readiness for college has implications that, like a long-lasting inoculation,
manifest themselves throughout a lifetime. Students who can cope with the vicis-
situdes of college and persist until receiving diplomas are more apt to get better
jobs, earn more money, steer clear of the justice system, not require public assistance, participate in civic activities, and raise children with more chance of suc-
ceeding in school.

Some Measures of Readiness

So how should advocates define college readiness? The Education Commission of
the States, a consortium of state governments, issued a report that considers three
approaches to answering this question: (1) states could align performance expectations with state standards, (2) they could establish ambitious cut scores on state
assessments, or (3) they could simply use scores on such tests as the SAT and ACT
as proxies of readiness.[14]

As it happens, 46 states and the District of Columbia had subscribed by 2013 to
a Common Core of curriculum standards developed subject by subject by panels
of experts. Twenty-two of the states collaborated as the Partnership for Assessment of Readiness for College and Careers (PARCC) to create assessments to mark
students' progress as they prepare for higher education. Presumably, assessments

tied to the Common Core will replace high school exit exams in many if not most of the 31 states with such exams. PARCC expects to have a test by 2015 to determine at the end of their high school math sequence whether students would need to take remedial math in college.

It remains to be seen how the states will implement the Common Core curriculum as a measure of college readiness. The report from the Education Commission of the States (ECS) said that many states were still working out their definitions of college readiness. Pass rates could be misleading if some states set their performance standards for readiness at low levels as they did in complying with the testing mandated by the No Child Left Behind law during the first decade of the twenty-first century.

The ACT views college readiness through the scores that high school students attain on the company's college-entrance examinations. Viewed in terms of scores on ACT's four subject-area tests, only one-quarter of test takers in the graduating class of 2011 proved ready for college in all four subjects. The percentage changed little during the years from 2007 through 2011, a period when educators increased their focus on readiness. The students most likely to meet ACT's benchmarks for readiness took four years of English and three years in each of the other major subjects. Similarly, the College Board's SAT college-entrance exam offers some indication of college readiness, and the outlook is not good either. From 2008 to 2012, scores declined four points in critical reading and five points in writing and remained about the same in math. Only 43 percent of those who took the SAT achieved the college- and career-readiness benchmark.[15]

The Bill and Melinda Gates Foundation took an interest in college readiness as well as in remedial testing. The Gates Foundation worked with the Annenberg Institute for School Reform at Brown University and the John W. Gardner Center of Stanford University to develop a College Readiness Indicator System. The system has three dimensions: (1) academic preparedness, (2) academic tenacity, and (3) college knowledge.[16]

This approach, in other words, predicates itself on the notion that mastering subjects in high school is not enough to get students through college. Academic preparedness, of course, refers to the knowledge and skills that students take with them from high school. Academic tenacity involves beliefs, attitudes, and behaviors that drive students to embrace their college-level work and to persist in the face of obstacles. College knowledge begins with the know-how to fill out applications for admission and financial aid and continues with navigating the ins and outs of campus life. Say Yes's work in Syracuse has been very much in sync with these three dimensions, though Say Yes has not explicitly defined its work as such.

The Effectiveness of Readiness Programs

Just how effective are formal readiness programs? One such effort in northern New Mexico provides some answers to this question. The program involved a collaboration between Engaging Latino Communities for Education (ENLACE), funded by the state of New Mexico, and GEAR UP, a federal program; the acronym stands for Gaining Early Awareness and Readiness for Undergraduate Programs. The U.S. Department of Education started GEAR UP as a result of an amendment in 1998 to the Higher Education Act. GEAR UP gives grants to states and to partnerships such as the one in northern New Mexico.

Researchers collected data on 866 students from five school districts, including Santa Fe and Taos. The students reported that the overwhelming obstacle to their academic success is a lack of support and encouragement from family, teachers, schools, and the community. Three other important obstacles, according to students, are negative peer pressure, their own lack of interest in school, and stress at home and outside of school.[17]

Among the report's recommendations are those for families—get involved in your children's lives, push your child and encourage hard work, get to know your child's teachers and track your child's academic progress, and talk to your child about school and how they are doing daily. The recommendations for schools and teachers are to motivate and encourage students, use a culturally relevant curriculum, explain lessons better, incorporate strategies that make learning fun, implement more intervention and support, set high expectations, never give up on students, and share best practices among other educators.

Some institutions of higher education have acted unilaterally to deal with readiness in order to assist underserved students who traditionally are least prepared. California's San Diego State University (SDSU) is one such school. It narrowed gaps in the graduation rates between low-income students and others. Among transfer students who come mostly from two-year colleges, San Diego State raised graduation rates for minority students. Of the students entering in 2003, more than 61 percent of those from underrepresented ethnic groups got their degrees in six years or less—almost double the rate during the 1990s.

Stephen L. Weber, who oversaw these accomplishments as president before retiring in 2011, said that the college's policies over this period led to better outcomes for underrepresented students. SDSU formed a compact to work with elementary and secondary schools in one of the city's poorest areas and managed enrollments so that sufficient funds would be available for services for at-risk students. By concentrating attention on students who might otherwise have faltered—and not taking in more of them than it was in a position to assist—the university more readily ensured that the time invested by faculty and staff would yield higher graduation rates. "Admitting more students than can properly be served does them no favors," Weber said.

12

Paying the Bills

Say Yes envisioned Syracuse as a model to demonstrate the possibilities of government working together at various levels to drive large-scale improvement in a school system. No longer, under this approach, would the schools stand alone, cut off from entities that, ideally, could emerge from their own isolation to act in concert with the school district to leverage resources for students. Furthermore, the model would ultimately boost the fortunes of the city. From the start, Say Yes knew it wanted a program that would eventually sustain itself and that the school system—with the support of its community—could institutionalize so as to outlast the midwives who brought it into the world.

Say Yes's role in picking up some of the costs that seem peripheral to the school system's usual expenditures—like those associated with meeting the social and emotional needs of students, for instance—could be shifted to other sources. The county government in Onondaga, among other agencies, quickly recognized these possibilities. And so it was that with a little ingenuity county expenditures for mental health were harnessed to the needs of the Syracuse school district's children and their families.

This move and others like it should be seen as simply a start in building a collaborative model with wide possibilities for replication. Schools employ nurses, but so do county governments. Schools employ security personnel, but so do police departments. Schools remove trash and maintain grounds, but so do cities. Schools fund after-school and summer programs for students, but so do philanthropies and community-based organizations. Say Yes sought to get people to consider more creative ways of supporting education.

Arkansas does just this with its joint use agreement grants that the state funds through its tobacco excise tax. The goal is to maximize resources while increasing opportunities for physical activity by children and adults. Municipalities, community-based organizations, recreation departments, and other nonprofit entities may obtain grants to support their proposals. The projects in a small state like Arkansas with a population of fewer than 3 million are admittedly on a more modest scale than might be possible in New York State with its population of almost 20 million. Nevertheless, the projects exemplify what can happen with leveraging. Springdale, Arkansas, for instance, built walking trails around its elementary schools when the city contributed the labor and construction equipment, and the school district donated and maintained the land.

The potential for something far more extensive exists in the Los Angeles Unified School District, which now promotes joint use agreements with local government agencies and nonprofit organizations. As in Arkansas, these agreements involve facilities for athletics and recreation. Among the main concerns in forging partnerships in Los Angeles are the maintenance of facilities, the oversight of operations, liability issues, ownership, and covering costs.

Thus Say Yes helped Syracuse move in a new direction by encouraging collaboration between the school district and other community entities. So it is that in leveraging more funds to hire mental health counselors for the city's schoolchildren through an organization known as Contact Community Services, Say Yes paid 38 percent of the cost, and the county government covered the other 62 percent. This was the pattern in the fiscal year 2012 budget as Say Yes tried to get local entities in Syracuse to take on an increasing portion of the expenses for services to schoolchildren.

The fiscal year 2012 budget, for instance, allocated $830,308 to pay the Say Yes student support specialists, formerly known as site directors, assigned to the individual schools. Huntington Family Centers employed the personnel, and a contract with Onondaga County's Department of Social Services called for that agency to cover $642,613 of the cost. Say Yes bore the remainder of the expense, using its own funds and grant money received through the Promise Zone, federal funds that flow through the state of New York. Under a similar arrangement, Syracuse University provided counselors for the summer program in the schools in conjunction with the county's Department of Social Services. The university paid the bulk of the $556,913 expense, and Say Yes covered the remainder. In total, Say Yes paid $1,188,803 in matching funds during 2012 to comply with various contracts with the Department of Social Services.

Covering Costs While Seeking Sustainability

Say Yes, holding to its goal of striving to get the community to assume fiscal responsibility in the long run to make the program sustainable, covered a decreasing percentage of the costs after 2008, when it provided 100 percent of the $1,754,465 in revenues. By 2011, Say Yes was the source of $6,739,793 of the $17,473,858, or 38.5 percent of the revenues. Amounts of more than a million dollars came from the school district's general fund, the county, the federal government, and the city.

The program received more than $50 million in operating funds since it started in 2008 through 2012, including $17,963,297 from Say Yes Inc. Skillful leveraging garnered substantial revenues over the same years from the Syracuse City School District ($20.2 million), Onondaga County ($8.9 million), the city of Syracuse ($3.48 million), and the state of New York ($1,000,000).

Issues of cost were paramount as Say Yes considered what form the program would take and where to situate it. The increase in state school aid scheduled for Syracuse over a four-year phase-in period, which happened as a result of the

Campaign for Fiscal Equity case in the courts of New York State, was to be approximately $3,500 per student. Coincidentally, Say Yes projected about the same cost per child for its program. The state and Say Yes were clearly reading from the same script. This would mean that the district could spend an additional $75 million annually.

Say Yes assumed the extra costs initially and proceeded with the program on the premise that the portion of added expense taken on by the school district and its allies would gradually increase by 20 percent annually for five successive years starting in the 2009–10 school year. The goal was that by the 2013–14 school year the district, using the state's fiscal equity funds and money from other sources, would cover the full cost of the enhancements introduced by Say Yes. In the meantime, Say Yes set out to raise the money needed to plug the gap while the state's contribution mounted. Say Yes knew from the outset that it did not want the program to remain entirely dependent on soft money, something likely to collapse like a balloon without air once the generosity ended. Say Yes wanted a program that the school system—with the support of its community—could eventually institutionalize. Individuals and businesses in Syracuse would have to be willing to reach for their checkbooks.

But largesse can be in short supply in Syracuse. The city has few sizable philanthropies other than the Central New York Community Foundation, which administers five hundred funds. Syracuse is a proud place that delights in a rich architectural heritage that left its neighborhoods with an unusually large number of houses in the Queen Anne and Arts and Crafts styles and a downtown that boasts buildings designed by prominent architects of the late nineteenth and early twentieth centuries.

The city, in other words, is in some ways locked into an earlier era and lacks the dynamism that once produced captains of industry and eager philanthropists. Individual donors were slow to come to the aid of Say Yes. "There's a dearth of capital here," said Peter A. Dunn, head of the Community Foundation. Say Yes's experience showed that such programs—even when they represent a thrust toward economic development—cannot necessarily count on the private sector to keep them afloat. Say Yes may have been overconfident about its ability to extract donations from the citizens and businesses of Syracuse, who, by and large, proved to be a parsimonious bunch.

This was a problem. The source of most philanthropy in the United States, according to the Foundation Center, a national group based in New York City, is individual giving, which provides 73 percent of all donations. Foundations and corporations rank far behind individuals. Moreover, of the $290.8 billion that Americans give away annually, 35 percent goes to religious groups and only 14 percent to education groups. Thus Say Yes must still find ways to stimulate individual giving in a place with "a dearth of capital" in the midst of a national recession.

Say Yes, though, can carve a niche among givers as it makes its case more widely known. Constellation Advancement, a fundraising consultant, found that Harlem Children's Zone and Teach for America, two of the most visible organizations devoted to education, raised $224 million and $143 million, respectively, in fiscal 2010–11, sums to which Say Yes can aspire. One of the most bantered-about phrases at a retreat that Say Yes held in Portland, Maine, in 2012 was "the elevator pitch." It is shorthand for the terse presentation that some advocates think Say Yes should develop to deliver to potential donors in the length of time it takes to ascend from the ground level to an office on a high floor.

Dealing with Tough Times

Most importantly, when it comes to financial needs, the recession intruded on Say Yes's plans, interrupting the state's anticipated funding levels after the second year of the program. Say Yes was mugged during what it expected to be a serene walk in the park. New York State froze its foundation aid for schools at the 2008–9 level, and the state legislature imposed a long-term cap on increases in state school aid. This ultimately led the district to implement various cutbacks and, finally, to borrow from the state against future budgets, a bit of legerdemain that allows for balancing the books without actually receiving money.

Michael A. Rebell of Teachers College, Columbia University, who studied the finances of the Syracuse City School District, praised the system's leaders for not backing down despite a budget gap of tens of millions of dollars from the full range of support services advocated by Say Yes in the 2010–11 school year. "Determined not to abandon or defer the pioneering urban reform program they had begun, Say Yes and school district leadership committed themselves to continue implementation of the Say Yes program and necessary instructional improvements," stated Rebell in an unpublished background paper he wrote for Say Yes.[1] Rebell was the moving force behind the Campaign for Fiscal Equity that had a major impact on school funding in New York State.

Say Yes retained Schoolhouse Partners to give the district advice for balancing its budget in 2011–12, a period during which aid from the state was reduced by $22 million. In turn, the teachers' union agreed to a reduction in salaries in exchange for an extension of the employment contract, and the district froze administrators' salaries. As it was, the Syracuse schools, compared with other districts, already spent less on central administration than five comparable school systems.[2]

"Poor school districts are being forced to cut electives, remedial tutoring, foreign languages, and other programs and services to balance budgets," Billy Easton, executive director of the Alliance for Quality Education coalition, wrote of the New York State situation in an op-ed column in *The New York Times*. "Many schools in less prosperous areas face what the state commissioner of education calls 'educational insolvency.'"[3] This concern about the plight of New York State's poor urban districts was registered in early 2012. Critics made much the same complaint in a report at the end of that year after looking at schools in some of the same districts. They found rising class sizes, minimum instruction devoted to science, and a failure to meet minimum academic standards—much of which the report attributed to financial shortfalls.[4]

New York State's financial crisis reflected what many other states experienced, except on a larger scale. Fiscal pressures affected not just school districts but entire cities. *The Wall Street Journal* described in 2012 how New York's state government might have to assume the oversight of cities, including specifically Syracuse and Rochester, by implementing financial control boards. Emergency assistance arrived in both cities in the form of one-shot advance payments in state aid.[5]

The school system in Syracuse deserves credit for striving mightily to protect and enhance its academic program even while cutting and consolidating expenditures in various areas. Contreras tried to minimize the impact on instruction as she eliminated positions. In 2012–13, she said only 13 percent of those who lost jobs were involved with instruction, and in 2013–14, the figure was only 6 percent, according to Contreras. The superintendent, with the encouragement of Say Yes, recognized the need to continue to bolster the portion of the budget most closely tied to instruction. Students coming out of the Syracuse schools had to be prepared to handle postsecondary studies if they were to make meaningful use of Say Yes's college tuition scholarships.

"Say Yes Syracuse's cost efficiency and cost effectiveness initiatives have tempered the impact of the major cuts in state aid that the district has experienced in recent years," Teachers College's Rebell said after studying the system's fiscal condition in 2012. He stated, "They have allowed Syracuse to continue to promote necessary instructional improvement, maintain the critical Say Yes comprehensive urban reform programs, and begin to implement properly the Common Core and APPR [Annual Professional Performance Review] mandates."[6]

Remaining Challenges

Some of the challenges that remain are as threatening as an ocean that has broken through a sea wall. Time and money for professional development are in short supply. Neither the after-school program nor the summer program, cornerstones of Say Yes's efforts in Syracuse, enrolls anywhere near all the students who might attend. Expenses would mount if more youngsters choose to participate in the two programs, which are voluntary. The system's preschool enrollment has increased, but many, many more children should be enrolled, and costs would rise accordingly.

Furthermore, most funding for the Syracuse public schools comes to the city from New York State, which provides more than three-quarters of the district's general operating fund. The school system got $288,500,564 from the state in the 2012–13 school year. Local funds from the city's property tax levy provided $64,617,911 to the public schools, which was the bulk of the entire amount collected through the levy.

The economic well-being of the school system is in jeopardy as it has no fiscal independence and operates as an arm of the city government, which Mayor Miner predicted in summer 2012 would be broke within three years. The extent of the city's burden can be appreciated by a careful reading of the statistics in a report issued in 2012. It showed that Syracuse, above all other municipalities in New York State, including New York City, theoretically carried the largest liability per household, $32,168, for the payment of health care coverage for its retired municipal and school employees.[7]

Local governments in New York State are responsible for these health care obligations to retirees. Syracuse was identified, along with Yonkers, by the State Budget Crisis Task Force in December 2012 as facing major fiscal problems.[8] Furthermore, the budget for the 2012–13 school year had to bear the burden of paying $26.3 million into the state's retirement systems for its employees. This obligation grew so fast that the figure came close to doubling in just three years.

The state government told localities that they were on their own in wrestling with their finances, a situation meaning that officials in Syracuse will probably have to juggle priorities to fund public education and the other services the city provides. "If you say to the municipality, 'You're going to have to figure out how to pay for it,'" Mayor Miner said of the city's wrenching financial obligations, "what you are saying is now bad people aren't going to be arrested. Snow will not be plowed from the roads. Trash will not be collected. And where are we going as a society if we cannot provide those basic, essential services?"[9]

Miner remained hopeful that the state would somehow ease the city's burden. So it was that when Governor Andrew M. Cuomo unveiled his budget in January 2013, proposing that hard-pressed municipalities deal with fiscal pressures by being allowed to delay their pension contributions, the disappointed mayor unreservedly criticized the budget and, by extension, the governor. It was a bold response on her part, playing Mother Hubbard to a political figure known to want to control the message. Mayor Miner doubled down in her criticism the next month, writing an op-ed column for *The New York Times* urging the legislature and the state comptroller to reject the governor's budget because it did too little to address the crises in the cities.[10]

Even after New York State stumbled into its own perilous fiscal times, Say Yes hoped that the city would be able to keep the plan on track. Say Yes projected the cost of each aspect of the Say Yes program—outlays for summer school, for instance, would grow from $738,003 to $3,939,592—and what it would mean in 2013–14. The program began without an ironclad financial guarantee of future revenues, only a vision of where the added funds would originate. Economic hardship left the school system flailing like a drowning person to continue its investment in the program. The district even cut student assistance counselors from its staff and depended on Say Yes and its partners to fill the void.

Making Fiscal Adjustments

An exhaustive review of the school system's budget by Schoolhouse Partners found that expenses rose from 2007 to 2011, while enrollment declined year by year. Schoolhouse Partners recommended that the district find savings through strategic reallocations. For example, eliminating high school study halls, which are duty periods of teachers, moving students into classes, and assigning one more class to each teacher could mean a reallocation of $1.9 to $3 million. Also, the consultant proposed combining smaller, less cost-effective high school classes on the same subject, a step that Contreras took in seeking to ensure that no general education course had fewer than 18 students.

Other expenditures, as well, appeared to Schoolhouse to be uneven and poorly planned. Spending on clerical staff, for instance, varied from 0.45 percent to 4.43 percent in the budgets of individual schools. The disparate spending patterns were reflected in average per student expenditures, which varied from $8,827 in the Henninger quadrant to more than $12,600 in the Fowler and Nottingham quadrants. These are direct costs attributed to each school and do not include such district-wide expenditures as supplies, transportation, professional development, curriculum, certain labor costs, and human resources. The school system spends $17,500 per student when taking into account all school and district-wide costs.

Examinations of individual departments revealed, for example, that information technology had 97 employees and received additional services from another seven people listed on the city's payroll. This bloated department typified the overstaffing found in some pockets of the district. This was an unusually large IT staff for a school system the size of Syracuse, a Jaguar XJ where a Nissan Versa might suffice. The district was told that it should eliminate and combine positions and turn over some work to vendors. Furthermore, a surfeit of managers in IT created a ratio of 1 per 5.3 staff members, a number that could easily be raised to 1 per 8 staff members by cutting some managerial positions, according to Schoolhouse Partners.

Consultants shone a bright light on special education as an area in which the Syracuse schools should seek cost savings. The district had identified more than 21 percent of its students as disabled, a figure about twice as large as the national average. In Syracuse, expenses were inflated by hiring a large number of teaching assistants in special education. The district made progress in cutting special education costs during the years after the arrival of Say Yes and Sharon Contreras. It reduced the number of teaching assistants, for instance, by 26 percent. Syracuse made these strides while, arguably, boosting the quality of the program. The number of teaching assistants was down to 540 by 2013, with 349 of them assigned to special education. Most of the others were in preschool and kindergarten classrooms.

Annually, like an overweight person who keeps going on diets and never seems to lose enough pounds, the district found itself eliminating staff into the 2013–14 school year. Each time, Contreras protected instructional staff so that they shed the least blood of any sector. Nonetheless, the general expenses budget projected for 2013–14 totaled more than $365 million.

Audits commissioned by Say Yes helped point the school system in a more viable direction. Gradually, the district adopted recommendations from these audits, and although enormous financial pressures remained, agencies in Syracuse learned that the synergy resulting from collaboration was a ray of sunshine breaking through an overcast sky. Say Yes's goal was to get everyone thinking in creative ways about how to support education, a form of thought that became more vital as resources shrank and district employees had to be more perspicacious in viewing expenditures. Of course, happiness did not prevail throughout the school system as it consolidated for survival. The teachers' union, for instance, thought the consultants did not paint an accurate picture and bemoaned the loss of many teaching assistants and other dues-paying members whose jobs were deemed superfluous by the consultants.

The nature of resource allocations goes a long way toward determining what school districts can accomplish for their students. Unlike for-profit businesses, public school systems cannot readily redirect allocations. An assortment of contractual obligations and political constraints tends to keep school districts from making some changes that might be advisable. Nevertheless, Stacy Childress, who gave much thought to such matters as deputy director of education at the Gates Foundation and as a faculty member at the Harvard Business School, thinks that public schools could find their way around such obstacles. She maintains that educational leaders generally have not developed a habit of weighing the relative impact of various activities so they can starve ineffective ones in order to feed promising ones. She concludes, after studying resource decisions in school districts, that the following measures could make a difference:

- Resource allocations should be a key part of a strategy.
- Superintendents should be prepared to make some top-down decisions when systemic barriers to improvement exist.
- Decisions should aim to add capacity to struggling schools without reducing capacity at stable or high-performing schools.[11]

Financing the Scholarships

The idea of paying for all of a town's high school graduates to attend college on tuition scholarships staggers the imagination and requires an exceedingly thick wad of dough. The more successful the school system becomes in preparing students for postsecondary education and the more ambitious young people grow in wanting to enhance their credentials, the more costly the venture. The mounting expense is so daunting that Say Yes trimmed back its original offer in Syracuse and scaled down its initial offer in Buffalo.

Say Yes set a goal of $20 million to endow tuition scholarships in Syracuse and had raised $7 million of the sum by 2012. The cost rose year by year in Syracuse as more students joined those already attending college. Most college-going students from the Syracuse school system attend public institutions of higher education in New York State. The Say Yes Higher Education Compact allows them to use the assistance at the two-year and four-year schools of the State University of New York (SUNY) and the City University of New York (CUNY). Students of all family incomes may use the scholarships at these institutions, where the $75,000 cap on income does not prevail. Say Yes will make up the difference—whatever is needed, if anything, beyond the aid from the institution—to cover the tuition.

Looking only at SUNY and CUNY schools, Say Yes spent $524,153 on scholarships during the 2009–10 academic year, supporting the first high school class to benefit from the scholarships. In 2010–11, when members of two high school classes used the tuition scholarships, the expense increased to $819,158. Then in

2011–12, the cost of the first three classes totaled $1,168,629. In addition, Say Yes supplements the tuition scholarships with money for books, fees, and—in some cases—room and board, having spent a total of $379,851 for these added costs from 2009 through 2013. Say Yes channels the money through Syracuse's Central New York Community Foundation.

Projections show that expenditures for students at SUNY and CUNY will rise to $1.6 million in 2014, $1.8 million in fiscal 2015, $1.9 million in fiscal 2016, and $2.1 million in fiscal 2017. Say Yes expects endowment income to rise from $40,000 annually in 2013 to $1 million in 2017. If these projections prove correct, Say Yes can increasingly rely on endowment revenues to finance the scholarships.[12]

Private institutions that belong to the Say Yes Higher Education Compact commit themselves to providing full tuition for students from families with incomes under $75,000. These colleges and universities make up the difference out of their own funds after students have gotten the financial aid for which they qualify. Say Yes does not have to pay the tuition for these students. The participating private institutions invested a total of $22,338,476 in scholarship aid for Say Yes students from 2009 through 2013. The annual figure rose quickly as more schools joined the Compact and more students went off to private colleges and universities, reaching $9,076,044 in 2012–13 alone.

Say Yes students at both private and public colleges and universities benefit from a host of state and federal aid programs. The largest of these sources and amounts they provided between 2009 and 2013 are Pell Grants ($8,128,119), the New York State Tuition Assistance Program ($5,796,929), the Higher Education Opportunity Program ($383,630), the Supplementary Educational Opportunity Grants ($299,953), and the federal Work-Study Program ($161,629).

As mentioned earlier, a small number of private schools provide tuition scholarships to all Say Yes students, regardless of family income. But the vast majority of participating institutions do not include students from families with incomes of more than $75,000 in their commitment. This prodded Say Yes to establish Choice Grants of $5,000 a year for students who do not qualify for the tuition scholarships provided by the private colleges and universities. Say Yes spent $1,184,274 on Choice Grants in 2012–13 and has invested $3,877,145 in such scholarships since 2009.

The increasing expenditures reflect the growing popularity of the scholarships and the expansion of postsecondary attendance among Syracuse's high school graduates. Onondaga Community College, given its proximity to the city, draws the most students from Syracuse by far. Among the most popular other public institutions that Syracuse students attend with scholarships are Buffalo State, Morrisville State, Oswego State, Monroe Community College, Mohawk Valley Community College, and Herkimer County Community College.

The portion of Syracuse students who enroll at private institutions is considerably smaller. Syracuse University, a private institution, waived the cap and is an important destination for students from the city's high schools. Among the most popular private schools are Bryant & Stratton, LeMoyne, Rochester Institute of Technology, Hobart and William Smith, and the University of Rochester.

In fall 2009, when graduates of Syracuse's public high schools benefited from the Say Yes scholarships for the first time, the school system sent 501 students off to college, 437 on Say Yes scholarships. The remainder attended schools that were not part of the Higher Education Compact or simply did not apply for scholarships. The number in postsecondary education on Say Yes scholarships reached 851 in fall 2010, after two high school classes had graduated. There were, at that point, an additional 79 students from the two classes attending college without the Say Yes scholarship. A total of 1,358 students from three high school graduating classes—1,241 of them on Say Yes scholarships—were enrolled in postsecondary schools in fall 2011.

The dollars spent on Say Yes's Higher Education Compact should be viewed as an investment. A definition of an investment holds that it is an asset or item purchased with the hope of generating income or appreciation in the future, much like purchasing stock in IBM or McDonald's. In this case, educated young people are the asset, and if they return to Syracuse, diplomas in hand, as productive members of the community, then the dividends will be on the blue-chip level.

Analysts examining another program with some of the characteristics of Say Yes, Communities in Schools (CIS), found that the payoff for every dollar spent by CIS was $11.60 in economic benefits created. Given that CIS worked with high schools in 113 school districts, the net value of the investment return was $2.6 billion. A report estimated that it would take nine years to amortize the investment costs of assisting the young people involved. Then everything would be gravy.

The disposable annual income of the students served by CIS would eventually be $63 million, meaning greater tax revenues for the communities and more purchasing power for the young people. Fewer of them would be high school dropouts, and more would be college graduates. The social savings involved would total $154.5 million due to reductions in smoking, alcoholism, crime, and welfare and unemployment costs.[13]

Say Yes has been the subject of no such study, but many of its procedures and goals track those of Communities in Schools. The study of CIS shows why it is shortsighted to consider the program in Syracuse as simply an educational one. Say Yes viewed the program from its inception as having as much to do with urban revival as with education reform. A more highly educated community would benefit Syracuse in the myriad ways mentioned in earlier chapters.

13

Lifting the City

The effort by Say Yes to give the city of Syracuse a boost by helping to improve its school system can only add luster to a town that has already won recognition in some circles. In 2010, *Forbes* magazine named Syracuse as one of the country's ten "Best Places to Raise a Family."[1] The ranking was based on cost of living, prevalence of home ownership, median household income, housing costs, commute time, incidence of crime, and percentage of young adults who graduate from high school.

While this accolade may surprise those who believe that Syracuse has slipped from the prominence the city attained by the middle of the last century, it indicates that in trying to revitalize Syracuse, Say Yes took on a project with real potential. That potential was recognized in the first half of the twentieth century by the many ethnic groups that built the neighborhoods that gave the city its character: Germans and Italians on the north side; African Americans on the south side; Jews on the east side; and Irish, Polish, and Ukrainians on the west side. Scattered among them were a host of other groups that constructed their futures in Syracuse. And before any of these people arrived, the area was home for generations to the five tribes of the Iroquois Confederation, remnants of which live on the nearby Onondaga and Oneida Indian reservations.

Historic Syracuse

This is a city that was an important depot on the Underground Railroad before the Civil War, boasted a station of the New York Central Railroad in the late nineteenth century, produced the first four-cylinder car in the United States at its Franklin Automotive Company in 1902, played a role in the nation's industrial expansion during World War II and emerged from the war with General Motors and Chrysler plants, and benefited from the Great Migration of blacks to the North in the 1940s and 1950s.

A walk through downtown Syracuse provides a rewarding glimpse of the city's rich physical heritage, which took shape on the drawing boards of prominent architects during the late nineteenth and the early twentieth centuries. The Syracuse Savings Bank from 1876, with the first elevator in town, exemplifies Victorian

Gothic. The Hills Building, erected in the 1920s, represents an attempt to adapt the Gothic style to a tall building. Two art deco gems—the State Tower Building with its setbacks and vertical strips of windows and the glass-and-steel Niagara Mohawk Building with its geometric styling—came just a bit later.

And then there is the Syracuse Landmark Theatre, rescued from demolition in 1977, with its grand staircase and Tiffany chandelier, representing the era of sumptuous movie palaces. Syracuse mayor Stephanie Miner saw the Landmark Theatre as a perfect example of an institution evolving and reinventing itself in turbulent times when she chose it as the site for her State of the City Address in 2012. "That's what city government, in fact, all levels of government, must do: evolve and reinvent," she said to an audience assembled during one of the toughest financial periods their city had faced since the Great Depression.

"Think of what happened right here," Miner continued. "Without taking a bold step, this theater was not going to survive. It needed a vastly expanded stage, more technical capabilities and more space to host events and bring in revenues . . . Like many projects, the Landmark had been stuck at the starting line for years. But with a new sense of urgency, the theater's resulting $16 million renovation now means this theater has more than just a rich history—it has a viable and promising future." Indeed, optimists see the Landmark and its revival as a symbol for the city itself.

Syracuse boasts not only historic buildings but its share of distinguished Americans, as well, especially in the entertainment world. It was the place whence the Schubert brothers went off to New York City to establish the chain of theaters that formed the spine of Broadway. Syracuse is where songwriter Jimmy Van Heusen, television science fiction writer Rod Serling, and actor Tom Cruise were raised. It was also the hometown of Theodore Hesburgh, who grew up to become a priest and arguably the most famous president that Notre Dame University has had.

The city also has been a kind of literary hive where some leading writers have swarmed. Authors Mary Karr and George Saunders teach at Syracuse University, once the home base for Tobias Wolff, Raymond Carver, and Tess Gallagher. David Foster Wallace lived in an apartment near the campus when he wrote *Infinite Jest*, Toni Morrison began her climb to the Nobel Prize as a textbook editor in Syracuse, and Joyce Carol Oates won her first recognition by capturing a fiction prize as an undergraduate at the university.

And while Syracuse no longer fields a major league professional sports team as it did when the Nationals were a founding member of the National Basketball Association, the city does have the Chiefs, a minor league baseball team. The city, of course, also features big-time college athletics at Syracuse University, where the basketball team made it to the Final Four in 2013.

Obviously, Syracuse lost some of its luster to the corrosion induced by the Rust Belt, and Say Yes arrived in the early twenty-first century to find a city very much in need of brightening. The attractions of life in a small urban center and most especially the job market, for example, had dimmed even by the 1980s. The school system was not helping enough of its students to fulfill their potential. One final inglorious kick in the head arrived at the end of 2012, when the local Newhouse newspaper, *The Post-Standard*, ceased printing a daily edition for home delivery and became essentially a three-day-a-week publication. Economics overcame civic pride.

Placing Say Yes's Role in Perspective

Change was already in the air when Lionel "Skip" Meno became the "boy superintendent" of the Syracuse public schools in 1979. In fact, he saw the city and its schools transform before his eyes. He joined the system as a teacher in 1970 and was promoted to deputy superintendent prior to assuming the top job at age 32. The city and the district were wrestling with the effects of urban flight. So many white families departed for the suburbs that the school enrollment became about one-third African American, many of whom were eligible for federally subsidized lunches.

The district tried to maintain high expectations. It was the state's only school system requiring every eleventh grader to take New York's English competency examination. And 85 percent of the students were passing. Students posted similarly favorable results on tests in reading and math. Meno, who eventually left Syracuse to serve as New York State's deputy commissioner of education and later became state education commissioner in Texas, didn't believe that the bar should be lowered for poor minority children. But the superintendent who followed him said that the district expected too much of some of its students, and gradually standards dropped.

Gerald Grant, an emeritus education professor from Syracuse University mentioned earlier, wrote in his book in 2009, *Hope and Despair in the American City*, of the decline of Syracuse and its public schools in the 1970s and 1980s. He depicted "the major emptying out of the city by middle-class whites" and the dismal plight of the system's minority students.[2] Grant, a sociologist of education, focused on the poverty and low test scores that afflicted many of Syracuse's students. He contrasted the situation with that in Raleigh, North Carolina, where the formation of a countywide school system relieved the racial isolation of the city schools. Grant's book instigated a discussion in Syracuse about whether school districts in Onondaga County should merge with the city system, an idea whose time clearly had not come and—like the end of poverty—is not apt to arrive anytime soon.

While there may not be the sort of school integration that would result from a merger with the county, Say Yes intended with its approach to make those schools more appealing to the very sort of families that Syracuse lost in the 1970s and 1980s. In part, Say Yes meant to do this with its college tuition scholarships. Say Yes hoped the opportunity would retain families in the city who might otherwise move out and draw in new families.

This is part of Say Yes's plan to revitalize Syracuse. Better schools would make the city more attractive to business and industry. Such schools could provide future employees for companies that want to call Syracuse home. Houses would be in demand. A more educated, more fulfilled population would almost certainly mean less crime. These are not abstract concepts. Research by RAND Corporation found that good schools affect the value of real estate and the quality of life in a community.[3]

Some of the strongest evidence of the potential benefits to Syracuse of sending more high school graduates to college may be the findings of researchers who examined the impact of the open admissions policy that the City University of New York (CUNY) adopted in the early 1970s. They first studied the results of the policy in its beginning years and then again in 2000 to determine the long-term effect on the females who participated. The researchers looked only at women because they were more apt to have had custody of their children as they grew up, and an ancillary goal was to determine the impact on the offspring of open-admissions students.

Seventy-one percent of the women who entered CUNY under open admissions got at least an associate's degree from a community college with three-quarters of that group continuing on to receive degrees at the baccalaureate level. Twenty-six percent of the group completed a master's degree or higher.[4] But just as importantly—and with great consequence to the city of Syracuse—college-educated females who came from underprivileged backgrounds had children who gained an advantage over their counterparts by dint of their parents' education.

"[T]he children of college-educated women fare much better educationally than children whose mothers did not go to college," the authors declare definitively,[5] calling their findings startling and unprecedented. They point out that attending college—and particularly persevering to a degree—changes the way that women raise their children and the expectations they have for those children. Sons and daughters end up accruing more social capital and cultural capital than do the offspring of non-college-educated mothers. If this turns out to be the experience in Syracuse, Say Yes will realize its fondest dream and leverage the accomplishment into the next generation.

The canaries in the mine for the school district might be the children of the faculty and staff at Syracuse University. An important measure of the acceptance of the schools is the extent to which the university community judges them desirable for their own youngsters. Gerald Grant, who has lived for many years in the near-downtown neighborhood that shares a zip code with the university, estimates that when he was a young faculty member, as many as 85 percent of the faculty resided in the neighborhood. Now he thinks that the portion of university people living in the area has dwindled to 35 percent and that even though they may use the district's elementary and middle schools, they pull out their children when they reach the high school level.

Say Yes's entry into Syracuse was fortuitous in that it came at a juncture when the city fathers and mothers were searching for ways to resuscitate the city. Some eighty of them, movers and shakers from all sectors, had gathered for a retreat just outside the city at Skyline Lodge at Highland Forest to explore the possibilities. Proposals ranged from building bike paths to razing Interstate 81, an elevated highway near downtown that had proved an impediment to development by dividing parts of the city.

Though Say Yes was still so new that not even everyone in this august group knew about it, some participants at the retreat kept mentioning Say Yes and its potential for promoting revitalization. Finally, Say Yes's Mary Anne Schmitt-Carey and Syracuse University's Nancy Cantor were asked to get up like a couple of kids at show-and-tell and describe Say Yes and what it sought to accomplish.

The two-day retreat contained many breakout sessions, and a member of each group reported out to the entire assemblage as the event drew to a close. One such person, Allen Galson, the retired founder of an industrial engineering company, felt that the proposals he heard were not sharply focused. So he rose and announced that the only idea with momentum, money, and enthusiasm behind it was Say Yes. He asked that everyone concentrate on that option and push it hard because that would make the greatest difference in Syracuse. The moment, like the spring's first robin, was a harbinger, and Say Yes did indeed continue to move ahead. But as if to show that no good deed goes unpunished, some people resented Say Yes's emergence as the darling and accused Say Yes of hijacking the retreat. For all the goodwill that came Say Yes's way as a result of the retreat, the event engendered some defensiveness that took a long while to dissipate.

Pursuing Similar Goals in Other Cities

The notion of desirable educational opportunities injecting a dose of vigor into cities has echoes around the country. Mayor Rahm Emanuel of Chicago called for his city's community colleges to modernize their approach to job training so that their training programs would more closely match the need for employees in such fields as welding, computer science, transportation, and health care.[6]

Also, in the Midwest, the resurgence of the University of Cincinnati with its updated campus is seen as a fillip for expanding the local medical research and health care industries.[7] Nearby, in downtown Louisville, Nucleus Innovation Park provides a home for research and innovation, particularly in health care and information technology. Similarly, the prospering higher education sectors in Pittsburgh, Pennsylvania, and Rochester, New York, have contributed mightily to the ability of those cities to survive the loss of major employers.

Steven Fulop, who was elected mayor of Jersey City, New Jersey, in 2013, is another public figure who views the public schools as the key to urban revival. While he was still a councilman, he helped lead a group in his town dedicated to overcoming the inertia created by old-time politicians who were notorious for running the city—the second largest in the state—and making the schools their fiefdom. "If Jersey City is to succeed, we know it starts with its schools. And today we are clawing our way back," he wrote in an op-ed. "Changing urban education is not easy, and a lot of what has happened . . . has to do with partnerships."[8]

Elsewhere, some two dozen city-based foundations, nonprofits, and mayors' offices have formed themselves into a group to create a network for school reform that extends well beyond the educational establishment in each of the respective communities. Calling itself the Cities for Education Entrepreneurship Trust, the organization, started by the Mind Trust in Indianapolis, sees such an approach as creating a kind of urban ecosystem to assist reform in each locale. This is in accord with the path that Say Yes followed, first in Syracuse and then in Buffalo.

It all does "start with the schools," as Fulop says. Educational institutions that enhance a community serve the public good. The work of Say Yes in Syracuse follows in this tradition, which was recognized early in the nation's existence. The Northwest Ordinance of 1787, pertaining to the territory that eventually was carved into the five easternmost states of the upper Midwest, provided public land for the building of schools. Without a properly educated populace—in Syracuse or anywhere else—civic betterment falters. Thus the ordinance stated, "Religion, morality and knowledge, being necessary to good government and the happiness of mankind, schools and the means of education shall forever be encouraged."

Say Yes's activities in Syracuse have implications for cities of similar size. They face many common problems and could shape their own approaches to solving them based on the experiences that Say Yes and Syracuse have had in seeking to reform the schools and renew the city. A list of some possible candidates for this kind of pursuit—all having populations within ten thousand of that of Syracuse— includes Sioux Falls, South Dakota; Elk Grove, California; Springfield, Massachusetts; Joliet, Illinois; Kansas City, Kansas; Dayton, Ohio; and Savannah, Georgia.

The fate of cities of this size is inextricably coupled to the perceived quality of their school systems. Such metropolises as New York, Philadelphia, Chicago, Dallas, and Los Angeles get by just fine despite low-achieving public schools. These are business and entertainment hubs where those who earn a living either have no public-school children or traipse off to bedroom communities, leaving intact the desirability of working and playing in the big city. These urban centers boast the critical mass to have shifted to economies driven by service and information technology. Small- and medium-sized cities like Syracuse, bereft of such advantages, suffer far more when their public schools lag.

Say Yes is a cornerstone of Syracuse's effort to attract and retain middle-class families so that it does not follow other postindustrial cities that have seen their middle class disappear as public schools faltered and economic reversals became the norm. Such Syracuse residents as Joanne Harlow, a principal at one of the city's public schools, said that she felt fortunate to raise her children in the city. One went off to college on a Say Yes tuition scholarship, and the other was a high school student for whom such a scholarship was in the offing. "My experience with my own children has been positive," she said. "I never considered moving my children out of the city."

The Impact on Business

Syracuse, like so many industrial towns—large and small—was once a place that employed people to "make stuff." This is no longer the case. Most of those jobs are gone, along with drive-in movies and dime stores. A major symbol of the city's manufacturing past is Carrier Corporation, which once had a huge building with a blue-and-white sign proclaiming it as the "World's Largest Air Conditioning Company." The Syracuse area was formerly to air conditioners as Detroit was to automobiles and Pittsburgh was to steel. It was here that Willis Carrier, inventor of the air conditioner in 1902, centered his production. As recently as 1980, Carrier employed 7,100 workers in Syracuse and its environs. The company still makes air conditioners, but not anywhere near Syracuse. The last of several factories in the area closed in 2004, leaving a complex of abandoned buildings.

Then in 2010, Carrier announced that it would spend $30 million to raze hundreds of thousands of square feet of unused space and to enhance the remaining structures to become the company's main center for research and development. The move came on top of Carrier's earlier investment in the locale for research and development. Conversion of the site was completed in 2011. Essentially, this meant that the largest blue-collar employer in the Syracuse area completed the transition to white-collar employer. The area's three largest local job providers became higher education, health care, and gambling (at an Indian-owned casino).

The new Syracuse, for which Say Yes hopes that the school system will produce employees, will require skills that were unnecessary in a job market in which Carrier and other manufacturers needed people to send into factories. Say Yes predicated its college tuition scholarships on the assumption that college graduates returning to the city must now have preparation that their parents and grandparents did not need.

Economic Development as a Component of Say Yes

Mary Anne Schmitt-Carey went to leaders of the Metropolitan Development Association (MDA), the local business and industry group, early in her search for allies. She projected a future in which the success of Say Yes would enhance property values, build a stronger tax base, and create a better workforce. This argument comported with a report by the Washington-based Alliance for Excellent Education, which maintains that if urban school systems could halve their dropout rates, it would have a positive effect on the economic, social, and civic health of their communities.[9]

Say Yes was an easy sell when its supporters approached MDA, a forward-looking group headed by Robert M. Simpson, a former aide to West Virginia U.S. Senator John D. Rockefeller IV. Say Yes and its intentions fit comfortably into the organization's ongoing dialogue about economic development. The MDA, now called CenterState Corporation for Economic Opportunity and serving a 12-county area, is not your run-of-the-mill group of small-town boosters.

The organization had secured three grants from the Ford Foundation to promote urban revitalization, and it ran the largest annual business event in upstate New York. It had commissioned a couple of reports earlier in the decade from big-name consultants—Battelle Memorial Institute and Richard Florida—about the future of business and industry in the region to fire up a dialogue about economic development.

The message from the consultants' reports was that Syracuse should invest in people, and the scenario put forward by Say Yes lent an opportunity to do so. Simpson and the businesspeople he represents readily saw Say Yes's potential for transforming the community. Syracuse and Onondaga County are part of a central New York region that contains 35 colleges and universities, 138,000 college students, and 65,000 employees of higher education institutions. "We have always been interested in the role of education in economic development," said Simpson. A healthy public school system in Syracuse would be a boon to the region. "She was looking for people who get it," Simpson said of his early meetings with Schmitt-Carey. Simpson and his group got it.

Enthusiasm for Say Yes in the private sector could be seen in the message tacked onto FOR SALE signs by some realtors: "This Is a Say Yes House." They hoped that the possibility of free college tuition for their children would draw buyers into the city. Realtors even invited representatives of Say Yes to address their meetings.

Say Yes arrived in a Syracuse that was at sea, grasping for a fiscal lifeline. The tax base was stagnant, and some residents feared that the city was fast becoming a financial ward of the state. "The reality of our marketplace and our economy," said Mayor Stephanie Miner, "is that students need a solid high school education and preparation beyond that. I was a labor lawyer, representing unions and employees. You can't be a journeyman electrician if you can't do math. All of the trades need a diploma to get in."

When Say Yes entered Syracuse, it provided the community with a report on the implications of the program for the city's educational and economic development. A bar graph in the report shows the difference that a college degree makes on the future earnings of young people from families in the bottom fifth of income. Not all the graduates of Syracuse's high schools are apt to stay in the city after completing college, but those who do remain—assuming that jobs are available—will become economically productive, taxpaying earners.

Calvin Corriders, a member of both the Syracuse school board and the banking industry, had no doubt about Say Yes's potential economic impact on the city and the surrounding county. He cited middle-class families moving into the city as an indicator of change. "I do see revitalization in the city," he said. By way of example, Corriders pointed to the success of Say Yes—however limited—in raising money from the private sector for its scholarships, a notable achievement during a time of dwindling resources. He sat on the board of the city's largest philanthropic foundation, which received far more funding requests than it could accept but looked favorably on Say Yes. "Say Yes has been able to get grants from both the public and private sectors," Corriders said. "It is a paradigm change." Say Yes, in other words, got Syracuse to start revising its view of philanthropy.

School board member Steven Swift, who became board president in 2012, saw education as the root of economic policy. Swift, who owned a small investment firm, maintained that a city lives or dies by its schools. His two oldest children had graduated from city high schools before the advent of the scholarship program, but he had a high-school-aged son who was poised to be the first in the family to benefit directly from the program. "Syracuse is the heart of the central New York region," Swift said. "If we have a cancer of education and economic policy it will diminish the ability of central New York to grow. If you have a city that is dying, it will affect the region. The success of the Syracuse City School District is paramount to the region."

Refurbishing the City's Fabric

Physical improvements in Syracuse cannot necessarily be attributed to Say Yes but attest to the sort of changes one might expect in a city that feels better about itself. At the downtown crossroads, Salina and Fayette Streets, four buildings that stood as a sign of decay in the heart of the commercial area were renovated as the Pike Block Project for retail, office, and residential use.

Nearby, at Bank Alley, redesign work was under way with help from the county in conjunction with the Syracuse Trust Building and the Label Shopper Building. Also downtown, Marriott has built a new hotel to anchor Armory Square and SUNY Upstate Medical University and SUNY College of Environmental Science and Forestry were erecting the Central New York Biotech Accelerator. In addition, SUNY Upstate unveiled plans to develop office, residential, and retail space on ten acres of a site transferred to it by the city and the county.

Syracuse was a main beneficiary in central New York of Governor Cuomo's plan for distributing state funds through regional economic development councils that compete for grants from Albany. The state in 2012 earmarked $103.7 million for 74 projects proposed by the Central New York Council, which is centered in Syracuse. The Kennedy Square site, which got $3.6 million, was just one of the recipients. The state also dedicated $3 million for redevelopment of the Syracuse Inner Harbor to transform 32 acres of waterfront property for housing, recreational, and commercial purposes. When Cuomo visited Syracuse in fall 2012, he led an entourage of officials on a tour of four projects financed partially by state funds.

One of the most visible signs of the city's need for rejuvenation that some in the Cuomo delegation may have glimpsed is the 790-room, downtown Hotel Syracuse, opened in 1924 and vacant since 2004. Despite a succession of announcements, including a scheme to convert much of the huge building to condominiums and rental apartments, the forlorn structure attests to the city's faded glory. Nearby, the ultimate testament to the city's victimhood is the elevated Interstate 81, a dagger through the heart of Syracuse bequeathed by misguided urban renewal policies that destroyed a neighborhood and erected a kind of Berlin Wall.

Keenly aware of the hurdles that the city still must clear in the race to improvement, William M. Ryan says that "any evidence that ties back to Say Yes is speculative at best" when it comes to recent economic development in Syracuse. In other words, Say Yes should be cautious about taking credit for upticks in the city. Ryan should know. He is a former council member, now chief of staff to the mayor and chair of the Syracuse Industrial Development Agency.

While a reversal of economic fortune in Syracuse will take time, CenterState Corporation's Simpson was able to say that the opportunity for Say Yes's college scholarships figured in his talks with a financial services company that considered creating several hundred jobs in the city. "They see a community that has made a long-term commitment to its workforce for many years to come," Simpson remarked. "My major point is that there remains a lot of enthusiasm for the Say Yes program." So the notion of embracing Say Yes, like finding the ideal romantic partner, has resonated throughout the business community. Collaboration with Say Yes represents a serendipitous combination of altruism and self-interest.

The Effect on Real Estate

When Susan Dutch's family was transferred to Syracuse in 1998 in connection with a job relocation, they contacted a realtor so that they could quickly look for a place to live. The obliging realtor picked them up at the airport and drove them directly to Manlius, one of the city's larger suburbs. The realtor was adamant that Manlius, a town that was 95 percent white, would be the place where the family would be happiest. She offered the family no alternative and certainly didn't take them to see homes in Syracuse. Manlius, she said, had the best school system in the county.

This family, originally from Kansas, didn't know the area and placed their trust in the realtor. In those pre-Internet days there were few other ways to find a home in a hurry. So they bought a house in Manlius and all three of their children graduated from the local high school and went on to earn college degrees. "I can only hope that if it were today that we were relocating to Syracuse," said Susan Dutch, "we'd be told about Say Yes to Education and the wonderful opportunity it offers families who buy a home in the city school district." She thought her family could have saved hundreds of thousands of dollars in college tuitions under the Say Yes tuition scholarship plan.

The Schools and Real Estate Values

Kim and Blair Frodelius had a rather different experience when they looked for a home. They lived in Solvay, a small suburb of Syracuse, and thought about moving. They probably would have bought a house in the country if not for the Say Yes tuition scholarship program. They were the parents of four grown children and two still in high school. Their son had a strong interest in music, and they envisioned him eventually attending Syracuse University on a Say Yes scholarship. Furthermore, the house they selected in the city was just minutes from campus.

They had begun their search for a home in Syracuse by scanning newspaper ads and attending open houses. They weren't pleased with the real estate agents whom they encountered, and they finally found a house by looking online and using an agent recommended by their credit union. Were they satisfied with their approach? "The community is better, the neighborhood is friendlier, and our commutes to and from work are easier," they said.

They also have the advantage of living close to both his and her parents as well as being near their four adult children. They like the idea of living close to Nottingham High School and expect that their son will have a "top notch" education. They consider Say Yes a major factor in their move. "I think it's a great program," said Blair Frodelius. "I hope it takes off not only here, but in other cities."

Say Yes's tuition scholarships have made homes in Syracuse more alluring. Presumably, the academic improvements that the school system is implementing in conjunction with the scholarships will add to the district's appeal. The Brookings Institution, a social science research center in Washington, DC, analyzed test scores in 84,077 schools across the country in 2010 and 2011, concluding that "housing costs an average of 2.4 times as much, or nearly $11,000 more per year, near a high-scoring public school than near a low-scoring public school." To some extent, the availability of the tuition scholarships in Syracuse is a proxy for high test scores. If education is a key contributor to regional prosperity, as the report by Brookings asserted,[10] then Say Yes has helped point Syracuse in the right direction.

Florida rates schools statewide based on test scores and other data, awarding each school a letter grade ranging from A to F. When Florida released grades for the schools at the end of the 2011–12 school year, the *South Florida Sun-Sentinel* studied the ratings in terms of the cost of homes in the highest-scoring districts. It reported, for instance, that while Palm Beach County exceeded the state average with 55 percent of its schools receiving grades of A, all eight of the schools in the county getting D grades and the single one rated F were in neighborhoods in which median home values were below the countywide median. The newspaper quoted realtors who said that homebuyers want to move into places with the best schools and avoid those neighborhoods with the worst schools.[11]

The Syracuse City School District's statistics are somewhat encouraging in regard to whether the advent of the Say Yes college tuition scholarships stirred an upsurge in enrollment. The school year of 2007–8, the year before Say Yes began operating in Syracuse, may serve as a base year for viewing enrollments. By the start of the 2011–12 school year, Say Yes's fourth year in the city, two of the city's four neighborhood high schools—Fowler and Nottingham—showed enrollment gains, Henninger essentially held steady, and only Corcoran had a significant drop in enrollment. These figures apparently reflect the decrease in dropouts that the school system experienced during this period and perhaps demonstrate some progress in retaining and attracting residents.

Statistics for elementary schools, which were the focus of Say Yes's early work in Syracuse, also indicated that the system was, by and large, not losing students. Third-grade enrollments in a sample of four schools showed gains in three of the four schools. Fourth-grade enrollments in a sample of four other schools revealed that one school gained students, one held steady, one declined by only a single student, and one suffered a sizable loss of fourth graders.

In terms of total enrollment, though, the size of the school system barely changed from the beginning of the 2007–8 school year (21,099) to the start of the 2011–12 school year (21,070). This was a time when many other urban districts were losing students. A case can be made that the Syracuse public schools stabilized enrollments. The total enrollment figures do not include preschool, as a special effort was made under the prodding of Say Yes to grow the preschools, a crucial element in preparing students for higher achievement.

The Role of Scholarships in Home Sales

The city school district still has a long way to go in drawing families to Syracuse. It is a hard sell even with the availability of the scholarships. Real estate agents in Onondaga County say that in almost half their transactions, neither the buyers nor the sellers mention the scholarships. The scholarships, in other words, don't seem to be a magnet pulling a great many residents of the county into the city. The situation is somewhat different in Syracuse itself.

Among those already living in the city, one out of four clients sought to find another home in Syracuse. But half of them said the scholarships were not a factor, perhaps because they no longer had school-aged children. These figures come from a survey conducted by the Greater Syracuse Association of REALTORS at my behest and with my assistance. On a scale of 1 to 10, with 10 as the highest, the respondents to the survey said that Say Yes college tuition scholarships rated a 4.5 as a sales incentive for them. More than 80 percent of the agents knew of the Say Yes to Education program in Syracuse. Some said that the survey served to remind them to mention the scholarships more frequently, and others said that they would like to hand out information to clients but didn't know where to obtain such information.

Given the chance to write anonymous comments about selling homes in Syracuse, the real estate agents repeatedly cited the perceived low quality of the public schools and fears of crime as main reasons why buyers avoid property in the city. "If the people I worked with had school-age children," one agent said, "none that I can remember wanted to remain in Syracuse due to Say Yes. All felt the school system was not good and the kids were getting a poor education. They all sought the suburbs."

Nevertheless, Say Yes is on the minds of many of the agents. "I bring up the program to any clients that have children, even if they are looking outside the city because it's a program that I don't believe many know about and the money for college is huge," said an agent. Another said that potential buyers lose interest when they learn about the income cap on the scholarships. "These are people interested in the program and in living in the city," she said. "However, finding out that there are income parameters pushes them away."

The situation poses a quandary for some people. They see a city with many problems waiting for solutions and a school system that has yet to make great strides. But they want to be loyal to Syracuse and its public schools, and they also want to gain from the scholarship offer. Ben Walsh personified those who are perplexed. Only 33 years old, he was deputy commissioner of the city's department of neighborhood and business development. In other words, Walsh was a guy responsible for selling Syracuse and its virtues, a job he approached with passion. He and his wife were also the parents of a three-year-old daughter who would be eligible for kindergarten in a couple of years, and they wanted to be sure that she embarked upon a quality education in a safe setting.

Walsh acknowledged a clash between the personal and the professional. In the pre–Say Yes era, by his account, he would have leaned toward an alternative to the city's public schools for educating his children, probably in the Catholic schools where his parents sent him. Now he was inclined—his wife apparently needed more convincing—to send his daughter to the neighborhood public school. "Say Yes gives people like me a reason to take a second look," he said. Whatever choice the Walshes make, he will continue to tell businesses about the benefits of Syracuse.

Crime as a Factor

Syracuse has gotten safer during Say Yes's time in town. And this is saying a lot given that Say Yes arrived just as the bottom was about to drop out of the economy, a period during which one might expect crime to increase as jobs grow scarce and people grow desperate. Say Yes came to a city struggling to deal with lawlessness through the early part of the 2000s. Drugs, gang violence, and other such blights threatened the community. The police department had to turn to the federal government and its RICO Act (Racketeer Influenced and Corrupt Organizations Act) for assistance. Then, by 2009 and 2010, crime statistics showed that the good guys were making headway.

Say Yes is not about law enforcement, and the organization takes no specific steps to counter crime. But it does have an impact on the lives of young people. Their social emotional needs get addressed. More is done to reach out to their families. A new superintendent brought new priorities to teaching and learning, and Say Yes gave students a shot at a higher education, a chance to grab opportunities that never before seemed possible. In sum, as Syracuse police chief Frank Fowler put it, people had hope. "Crime has a preventive side," said Fowler, "and what better way is there to prevent crime than to give people opportunity through education?"

This is not to say that people in Syracuse should cease their vigilance. One measure of crime in the city is the level of safety in the university community. A rash of robberies near the campus in fall 2012 raised concerns and underscored the role of the University Area Crime-Control Team, a collaboration between the Syracuse police and the university's public safety department.

What the Statistics Say

One must be chary in attributing cause and effect. Nevertheless, there is no ignoring the favorable signs reflected in the city's crime statistics. Most categories of crimes, both violent and property, dropped in Syracuse between 2009 and 2012. Drug arrests also declined year by year from 2010 to 2011 to 2012. There were, however, some troubling increases between 2011 and 2012 in such categories as robbery, burglary, larceny, and motor vehicle theft as the recession continued its grip on the city. These overall figures pertain to crimes by perpetrators of all ages.

Something dramatic appears, though, when the numbers are broken out for juveniles, those aged 15 and younger, who are the residents of Syracuse most affected by the school system and by Say Yes. Juvenile arrests fell year by year, from 2010 to 2011 to 2012, for robbery, larceny, motor vehicle theft, marijuana possession, possession of other drugs, stolen property, offenses against family, local law violations, and warrant arrests. In other categories, juvenile arrests increased from 2010 to 2011 but dropped from 2011 to 2012. These were sex offenses, stolen property, simple assault, liquor law violations, disorderly conduct, and vehicle and traffic offenses.[12]

Say Yes can hardly claim credit for favorable crime figures, but one can't ignore the possible impact that the organization's work in the public schools played in giving young people in Syracuse hope and a sense of purpose. The improved statistics merit attention. "If Say Yes stays the course," Chief Fowler said, "the City of Syracuse and the County of Onondaga will continue to enjoy a reduction in Part I crime [violent]. This will make the city and the county more attractive to people who want to buy homes and raise their children in a safe environment. Our young people will become productive members of society and will return as well trained adults ready to move the city and the county forward. We'll be better off."

Frank Fowler

Syracuse Police Chief Frank Fowler's interest in young people predated his tenure on the police force. He spent two years as a counselor in a residential facility for juveniles, where he said he found fulfillment and thought he made an impact. He might still be working in that field if he hadn't wondered about whether he could pass the examination to become a police officer. So he took the test on a whim and, after passing, gave the idea further consideration.

He joined the Syracuse Police Department at the age of 27 in 1989, a decision about which he was somewhat conflicted. In Fowler's neighborhood in St. Louis, where he was born and raised, the police were not held in high esteem. He had some explaining to do to the folks back in Missouri after they heard that he joined the force in Syracuse. "They were confused by my decision," he recalled. Fowler, responding to the show-me mentality in his native state, told the doubters that he believed that he could bring about changes in police conduct from the inside.

Like most recruits, Fowler began as a patrolman. Nineteen months later, he was a detective, working for eight and a half years in narcotics, a period he looks back on as one of the most rewarding in his life. He felt that he contributed to the community and accomplished a great deal. In 2000 he was promoted to sergeant, and the next year he rose to commanding officer for recruitment and community relations. Fowler was promoted to deputy chief in 2005 and placed in charge of community service. This role put him closer to education, giving him supervision of police officers assigned to the schools. There are now two such officers in each of the city's high schools. One of the programs under his jurisdiction was D.A.R.E., Drug Abuse Resistance Education, which police departments across the country operate in collaboration with schools.

Then, in 2010, Mayor Stephanie Miner tapped Fowler to become chief, making him the second African American in the post. This placed him in charge of 484 sworn police personnel and a nonpolice staff of 200. As chief, he tried to follow the philosophy that leaders can benefit by being receptive to the ideas of others. "If someone is knowledgeable on a subject, why not get their viewpoint?" he asked.

Perhaps the main point of contention during Fowler's time as chief was his running battle with William Fitzpatrick, the Onondaga County district attorney. They clashed several times over the police department's handling of an investigation of the alleged child-molesting case involving an assistant basketball coach at Syracuse University. Given the various pressures on him, Fowler welcomes the chance to enjoy some tranquility, and he finally found an ideal outlet as he moved into middle age. He had never been on a golf course until he was assigned to head a security detail for a celebrity tournament. The crowds of spectators lining the fairways to watch pros such as Phil Mickelson and Fred Couples intrigued him.

Fowler was impressed to see Couples, a man of about his age and stature, drive a ball off the tee straight down the middle of the fairway, reach the green with just one more shot, and sink a putt from three feet in order to stay one under par on a four-stroke hole. "I thought there was no way this little guy would hit the ball all that distance, be able to find it, and do it all in four strokes, let alone three." Fowler was hooked, and playing golf became a regular part of his life.

14

Putting It All in Perspective

Say Yes President Mary Anne Schmitt-Carey and her lieutenants largely under-stood from the outset the challenges facing them in helping to create a program of whole-system educational reform to serve as a demonstration model for other cities. Most of their steps were surefooted and carried the undertaking forward with distinction. There were occasional stumbles and some moves in unproductive directions that required U-turns. Schmitt-Carey conceded that "the community took a calculated risk" in giving entrée to Say Yes. Mostly, though, Say Yes readily acknowledged its mistakes and learned from them. As a result, it was able to apply the lessons when the organization added Buffalo to its portfolio in 2012.

This does not mean that Say Yes's approach is the only one possible. Surely there are other ways to embark on this journey of improvement, and some observers may decide that Say Yes's methods could have been different. Make no mistake, though. Whatever the result in Syracuse, Say Yes attempted something unprecedented. Those who want to see a better future for America's children should study Say Yes to Education in Syracuse.

Laying the Groundwork for Community Support

Sometimes a community can be sensitive to perceived slights from newcomers who may forget that the path of good intentions exists simply because countless others have trod the same route. In such an effort as Say Yes undertook in Syracuse in conjunction with the university, there was an ever-present danger of being seen as trying to play big brother to those who wanted to be equal members of the family. "We've always had this thing with Syracuse University," said an educator in the city, "that they will come down and fix us. We don't need to be fixed. We need to work collaboratively—the staff of the Syracuse City School District and the university."

Say Yes and Syracuse University sometimes had to cope with the perception that they sought to take control of the school system, as, for instance, during a two-day retreat at the teacher center. Some teachers and principals at the event did not feel that they were equal partners. "The intent was right," said one participant. "The problem was that they talked at us rather than all of us talking together."

At the outset, Say Yes thought that its role in Syracuse as an honest broker in convening the various individuals and organizations would be less crucial after the project got off the ground and established itself. Mary Anne Schmitt-Cary and Gene Chasin, the chief operating officer, each spent several days a week in Syracuse, existing as long-distance commuters, to ensure that a neutral party with no entanglements was generally on the scene to stand above the fray, whatever arose.

They eventually became aware, though, that someone who personally represented Say Yes exclusively would have to remain in Syracuse as they disengaged. Chasin felt the pressure of this need as one person after another continually sought him out to act as "counselor" when sticky issues arose. He and Schmitt-Carey sometimes overextended themselves, two industrious individuals who occasionally were so swamped that they lost track of the many irons that Say Yes had put in the fire. Thus they looked for a person from the outside to hire as executive director of operations for Say Yes to Education in Syracuse: someone separate from those with links to the university, or the school system, or government, or any other entity. Patrick Driscoll was this person.

Gene Chasin

As chief operating officer of Say Yes to Education, Gene Chasin was the head liaison for the academic side of the organization. His career prepared him well for this role. He knew early that he wanted to make a living serving kids, though he was not certain which field would give him the best opportunity to do so. Education proved to be that venue. A native of Southern California who earned a master's degree in educational administration from the University of San Francisco, he began his work as an elementary school teacher and reading specialist. His rise through the ranks put him in two separate principalships in California and then placed him as an assistant superintendent in North Carolina and as a superintendent in Massachusetts.

He gravitated to a larger stage in 2000 at the University of Connecticut, where he directed the Institute for Urban School Improvement until 2008. It served as the base for the ComPact School Project and for the Accelerated Schools Project, which had originated out of Stanford University.

Chasin was steeped in school reform by the time he joined Say Yes in 2008. The demands of his job limited the amount of time he spent with his family in Connecticut. "Being on the road has been a challenge," he said in 2012 as he shuttled between Syracuse and Buffalo. "I still have a child at home and to see him only three days a week has been really tough on him and me. My wife is amazing and has adjusted."

Chasin, like a traveling salesman, found that trying to have a social life back in Connecticut was nearly impossible, and he lost count of the times that he missed events for which he and his wife had purchased tickets in advance. On his few days of unscheduled leisure, Chasin enjoyed golfing, cycling, and reading.

Following Through

For Chasin and other leaders of Say Yes, the prospect of blazing a trail to postsecondary education for students who felt dispossessed—even if some youngsters didn't have the advantage of strong early preparation in elementary and middle school—was both shrewd and logical. This program, after all, is meant to change life outcomes, and it probably would have been unreasonable to ask Syracuse to wait until third graders in the first quadrant finished high school before implementing the tuition guarantee. The goal of going to college captured the imagination of people and made the new reality that Say Yes wanted to inculcate in the community almost palpable.

Say Yes sought to keep policymakers and the public at large aware of the twists and turns as it worked its way over and around mountains of demands. But the goal of transparency was sometimes elusive given the swiftness and complexity of what Say Yes set out to accomplish and the many people it tried to pull into the loop. How can everyone be fully informed when there are so many separate gatherings with shifting casts of characters? Even in the fourth year of operations, some observers still complained that not enough was done to inform the public about the evolving status of the program.

"They talked about transparency, but I'm not sure it was all that transparent in the beginning," the principal union's Brian Nolan said. While Say Yes may not have always achieved its goal of openness, the very fact that it commissioned a succession of audit reports on important aspects of the school system's operations and made the findings public exerted pressure for change. It was olly, olly, oxen free, and many of the hiding places in the intricacies of the school bureaucracy were revealed.

Say Yes sought to develop a funding stream that would institutionalize the program and make it self-sufficient. "We need to raise a lot of money in a relatively short period of time," Schmitt-Carey said early on. "This is about our ability to deliver on a promise to kids. We need $20 million to assure a permanently sustainable program." She was referring to the endowment required to maintain the free-tuition feature.

Bill Ryan, who worked at the Syracuse Fire Department Federal Credit Union and was a member of the Common Council when Say Yes arrived in Syracuse, fretted about the extra funding that the school system needed in order to deliver a better and more comprehensive education. "Continued funding is vital, and we don't know with any degree of certainty that this will be funded in the way it needs to be for the period required," said Ryan, who followed Stephanie Miner to the mayor's office as a top aide. The recession that began shortly after Say Yes launched its program was a conflagration that threatened to burn indefinitely in Syracuse, putting sustainability at risk. The heart of the enterprise, after all, is the instructional program. Teaching and learning could be devastated if Syracuse becomes so hard-pressed that the school district must continually slash personnel and boost class sizes.

Nancy Cantor and Mary Anne Schmitt-Carey were the mighty dynamos generating a considerable amount of the power for Say Yes in Syracuse. Any discussion of sustainability led to the inevitable issue of how the program could operate without them. Commissioner David Steiner posed the following question during his visit: "To what degree does it depend on extraordinary leadership?" No doubt the leadership was extraordinary, yet Say Yes premised its efforts on the idea that carefully constructed scaffolding would sustain the program when inevitable changes in leadership occurred.

The first major change in leadership was the retirement of Dan Lowengard, the superintendent at the time that Say Yes entered Syracuse. He observed in retrospect that the institutional transformation that Say Yes sought could not rely in the long run on the personalities that were originally in place and that eventually he, Schmitt-Carey, and Cantor would all pass from the scene. "This has to be bigger than three people," he said. And, indeed, Lowengard retired, Cantor announced that she would give up her position, and Schmitt-Carey, along with Chasin, gradually transitioned major portions of their time to Buffalo.

From the beginning, Say Yes itself had to win confidence that the venture merited support. When Say Yes capped the tuition assistance plan, some backers felt betrayed. When test scores were slow to rise, the value of Say Yes's role was called into question. When Say Yes promulgated audit reviews of the school system's human resources, curriculum and instruction, finances, special education, technology, and mental health supports, some critics felt that Say Yes predetermined the outcomes. Syracuse was conditioned to skepticism by previous interventions that promised the stars and delivered barely a twinkle.

Any program such as that pursued by Say Yes must strike a delicate balance between instilling confidence and overpromising—the same challenge that faces a coach who takes over a losing team and wants fans to support it but hopes not to raise expectations to an unattainable level. It's a matter of managing expectations and cultivating patience.

Using Research

Many aspects of Say Yes's program are research driven, which attracted a number of backers inside and outside the school system. "The only way we can know what works and does not work to improve student performance is to more effectively link basic research to applied research . . . to improve schools and significantly increase student learning," Mary Anne Schmitt-Carey stated in testimony to a congressional committee in 2001, when she was still with New American Schools. In that testimony, an uncanny hint of the philosophy that would guide her in Syracuse, Schmitt-Carey said that quality research underpinned successful reform. She cautioned policymakers on the use of shoddy research.[1] Schmitt-Carey went on to become a vice president of the American Institutes for Research (AIR) and leveraged that relationship when she took Say Yes into Syracuse.

AIR lent its prestige to Say Yes—some of it on a pro bono basis—in a close relationship that the two groups forged. This was not a seat-of-the-pants operation as so often occurs in the name of school reform. AIR's research expertise resulted in the student monitoring system, individual school reviews, outcome studies, a district-level report, a case study of the after-school program, an analysis of Say Yes's relationship to the Huntington Family Centers, and a study of the implementation of the system's reforms. But the pro bono portion of AIR's contribution sometimes came back to bite Say Yes, which discovered that getting something for free could mean waiting at the back of the line.

Additional research came from Cross & Joftus, Schoolhouse Partners, Education Resource Strategies, Schaffer Consulting, and Collier Education Consulting. Seldom has a school reform effort relied so extensively on research to determine the course of action, to gain data for recalibrating the work, and to evaluate outcomes. Research drove a considerable amount of the change in Syracuse, though ultimately it was up to educators in the district to decide how to use the research. What is that adage about leading a horse to water?

Say Yes is in the vanguard in its attempt to unite research and practice. The William T. Grant Foundation convened a gathering of educational researchers and urban school leaders in May 2012 to explore this very topic. Participants agreed that the researchers would study problems over time and help districts use research to improve. The need for research to promote more effective teaching of middle school mathematics was one such area that they discussed. As an objective, they pointed to the need for researchers to improve their communication, distribution, and marketing of research to practitioners and for practitioners to adopt and implement evidence-based programs. Say Yes set itself on a similar path with educational researchers. Successful practices in Syracuse, and eventually in Buffalo, may serve as evidence to other urban school systems of the possibilities of reform guided by research.

The huge role filled by Syracuse University, a major research institution, raises the question of the degree to which such a program requires a single major local institution as a key player. In a twist on the advertisement for the now defunct E. F. Hutton brokerage house, one might say, "When Syracuse University talks, people in Syracuse listen." Engaging such a partner for a venture of this kind can be crucial. Resources, personnel, and influence flow from the arrangement.

But there came points at which the two organizations, like a couple of Type A's competing for dominance, could not agree on who should have the greater say in this or that matter. It was probably inevitable that strains would develop in the relationship between Say Yes and Syracuse University. They share many goals and, by and large, work well together. Despite an abundance of goodwill, though, their operational approaches and their aims could not possibly mesh all the time. It was more than coincidental that when Say Yes chose Buffalo as its second site, it relied on a consortium of area colleges and universities rather than anointing a single institution as its primary partner.

The Issue with the Site Directors

There was also the change in the site directors' position that removed them from the aegis of Syracuse University, altered their function, and made their employer Huntington Family Centers, which provides a range of social services in Onondaga

County. Huntington was to pay 75 percent of the salary with money from the county that originated with the state. Say Yes was to provide the rest, designating that portion to cover the administrative duties that remained with the position. Site directors became student support specialists and, as such, would be mostly case managers.

There were several reasons for the move, indicating that Say Yes had not put enough forethought into the position that it created at each elementary school. A feeling arose that the role of the site directors was fuzzy. Some of them thought that they had been inserted in the schools as change agents, occupying a stratum equal to that of the principal. Others performed duties beyond their scope, and still others failed to render the services expected of them. Principals had mixed reactions to the site directors and wanted more input in their selection. Say Yes had ceded much of the control of the position to the university, an arrangement that made Say Yes increasingly uneasy.

Finally, during summer 2012, four years into the project, Say Yes ordered the 18 site directors to reapply for the positions and retained only half of them as student support specialists. In addition, Say Yes moved to appoint four more support specialists in anticipation of expanding into the middle schools. In changing the position's title and role, Say Yes bolstered the relationship that they would have with students and their families. Support specialists would serve as case managers for up to 25 students in each building. They would, in effect, supplement the social workers already in the schools.

No longer, though, would each building have a lead person to represent Say Yes in conjunction with the entire school program, and that was a loss, no matter how much Say Yes did not want to admit it. Say Yes also severed the connection that site directors had to the after-school program. The changes seemed in keeping with a recommendation by a consultant who said that Say Yes—in collaboration with school personnel—should rewrite the job description to aid the school's student support team.[2] Say Yes strived to put the best face on the shift, which would appeal to principals who felt that the site directors had intruded on their domain. Moreover, the new position was potentially more fiscally sustainable than the site director position had been.

Certainly a program as wide ranging as the one that Say Yes took to Syracuse had to adjust its approach as it went along. The episode with the site directors—conceived as prime players in this drama—illustrates the need for flexibility each step of the way in school reform. It is not a sign of failure to feed the players new lines as the action unfolds and the roles grow more defined. But one must hope that changes, often driven in part by economics, will serve the best interests of the entire production in the long run.

Lessons Learned

Say Yes, like a diligent student, took to heart the lessons that it learned in Syracuse. While every school system has its own personality, there are sufficient commonalities so that school reform need not be totally reinvented each time someone pursues it in a new place. The similarities between the Say Yes experience in Syracuse and what other reformers have encountered are striking—and instructive.

School Reform Elsewhere

School reform has proved itself more difficult than getting a man on the moon. Failures and mixed results predominate. It puts one in mind of the exploits of Don Quixote, with reformers at times seemingly tilting at imaginary windmills. The Edna McConnell Clark Foundation early in the twenty-first century abandoned its efforts to change outcomes for poor children by improving their schools, concluding that it was too difficult to alter the attitudes and behaviors of people in a whole school system. Around the same time, the Chicago Annenberg Challenge, which absorbed more than $100 million from 1995 to 2001, was found to have had little impact on student achievement, classroom behavior, or social competence. Just a few years later, Bill Gates conceded that his foundation's investment of $2 billion to create smaller high schools had produced "achievement scores below district averages in reading and math" and "graduation rates no better than the statewide average."[3]

In Syracuse, Say Yes succeeded in rounding up backers for its interventions. This may not be enough, though. A study of school reforms over the last century led the authors to declare that "even reforms with strong supporters do not always become embedded in the schools." They argue that schools are "in some respects autonomous, buffered institutions."[4] As such, they represent a culture built to resist reform.

The Chicago Annenberg Research Project conducted one of the most exhaustive studies ever of a school reform project. It found the greatest success in schools that brought together the synergy of a combination of supports, rather than relying on a single intervention. "The supports that represent key organizational capacities—school leadership, professional community, and parent and community support—are crucial for developing and supporting school practices—student learning climate and quality instruction—that in turn are instrumental for promoting student learning," the report states.[5] Such findings validate the approach taken by Say Yes.

Similarly, the best results among the small high schools supported by Gates tended to come at schools that could carry out many proven reforms well, all at once. This included a longer school day, better relationships within the school, and "college-ready standards aligned with a rigorous curriculum, with the instructional tools to support it, effective teachers to teach it, and data systems to track the progress."[6] This approach, too, resembles Say Yes's multipronged efforts in Syracuse, and the question after five years is whether the city's public school system can sustain these taxing all-at-once efforts.

The improvements pursued in Syracuse proceed on the assumption that the basic educational structure, very much resembling what exists in most places in the country, is sufficient for the future. No one seems to ask whether the city's public schools require more drastic change. The style of teaching and learning remains pretty much as it was five years ago and is likely to be similar five years from now. Will that be enough to equip urban students for a productive postsecondary education? It is great that more of them will go off to college, but what will they make of the experience? One reason school reform has faltered in so many instances is that life in the classroom—in terms of the behaviors of both teachers and students—stays relatively the same. But this is a question for another book.

A Current Reform Network

The Cities for Education Entrepreneurship Trust (CEE-Trust), mentioned in the previous chapter, is a network of school reformers formed in 2010 that seeks transformative educational change in urban settings. A report[7] on work in three of those cities—Indianapolis, New Orleans, and Detroit—offers these lessons familiar to those who observed Say Yes's work in Syracuse:

- Find the right leader or leadership team. As should be clear to any reader of this book, Say Yes placed great importance on this point. The CEE-Trust report recommended that the leaders have deep ties to the community and that they understand the leverage points in the educational reform world.
- Develop a comprehensive plan for reform. Say Yes based its plan for Syracuse on the results of years in the field in other cities. Then Say Yes spent a year gearing up to roll out the program in Syracuse.
- Grow talent pipelines. From the superintendent that Say Yes helped Syracuse recruit to local talent like Pat Driscoll, Monique Fletcher, and Kristi Eck to the site directors to the community-based organization (CBO) representatives, Say Yes recognized that sustainability meant that the program had to cultivate local roots.
- Engage stakeholders in the community to accelerate reform. Such engagement is vital to the long-range success of Say Yes in Syracuse and may be an area in which Say Yes has had to struggle. In some ways, Say Yes did not do enough to get the initial buy-in of stakeholders, and in other ways, it had to deal with intractable skepticism and even cynicism in a city that critics say has an inferiority complex.

All in all, Say Yes absorbed such lessons and applied them when it moved into Buffalo. Syracuse, after all, was the first try at whole-district school reform, and nobody said it would be easy.

Shuffling Off to Buffalo

Say Yes had eyes on other places even as it refined its venture in Syracuse. There was a sense that what it had in mind for one city could be tailored to suit another locale. Replication, in other words, always loomed as a likelihood and, quietly, the search for a second city was under way.

The $4,265,000 grant from the Wallace Foundation, awarded in 2011, contained a half-million dollars for work that Say Yes would carry out in Buffalo. Drawing on experiences in Syracuse, Say Yes prepared to undertake some initiatives earlier in the process the second time around. Say Yes used what it learned in Syracuse to place some of the work on a faster track in Buffalo. In January 2012, for instance, just weeks after publicly announcing the move into Buffalo, Say Yes—in collaboration with the Buffalo Public Schools and with the aid of consultants—began a fiscal review of the school system, as well as reviews of the district's curriculum, information technology, and mental health provisions.

At that time, Say Yes also established a due diligence process with the aid of the American Institutes for Research in order to identify community-based organizations to bring into the program as partners, taking this step earlier in the process than it had in Syracuse. CBOs weren't identified as partners in Syracuse until after Say Yes had launched its services to students. Say Yes didn't even have a fully developed framework for its after-school offerings in Syracuse when the programs began. By comparison, the planning for the after-school part in Buffalo occurred before the rollout.

In February and March 2012, prior to the fall 2012 start-up, Say Yes hired an executive director and staff for Buffalo, developed a student monitoring system and a plan for implementing it, and conducted due diligence reviews of specific CBOs identified by the process just two months earlier. Say Yes had letters of commitment in hand from the city, county, school district, and teachers' union before it even announced its program for Buffalo. In Syracuse, such commitments did not entirely materialize until after the program started.

The student monitoring system is supposed to play a major role in ensuring that students remain on track to benefit from the college scholarships. The monitoring system was mostly in place when school opened in Buffalo in September 2012. It took Say Yes four years to get the public schools in Syracuse to implement the monitoring system, and even then it was not fully operative.

Say Yes entered Buffalo with $15 million already pledged toward a projected endowment of $100 million in support of its free-tuition program, starting this fundraising earlier than it did in Syracuse. There was also news that the federal government would award Buffalo a grant from its Promise Neighborhoods program to dovetail with Say Yes's work by making funds available for specific neighborhoods in the city to engage families and communities in efforts to prepare young people for higher education. The Community Foundation for Greater Buffalo assumed a major responsibility for raising money for Say Yes's efforts in the city. "We're trying to impact an entire generation," said Alphonso O'Neil-White, chairman of the community foundation. He told the *Buffalo News* that up until that point no potential donor had turned down a request for a donation.[8]

But roses did not bloom throughout Buffalo for Say Yes, and the severe winter weather was not the problem. A few weeds sprouted into view. During the first school year of operation in the city, 2012–13, a *Buffalo News* article accused Say Yes of exaggerating its impact on Syracuse. The daily newspaper story raised questions about statistics in Syracuse regarding such matters as high school graduates going to college, enrollment growth in the school system, increases in home sales, and results on New York State Regents Examinations. The article wondered why, in light of "remarkable results," Say Yes felt the need to inflate claims about its accomplishments.[9]

I, too, found a tendency by Say Yes representatives sometimes to give the program credit for achievements in which its role was limited. Furthermore, as the *Buffalo News* said, the statistics that Say Yes cited as evidence of progress were occasionally a comparison of apples and oranges or, at least, Granny Smiths and McIntoshes. I discovered, for instance, a discrepancy between the less-than-stellar attendance statistics I obtained for the high schools and the more impressive numbers handed out by Say Yes.

It is understandable if Say Yes officials are driven by concern about losing support for their work. So many efforts at school reform around the country have been washed away by a tide of disappointment that Say Yes rightfully worried that its results in Syracuse would not appear on the balance sheet quickly enough. This phenomenon resembles the push by America's corporate chieftains to emphasize growth in quarterly earnings rather than waiting for the painstaking, less glamorous results that show up only in the long run. Say Yes faced the ever-present challenge of maintaining the confidence of funders; continuing to please various constituencies in Syracuse (and now in Buffalo); and not losing the support of backers in city, county, state, and federal government.

A major test of supporters' confidence in Buffalo came halfway through Say Yes's first school year in that city, in January 2013. A report by an independent education expert working in conjunction with the state education department found that conditions had hardly changed in the public schools during the first six months in office of Superintendent Pamela C. Brown—whom Say Yes touted for the position. The report pointed to many areas in which progress was slow or nonexistent. "There appears to be a lack of systemic coordination and communication across the 28 schools," the report said of the priority schools. "Principals across different levels (elementary and secondary) report little to no change." It said of professional development: "There is not yet evidence of continuous training or follow up on the initial November training for priority schools."[10]

But as Say Yes continually reminds all who will listen, school reform in an urban setting is, in effect, a job for Sisyphus. Only the foolhardy would try to roll that boulder up a hill. The statistics in places like Syracuse and Buffalo have been dismal for so long that it requires patience to appreciate the time it will take to produce lasting improvement. That is a better story for Say Yes to tell than one that may make listeners distrust the exemplary work it does.

Next Steps

Syracuse and its school system are just about the right size for Say Yes's venture, kind of like Baby Bear's bed was for Goldilocks. There is also the matter of need, which made the advent of Say Yes compelling to the locals. Both the city's public schools and its economy require the reform and revitalization that a successful Say Yes can provide. If Say Yes has the right stuff, it will likely prevail in building its model. The other side of the coin, though, is that in such a place—a small postindustrial urban area—finances these days are as shaky as a table with three legs. The very reasons that make Syracuse an attractive proving ground can cause the experiment to blow up. "The outlook was good on paper and all of the assumptions had real substance but the world has changed and that's the most precarious part," said Mayor Miner.

As already noted, the classroom is the cockpit in which Say Yes does not have its hands on the controls. But such a person as Kevin Ahern, the teachers' union president, believes that even without piloting the plane, Say Yes can affect the flight pattern. "Say Yes can have an enormous impact on student achievement," he said during the fifth year of the program. "The longer we do this, we see a greater potential for that to happen." This may be increasingly true as forces beyond Syracuse exert influence on the classroom. The Common Core curriculum, shaped by national authorities, that the district adopted leaves less of the content to chance than previously. New York State's demand for teacher evaluation, under pressure from the federal government, can make instructional quality less problematic.

Nevertheless, some teachers and principals in the city continue to worry that scholastic achievement in Syracuse, especially among low-income students and English language learners, is so deficient that even extra resources and new approaches encouraged by Say Yes might not be up to the enormity of the task. Then there is the perception among the system's educators that some students seem to shut down their aptitude for learning once they reach middle school. On top of this, the large special education enrollment requires greater financial outlays and more attention than that required for other students.

The Syracuse public schools have been long mired in low expectations, and many students are bereft of the kinds of experiences that enhance academic achievement. It need not follow, though, that this situation becomes a self-fulfilling prophecy of failure. There is lots of room in Syracuse for better instruction, closer alignment between curriculum and learning goals, greater collaboration among educators, improved professional development, and programs to compensate for what has been missing in the lives of some of the city's young people. The school system, in other words, needs a cultural shift, and this means expecting more of students and teachers—and parents, too, I might add—and providing the tools to help.

What Say Yes assumed would happen in the schools did not always happen, especially in the early years. One level sometimes did not disseminate goals and expectations down to the next level. Results were not necessarily monitored. Frequently, there was little accountability for actions not taken and for outcomes not attained. Unimplemented plans for school improvement, in Syracuse or anywhere else, have no more effect than pennies flipped into a wishing well.

Say Yes was aware of these and other challenges. Before the second year had ended, the analyses conducted by the American Institutes for Research in the system's 32 schools had identified at least three areas of priority in which the district urgently required help to improve instruction: the teaching of math, differentiation of instructional approaches, and a rigorous curriculum with multiple pathways to send graduates in various directions.

The district, according to this report, had to work more assiduously to give students a mathematical foundation for courses such as algebra that push open the gate to success in high school and beyond. Students had to be better prepared to choose their courses, whether they want to attend a two-year college, a four-year college, or a proprietary school or go directly to a job. In general, the findings of reports two years later were much the same. Restless with the pace of change and not wanting simply to wait for existing schools to make a cultural shift, Contreras got the school board in 2013 to create Syracuse Latin, which will take over an existing building. It will offer a rigorous, classical education, including the study of Latin. The school is scheduled to open in 2014 with a kindergarten and first grade and will add a grade each year.

Say Yes's goal for students is not simply higher test scores, but postsecondary completion. That dictates a laser-like focus by teachers and a greater willingness to work hard by their students. The implications for staff development are enormous and potentially costly. Say Yes wants educators in Syracuse to have the opportunity for technical assistance and to be able to attend single-day and multiday institutes. Such institutes would draw on experts from AIR and Syracuse University as well as those from across the country. Sharon Contreras gave promise of responding to these needs.

Given all that Say Yes accomplished in Syracuse in the first five years, one hesitates to quibble. Bolstered by its influential supporters, Say Yes gained a following in a community looking for a "game changer," as people in the city tended to put it. The kind of goodwill generated by Say Yes extended beyond the movers and shakers. When Dan Trivison, a school custodian, went on jury duty, he and his fellow jurors were confronted by a case involving a juvenile offender. Trivison used the occasion to assure his fellow jurors that with Say Yes in Syracuse, people would see a decline in juvenile delinquency. That is the sort of confidence and hope that the program inspired.

Appendix A

These private colleges and universities belong to the Say Yes Higher Education Compact, having agreed—some with certain conditions—to provide Syracuse City School District graduates who meet entrance requirements with a financial aid package that will cover tuition.

Private Institutions

Bryant and Stratton College, Syracuse campus
Canisius College
Clarkson University
Colgate University
Columbia University
Cooper Union
Crouse Hospital College of Nursing
D'Youville College
Daemen College
Drexel University
Fordham University
Goodwin College
Hartwick College
Harvard College
Hilbert College
Hobart and William Smith Colleges
Houghton College
LeMoyne College
Lesley University
Manhattanville College
Marist College
Medaille College
Molloy College
New York Institute of Technology
New York University
Niagara University
Northwestern University
Rensselaer Polytechnic Institute

Rochester Institute of Technology
Sarah Lawrence College
St. Bonaventure University
St. Joseph's College of Nursing
Syracuse University
Trocaire College
Tufts University
University of Pennsylvania
University of Rochester
Vassar College
Villa Maria College

Say Yes supplements the financial aid that Syracuse high school graduates receive from these publicly-supported institutions to cover the balance of what is needed for a full-tuition scholarship.

City University of New York (CUNY) Senior Colleges

Baruch College
Brooklyn College
City College
College of Staten Island
Hunter College
John Jay College of Criminal Justice
Lehman College
Medgar Evers College
New York City College of Technology
Queens College
Sophie Davis School of Biomedical Education
York College

CUNY Community Colleges

Borough of Manhattan
Bronx
Hostos
Kingsborough
LaGuardia
Queensborough

State University of New York (SUNY) University Centers

Binghamton University
Stony Brook University

University at Albany
University at Buffalo

SUNY Technical Colleges

Alfred State College of Technology
Canton
Cobleskill
College of Environmental Science and Forestry
Delhi
Farmingdale State College
Institute of Technology (IT)
Maritime College
Morrisville State College

SUNY University Colleges

Buffalo State College
The College at Brockport
College at Old Westbury
College at Oneonta
Cortland
Fredonia
Geneseo
New Paltz
Oswego
Plattsburgh
Potsdam
Purchase College

SUNY Community Colleges

Adirondack
Broome
Cayuga County
Clinton
Columbia Greene
Corning
Dutchess
Erie
Fashion Institute of New York
Finger Lakes
Fulton Montgomery
Genesee

Herkimer County
Hudson Valley
Jamestown
Jefferson
Mohawk Valley
Monroe
Nassau
Niagara County
North Country
Onondaga
Orange County
Rockland
Schenectady County
Suffolk County
Sullivan County
Tompkins Corland
Ulster County
Westchester

Appendix B

Say Yes to Education has been involved in the Syracuse City School District in many ways. These are some of the actions that Say Yes has taken and/or facilitated:

Systemwide Supports

1. Audits on the district's finances, human resources, technology, special education, curriculum and instruction, and mental health, family support, and social-emotional services
2. Support for creation and implementation of a long-term strategic plan built on the external reviews
3. Facilitation of the board of education's search for a new superintendent
4. Creation of a college tuition scholarship program for high school graduates
5. Establishment of the Higher Education Compact of institutions in the scholarship program
6. Use of community-based organizations for delivery of after-school activities
7. Support of certain programs to support specific neighborhoods

Elementary and Middle School Supports

1. A student monitoring system
2. More social workers in the schools
3. School-based mental health clinics
4. School-based health clinics (for elementary schools)
5. Student support specialists
6. Family support specialists
7. Pro bono legal clinics for all families with students in the school system
8. Extended day programming available for all elementary school students
9. Summer program available for all elementary school students
10. Naviance system to help students in their college preparation (for middle schools)

High School Supports

1. A student monitoring system
2. More social workers in the schools
3. School-based mental health clinics
4. Student support specialists
5. Family support specialists
6. Pro bono legal clinics for all families with students in the school system
7. A regional financial aid counseling network
8. Improvement of college counseling in the high schools (development of a comprehensive guidance plan shifting the role from crisis counseling and scheduling to postsecondary advisement)
9. Tutoring of high school students
10. Coaching for the SAT exam
11. Naviance system to help students in their college preparation
12. Support for a summer leadership development program for refugee and native Syracuse high school students

Postsecondary Supports

1. Creation of a college tuition scholarship program for high school graduates
2. Establishment of the Higher Education Compact of institutions in the scholarship program
3. On Point for College Inc. to help in the transition to college
4. Summer bridge programming to assist students in the transition to two-year colleges

Notes

Chapter 1

1. David Tyack and Larry Cuban, *Tinkering toward Utopia: A Century of Public School Reform* (Cambridge, MA: Harvard University Press, 1995), 1.
2. Mark Berends and Roberto Penaloza, "Increasing Racial Isolation and Test Score Gaps in Mathematics: A 30-Year Perspective," *Teachers College Record* 112, no. 4 (April 2010): 979.
3. Dennis J. Condron, "Social Class, School and Non-School Environments, and Black/White Inequalities in Children's Learning," *American Sociological Review* 74, no. 5 (October 2009): 699.
4. Gerald Grant, *Hope and Despair in the American City: Why There Are No Bad Schools in Raleigh* (Cambridge, MA: Harvard University Press, 2009), 140–41.
5. Liana Heitin, "Gallup Poll: Student Success Linked to Positive Outlook," *Education Week*, August 29, 2012, 11.
6. *Public School District Total Cohort Graduation Rate and Enrollment Outcome Summary, 2010–11 School Year* (Albany: New York State Education Department, 2011), 713.
7. Alan Vanneman et al., *Achievement Gaps: How Black and White Students in Public Schools Perform in Mathematics and Reading on the National Assessment of Educational Progress* (Washington, DC: National Center for Education Statistics, Institute of Education Statistics, July 2009).
8. F. Cadelle Hemphill et al., *Achievement Gaps: How Hispanic and White Students in Public Schools Perform in Mathematics and Reading on the National Assessment of Educational Progress* (Washington, DC: National Center for Education Statistics, Institute of Education Statistics, June 2011).
9. *The Nation's Report Card: Vocabulary Results from the 2009 and 2011 NAEP Reading Assessments* (Washington, DC: National Assessment of Educational Progress, National Center for Education Statistics, December 2012).
10. *The Nation's Report Card: Mathematics 2011* (Washington, DC: National Assessment of Educational Progress, National Center for Education Statistics, November 2011).
11. *The Nation's Report Card: Civics 2010* (Washington, DC: National Assessment of Educational Progress, National Center for Education Statistics, May 2011).
12. Paul E. Barton and Richard J. Coley, *Parsing the Achievement Gap II* (Princeton, NJ: Educational Testing Service, 2009).
13. *The CEO Poverty Measure, 2005–2010* (New York: NYC Center for Economic Opportunity, April 2010).
14. *Pursuing the American Dream: Economic Mobility across the Generations* (Philadelphia, PA: Pew Charitable Trusts, July 2012), 1–2.

15. Raj Chetty, John N. Friedman, and Jonah Rockoff, "The Long-Term Impacts of Teachers: Teacher Value-Added and Student Outcomes," NBER Working Paper 17699, National Bureau of Economic Research, Cambridge, MA, December 2011.

16. Carrie Hahnel and Orville Jackson, *Learning Denied: The Case for Equitable Access to Effective Teaching in California's Largest School District* (Washington, DC: Education Trust–West, January 12, 2012), 2.

17. Sarah D. Sparks, "Gaps Found in Access to Qualified Math Teachers," *Education Week*, April 3, 2013, 6.

18. Robert Rosenthal and Lenore Jacobson, "Pygmalion in the Classroom," *The Urban Review* 3, no. 1 (September 1968): 16–20; Christine Rubie-Davies, John Hattie, and Richard Hamilton, "Expecting the Best for Students: Teacher Expectations and Academic Outcomes," *British Journal of Educational Psychology* 76, no. 3 (2006): 429–44; Clark McKown and Rhona Weinstein, "Teacher Expectations, Classroom Context, and the Achievement Gap," *Journal of School Psychology* 46, no. 3 (2008): 235–61; Linda van den Bergh et al., "The Implicit Prejudiced Attitudes of Teachers: Relations to Teacher Expectation and the Ethnic Achievement Gap," *American Educational Research Journal* 47, no. 2, 2010, 497–527.

19. Ronald F. Ferguson, "Teachers' Perceptions and Expectations and the Black-White Test Score Gap," *Urban Education* 38 (July 2003): 460.

20. Ibid., 494.

21. Stuart Luppescu et al., *Trends in Chicago's Schools across Three Eras of Reform: Summary of Key Findings* (Chicago, IL: Consortium on Chicago School Research, September 2011).

22. Fernanda Santos, "Regents Chancellor Minces Few Words on the City's Schools," *New York Times*, December 7, 2011, A25.

23. Claudia Vargas, "Metal Thieves Ravage Camden School Buildings," *Philadelphia Inquirer*, August 18, 2012.

24. *Needs Analysis: Camden City Public Schools* (Bethesda, MD: UPD and Cross & Joftus, August 21, 2012).

25. Office of the Governor, "Gov. Malloy Rolls Out Education Reform Package to Improve Low-Achieving Schools," news release, February 6, 2012.

26. *Connecticut Mastery Test, Fourth Generation, Percent Meeting State Goal* (Hartford, CT: Connecticut Department of Education, 2010–11).

27. *Report on Student Cohort Growth in Hartford* (Hartford, CT: Achieve Hartford, October 11, 2012).

28. *Hartford Public Schools 2012 CMT and CAPT Scores: What Do the Results Tell Us?* (Hartford, CT: Achieve Hartford, August 16, 2012).

29. *U.S. Education Reform and National Security* (New York: Independent Task Force Report No. 68, Council on Foreign Relations, 2012), 7 and 46.

30. *Education at a Glance 2011* (Washington, DC: Organization for Economic Cooperation and Development, September 2011).

31. Michael Fullan, *Choosing the Wrong Drivers for Whole System Reform* (East Melbourne Victoria, Australia: Centre for Strategic Education, April 2011), 3–4.

32. Denver Summit Schools Network, Far Northeast Regional Information, Denver Public Schools, http://fne.dpsk12.org/dssn.

33. Jacob Mishook, Elsa Dure, and Norm Fruchter, *Districts Play a Critical Role in School Turnaround—but They Need to Do It Right* (Providence, RI: Annenberg Institute for School Reform, related commentary, August 23, 2012).

34. Greg J. Duncan and Richard J. Murnane, eds., *Whither Opportunity: Rising Inequality, Schools, and Children's Life Chances* (New York: Russell Sage Foundation, 2011), 5.

35. Sean F. Reardon, "The Widening Achievement Gap between the Rich and the Poor: New Evidence and Possible Explanations," in *Whither Opportunity: Rising Inequality, Schools, and Children's Life Chances*, eds. Greg J. Duncan and Richard J. Murnane (New York: Russell Sage Foundation, 2011).

36. Paul E. Peterson, "Neither Broad nor Bold," *Education Next*, Summer 2012, http://educationnext.org/neither-broad-nor-bold.

37. Steve H. Murdock, "Population Change in Texas and San Antonio: Implications for Economic Development, the Labor Force and Education" (presentation to San Antonio Manufacturers Association, Hobby Center for Study of Texas at Rice University, slides 116 and 120, Houston, TX, October 18, 2012).

38. Paul Tough, "The Birthplace of Obama the Politician," *New York Times Magazine*, August 19, 2012, 31.

39. Barack Obama, "Remarks by the President on College Affordability, Syracuse NY" (speech, Henninger High School, Syracuse, NY, August 22, 2013), http://www.whitehouse.gov/the-press-office/2013/08/23/remarks-president-college-affordability-syracuse-ny.

Chapter 2

1. George Weiss, "A Passion for Learning and Helping the Underserved Succeed," *Central New York Magazine*, October 10–November 10, 2010, 42–43.

2. *An Imperiled Generation: Saving Urban Schools* (Princeton, NJ: Carnegie Foundation for the Advancement of Teaching, Princeton University Press, 1988).

3. Stephen Moore, "From the Fab Five to the Three Rs," *Wall Street Journal*, December 31, 2011, A13.

4. "Say Yes to Education Organizational Planning Discussion" (unpublished discussion, Schoolhouse Partners and American Institutes for Research, Washington, DC, November 13, 2006).

5. John Kania and Mark Kramer, "Collective Impact," *Stanford Social Innovation Review*, Winter 2011, 36.

Chapter 3

1. "Urban School Superintendents: Characteristics, Tenure, and Salary" The Council of the Great City Schools, *Urban Indicator*, Fall 2010.

2. Michael Casserly, remarks at Common Core Publishers Criteria event, New York City, June 28, 2012.

3. Kathy Christie and Stephanie Rose, *A Problem Still in Search of a Solution* (Denver, CO: Education Commission of the States, September 2012), 3.

4. "Quality Counts 2008: Tapping into Teaching," *Education Week*, January 10, 2008.

5. Paul E. Peterson et al., *Globally Challenged: Are U.S. Students Ready to Compete?* (Cambridge, MA: Harvard Kennedy School, 2012), 10.

6. Jeffrey R. Henig and S. Paul Reville, "Why Attention Will Return to Nonschool Factors," *Education Week*, commentary page, May 25, 2011.

7. Michael D. Usdan, "Mayoral Leadership in Education: Current Trends and Future Directions," *Harvard Educational Review* 76, no. 2 (Summer 2006): 148.

8. Gene I. Maeroff, *School Boards in America: A Flawed Exercise in Democracy* (New York: Palgrave Macmillan, 2010), 179.

9. Robin Wilson, "Syracuse's Slide: As Chancellor Focuses on the 'Public Good,' Syracuse's Reputation Slides," *Chronicle of Higher Education*, October 2, 2011.

10. Letters to the editor, *Post-Standard*, October 30, 2011, E3.

Chapter 4

1. Andrew P. Kelly and Patrick McGuinn, "Mobilizing Parent Power for School Reform," *Education Week*, September 25, 2012.

2. Keith Catone and Alexa LeBoeuf, *Student-Centered Education Starts with Student-Led Reform* (Providence, RI: Annenberg Institute for School Reform, Brown University, November 12, 2012).

3. Laini Fertick, "Say Yes to Education Perceptual Study Report" *CRITICALMASSMEDIA*, Spring/Summer 2011, 15–16.

Chapter 5

1. *Syracuse City School District: Talent Management Assessment and Review* (Bethesda, MD: Cross & Joftus, December 5, 2011), 4.

2. Richard Elmore, "The (Only) Three Ways to Improve Performance in Schools" (Cambridge, MA: Harvard Graduate School of Education: Usable Knowledge, 2009), http://www.uknow.gse.harvard.edu.leadership/leadership001a.html.

3. Jacquelyn Thompson et al., "Executive Summary: Syracuse City School District: Special Education System Review" (Bethesda, MD: Cross & Joftus, November 30, 2011).

4. Steven M. Ross and Laura Rodriguez, *Student Achievement in Syracuse City School District* (paper commissioned by Say Yes to Education, New York, October 2012), 8.

5. *Public School District Total Cohort Graduation Rate and Enrollment Outcome Summary, 2010–11 School Year* (Albany: New York State Education Department, 2011), 712–14.

6. Gary L. St. C. Oates, "An Empirical Test of Five Prominent Explanations for the Black-White Academic Performance Gap," *Social Psychology of Education* 12, no. 4 (December 2009): 415–41.

7. Sharon Contreras, *Great Expectations: Syracuse City School District Strategic Plan 2012–2017* (Syracuse, NY: Syracuse City School District, August 24, 2012).

8. "How Do You Measure College Readiness?" (Providence, RI: Consortium on Chicago School Research, College Readiness Indicator Systems, Annenberg Institute for School Reform, Fall 2011).

9. *How the World's Most Improved School Systems Keep Getting Better* (New York: McKinsey & Company, November 2010).

10. Kimberly Kendziora and David Osher, *Say Yes to Education Research Report: Student Assessment System* (Washington, DC: American Institutes for Research, August 21, 2007).

Chapter 6

1. David Tyack and Larry Cuban, *Tinkering toward Utopia: A Century of Public School Reform* (Cambridge, MA: Harvard University Press, 1995), 10, 57–58.

2. "High Performing School Systems to Close Achievement Gaps in NEA Foundation-Funded Communities" (Washington, DC: The NEA Foundation Issue Brief, November 2012), 7–8.

Chapter 7

1. *Reimagining the School Day: More Time for Learning* (New York: Wallace Foundation, 2011), 13.
2. Shaver Jeffries, "After-School Programs Save Kids (Including Me)," *Star-Ledger*, Newark, NJ, July 8, 2012, 5, sect. 2.
3. Beth Sinclair et al., *Approaches for Integrating Skill-Based Activities in Out-of-School Time Programs* (Washington, DC: Policy Studies Associates, February 2012).
4. Nora Fleming, "Push Is On to Add Time to School Day, Year," *Education Week*, October 26, 2011, 1.
5. David Tyack and Larry Cuban, *Tinkering toward Utopia: A Century of Public School Reform* (Cambridge, MA: Harvard University Press, 1995), 57.
6. *Afterschool Implementation Summary Report 2012, Say Yes to Education and the Syracuse City School District.* (Washington, DC: American Institutes for Research, 2012).
7. "Afterschool Programs: Making a Difference in America's Communities by Improving Academic Achievement, Keeping Kids Safe and Helping Working Families," Afterschool Alliance, January 2013, http://www.afterschoolalliance.org/documents/outcomes_0208.pdf.
8. Jennifer S. McCombs et al., *Making Summer Count: How Summer Programs Can Boost Children's Learning* (Arlington, VA: RAND Education, 2011), 20–23.
9. Barbara Heyns, *Summer Learning and the Effects of Schooling* (New York: Academic Press, 1978); Harris Cooper, "Summer Learning Loss: The Problems and Some Solutions" (Washington, DC: ERIC Clearinghouse in Elementary and Early Childhood Education, ERIC Digest, EDO-PS-03-5, 2003); Karl L. Alexander et al., "Summer Learning and Its Implications: Insights from the Beginning School Study," *New Directions for Youth Development* 114 (July 2, 2007): 11–32.
10. Jean Grossman, Margo Campbell, and Becca Raley, *Quality Time after School: What Instructors Can Do to Enhance Learning* (Philadelphia, PA: Private/Public Ventures, 2007).

Chapter 8

1. Amy Checkoway et al., "Evaluation of the Massachusetts Expanded Learning Time (ELT) Initiative: Year Five Final Report: 2010–11, Volume I" (executive summary, Abt Associates, Cambridge, MA, February 2, 2012), xvii.
2. Joseph Epstein, "Striking Teachers, Divided Antipathies," *Wall Street Journal*, September 13, 2012, A15.
3. "French Teachers Strike over Having to Work Five-Day Week," *AsiaOne*, Singapore Holdings, January 22, 2013.
4. Alan Ginsburg and Naomi Chudowsky, *Time for Learning: An Exploratory Analysis of NAEP Data* (Washington, DC: National Assessment Governing Board, Dec. 2012).
5. Hedy Chang and Robert Balfanz, "Let's Focus on Chronic Absenteeism," *Education Week*, January 18, 2012.

6. Martha Philbeck Mussa, *Taking Attendance Seriously: How School Absences Undermine Student and School Performance in New York City* (New York: Campaign for Fiscal Equity, May 2001).

7. James Vaznis, "Absenteeism Rife at Boston High Schools," *Boston Globe*, January 15, 2012.

8. Gene I. Maeroff, *Altered Destinies: Making Life Better for Schoolchildren in Need* (New York: St. Martin's Griffin, 1998), 23–90.

9. Finley Edwards, "Do Schools Begin Too Early?" *Education Next*, Summer 2012, 53–57.

10. John Carroll, "A Model of School Learning," *Teachers College Record* 64, no. 8 (1963): 723–33.

11. Jane Stallings, "Allocated Academic Learning Time Revisited, or Beyond Time on Task," *Educational Researcher* 9, no. 11 (December 1980): 11–16.

12. Laura M. Desimone and Daniel Long, "Teacher Effects and the Achievement Gap: Do Teacher and Teaching Quality Influence the Achievement Gap between Black and White and High- and Low-SES Students in the Early Grades?" *Teachers College Record* 112, no. 2 (December 2010): 3061.

13. Kenneth Goldberg, "The Homework Trap and What to Do about It," *Washington Post*, April 6, 2012.

14. Adam V. Maltese, Robert H. Tai, and Xitao Fan, "When Is Homework Worth the Time?: Evaluating the Association between Homework and Achievement in High School Science and Math." *The High School Journal* 96, no. 1 (Fall 2012): 52–72.

15. Harris Cooper et al., "Does Homework Improve Academic Achievement? A Synthesis of Research, 1987–2003," *Review of Educational Research* 76, no. 1 (Spring 2007): 1–62.

16. Ibid.

17. Raegen Miller, *Teacher Absence as a Leading Indicator of Student Achievement* (Washington, DC: Center for American Progress, November 2012), 1–2.

18. Charlene True, Kyle Butler, and Rachel Sefton, "Substitute Teachers: Making Lost Days Count," *International Journal of Educational Leadership Preparation* 6, no. 1 (January–March 2011).

Chapter 9

1. John Fantuzzo et al., "Academic Achievement of African American Boys: A City-Wide, Community-Based Investigation of Risk and Resilience," *Journal of School Psychology* 50, no. 5 (June 2012): 573.

2. Ibid., 572.

3. "Youth Risk Behavior Surveillance: United States, 2011." Centers for Disease Control and Prevention, U.S. Department of Health and Human Services, *Surveillance Summaries* 61, no. 4 (June 8, 2012): 2.

4. *The Critical Connection between Student Health and Achievement: How Schools and Policymakers Can Achieve a Positive Impact* (San Francisco: WestEd and the Philip P. Lee Institute for Health Policy Studies, University of California, April 2009), 6.

5. Michael E. Bernard, Andrew Stephanou, and Daniel Urbach, *The State of Student Social and Emotional Health* (Victoria, Australia: Australian Scholarship Groups, 2007).

6. Terry B. Grier, "A Healthy Partnership Makes a Visible Impact in Houston," *American School Boards Journal*, June 2012, 15.

7. Carol Nixon, "Keeping Students Learning: School Climate and Student Support Systems" (Charleston, WV and Nashville, TN: Edvantia Inc., n.d.).

8. *Resources for Children: Findings and Recommendations for Better Integration and Capacity Development* (New York: Turnaround for Children Inc., June 4, 2010).

9. Mary Jane England and Leslie J. Sim, *Depression in Parents, Parenting, and Children: Opportunities to Improve Identification, Treatment and Prevention* (Washington, DC: National Academies Press, 2009).

10. Susan F. Cole, letter to the editor, "Overcoming Hurdles to a Child's Success," *New York Times*, October 3, 2012, A26.

11. *Improving the Children's Mental Health System* (District of Columbia: Children's Law Center, May 2012), 5.

12. Michael Winerip, "Trying to Keep Students' Mental Health Care out of the E.R.," *New York Times*, April 9, 2012, A19.

13. Kim Nauer, Andrew White, and Rajeev Yerneni, *Strengthening Schools by Strengthening Families* (New York: Center for New York City Affairs, The New School, 2008), 27.

14. David Osher et al., *Syracuse City School District: Academic, Social Emotional, and Behavioral Indicators* (Washington, DC: American Institutes for Research, August 15, 2011), 12.

15. *Realizing the Promise of the Whole-School Approach to Children's Mental Health: A Practical Guide* (Waltham, MA: SAMHSA-funded National Center for Mental Health Promotion and Youth Violence Prevention, Educational Development Center Inc., Health and Human Development Division, February 2011).

16. Ibid., 13.

17. "View of Climate," *Education Week Quality Counts* (January 10, 2013): 14.

18. *2011 Annual Report* (Syracuse, NY: Huntington Family Services, 2011).

19. *High School and Youth Trends* (Bethesda, MD: National Institute on Drug Abuse, National Institutes of Health, U.S. Department of Health and Human Services, March 2011).

20. Joseph A. Durlak et al., "The Impact of Enhancing Students' Social and Emotional Learning: A Meta-Analysis of School-Based Universal Interventions," *Child Development* 82, no. 1 (January/February 2011): 405–32.

21. *2013 CASEL Guide: Effective Social and Emotional Learning Programs, Preschool and Elementary School Edition* (Chicago, IL: Collaborative for Academic, Social, and Emotional Learning, 2012), http://www.casel.org/guide.

Chapter 10

1. Dale J. Cohen, Sheida White, and Steffaney B. Cohen, "Mind the Gap: The Black-White Literacy Gap in the Assessment of Adult Literacy and Its Implications," *Journal of Literacy Research* 44, no. 2 (June 2012): 123–48.

2. *Trends in College Pricing 2012* (New York: College Board, October 24, 2012).

3. Caroline M. Hoxby and Christopher Avery, "The Missing 'One-Offs': The Hidden Supply of High-Achieving Low-Income Students," NBER Working Paper No. 18586, National Bureau of Economic Research, Washington, DC, March 19, 2013.

4. "Affluent Students Have an Advantage . . . and the Gap Is Widening," Chart in *New York Times*, December 23, 2012, 31.

5. *How America Pays for College 2012: Sallie Mae National Study of College Students and Parents* (Washington, DC: Sallie Mae, 2012), 7.

6. *Student Debt and the Class of 2011* (Washington, DC: Institute for College Access & Success, 2012).

7. *Private Student Loans* (Washington, DC: report to Congressional committees by the U.S. Department of Education and the Consumer Protection Financial Bureau, August 29, 2012), 4.
8. "The American Freshman: National Norms Fall 2010" (Los Angeles, CA: research brief, Higher Education Research Institute at UCLA, January 2011), 2.
9. Timothy J. Bartik and Marta Lachowska, "The Short-Term Effects of the Kalamazoo Promise Scholarship on Student Outcomes," Upjohn Institute Working Paper 12-186, Kalamazoo, MI, August 29, 2012, 3.
10. Jean Johnson and Jon Rochkind, "Can I Get a Little Advice Here?" *Public Agenda*, March 3, 2010, 5–7.
11. John Bridgeland and Mary Bruce, *2011 National Survey of School Counselors: Counseling at a Crossroads* (New York: College Board, 2011), 5.
12. *Knocking at the Door: Projections of High School Graduates* (Boulder, CO: Western Interstate Commission for Higher Education. December 2012), xii.
13. *True North: Charting the Course to College and Career Readiness* (New York: 2012 National Survey of School Counselors, College Board, October 2012), 5.
14. Eric P. Bettinger et al., "The Role of Simplification and Information in College Decisions: Results from the H&R Block FAFSA Experiment," NBER Working Paper No. 15361, National Bureau of Economic Research, Cambridge, MA, September 2009.
15. David Osher et al., *Syracuse City School District: Academic, Social Emotional, and Behavioral Indicators* (Washington, DC: American Institutes for Research, August 15, 2011), 31–35.
16. *2009–2012 SCSD Student Performance Comparison AVID vs. Non-AVID* (New York: Data Analysis, Evaluation and Research Team, Office of Shared Accountability, Syracuse City School District, January 18, 2013).
17. Charley Stone, Carl Van Horn, and Cliff Zukin, *Chasing the American Dream: Recent College Graduates and the Great Recession* (New Brunswick, NJ: John J. Heldrich Center for Workforce Development, Rutgers University, May 2012).
18. Ibid.
19. U.S. Census Bureau, "Bachelor's Degree Attainment Tops 30 Percent for the First Time, Census Bureau Reports," news release, February 23, 2012.
20. *How Much Protection Does a College Degree Afford?* (Washington, DC: Pew Charitable Trusts, January 2013).
21. Anthony P. Carnevale, Tamara Jayasundera, and Ban Cheah. *The College Advantage: Weathering the Economic Storm* (Washington, DC: Georgetown Public Policy Institute, Georgetown University Center on Education and the Workforce, 2012).
22. Anthony P. Carnevale, Jeff Strohl, and Michelle Melton, *What's It Worth?: The Economic Value of College Majors* (Washington, DC: Georgetown Public Policy Institute, Georgetown University Center on Education and the Workforce, 2011).

Chapter 11

1. Steven M. Ross et al., *First-Year Evaluation of the Say Yes Summer Success Academy* (Syracuse, NY: Say Yes to Education, October 2011), 3, 17.
2. *Remediation: Higher Education's Bridge to Nowhere* (Washington, DC: Complete College America, April 2012), 6.
3. Elizabeth A. Barnet et al., *Bridging the Gap: An Impact Study of Eight Developmental Summer Bridge Programs in Texas* (New York: National Center for Postsecondary Research, Teachers College, Columbia University, July 2012).

4. Heather D. Wathington et al., *Getting Ready for College: An Implementation and Early Impacts Study of Eight Texas Developmental Summer Bridge Programs* (New York: National Center for Postsecondary Research, Teachers College, Columbia University, November 2011).

5. Ibid.

6. "Key Facts on Developmental Education," Bill and Melinda Gates Foundation, http://gatesfoundation.org/postsecondaryeducation/Pages/key-facts-on-developmental -education.

7. Paul Attewell and David Lavin, *Passing the Torch: Does Higher Education for the Disadvantaged Pay Off across the Generations?* (New York: Russell Sage Foundation, 2007), 7.

8. Community College Research Center.

9. *Remediation: Higher Education's Bridge to Nowhere* (Washington, DC: Complete College America, April 2012), 2.

10. Robert Stillwell and Jennifer Sable, *Public School Graduates and Dropouts from the Common Core of Data: School Year 2009–10* (Washington, DC: National Center for Education Statistics, Institute of Education Sciences, January 2013), 4.

11. Janis Brown et al., *Algebra I and Geometry: Results from the 2005 High School Transcript Mathematics Curriculum Study* (Washington, DC: National Assessment of Educational Progress, March 2013).

12. *College Completion Must Be Our Priority* (Washington, DC: National Commission on Higher Education Attainment, American Council of Education, January 2013).

13. "Beyond the Rhetoric: Improving College Readiness through Coherent State Policy" (Atlanta: National Center for Public Policy and Higher Education and Southern Regional Education Board, June 2010).

14. "Defining College Readiness: Where Are We Now and Where Do We Need to Be?" *The Progress of Education Reform, Educational Commission of the States* 13, no. 2 (April 2012).

15. *SAT Report on College and Career* (New York: College Board, 2012).

16. *College Readiness: A Guide to the Field* (Providence, RI: Annenberg Institute for School Reform of Brown University, 2012).

17. Kristen Krell and Alma Rivera, *Challenges and Solutions to Closing the Achievement Gap* (Santa Fe: Santa Fe Community College, July 2010), 5.

Chapter 12

1. Michael A. Rebell, *Attempting to Do Better with Less* (New York: Campaign for Educational Equity, Teachers College, Columbia University, August 24, 2012).

2. "SCSD Budget Analysis: Board Summary Presentation." Schoolhouse Partners, Alexandria, VA, December 8, 2011.

3. Billy Easton, "Albany's Unkindest Cut of All," *New York Times*, May 26, 2012, A21.

4. Michael A. Rebell, Jessica R. Wolff, and Joseph R. Rogers Jr., *Deficient Resources: An Analysis of the Availability of Bare Educational Resources in High-Needs Schools in Eight New York State School Districts* (New York: Campaign for Educational Equity, Teachers College, Columbia University, December 2012).

5. Jacob Gershman, "Governor Feels Squeeze," *Wall Street Journal*, April 14, 2012, A17.

6. Michael A. Rebell, *Attempting to Do Better with Less*, 17.

7. *Iceberg Ahead: The Hidden Cost of Public Sector Retiree Health Benefits in New York* (Albany, NY: Empire Center for New York State Policy, September 5, 2012).

8. *Report of the State Budget Crisis Task Force: New York Report* (Albany, NY: State Budget Crisis Task Force, 2012).

9. Thomas Kaplan, "Experts Warn of Budget Ills for the State Lasting Years," *New York Times*, December 19, 2012, A27.

10. Stephanie Miner, "Cuomo to Cities: Just Borrow," *New York Times*, February 14, 2013, A27.

11. Stacey Childress, "Investing in Improvement: Strategy and Resource Allocation in Public School Districts," working paper 10-057, Harvard Business School, Cambridge, MA, January 11, 2010.

12. *Say Yes Leadership Planning Retreat* (New York: Constellation Advancement, August 6–7, 2012), 6.

13. *The Economic Impact of Communities in Schools* (Moscow, ID: Economic Modeling Specialists Inc., May 2012).

Chapter 13

1. Francesca Levy, "America's Best Places to Raise a Family 2010," *Forbes*, June 7, 2010, http://www.forbes.com/2010/06/04/best-places-family-lifestyle-real-estate-cities -kids.html.

2. Gerald Grant, *Hope and Despair in the American City: Why There Are No Bad Schools in Raleigh* (Cambridge, MA: Harvard University Press, 2009), 143.

3. Stephen J. Carroll and Ethan Scherer, *The Impact of Educational Quality on the Community* (Santa Monica, CA: RAND Corporation, 2008).

4. Paul Attewell and David Lavin, *Passing the Torch: Does Higher Education for the Disadvantaged Pay Off across the Generations?* (New York: Russell Sage Foundation, 2007), 5.

5. Ibid., 72.

6. Rahm Emanuel, "Chicago's Plan to Match Education with Jobs," *Wall Street Journal*, December 19, 2011, A19.

7. Keith Schneider, "An Ohio River City Comes Back to Its Shoreline," *New York Times*, June 6, 2012, B8.

8. Steven Fulop, "Turning Around Jersey City's Schools," *Star-Ledger*, September 12, 2012, 18.

9. *The Economic Benefits from Halving the Dropout Rate: A Boon to Business in the Nation's Largest Metropolitan Areas* (Washington, DC: Alliance for Excellent Education, January 12, 2010).

10. Jonathan Rothwell, *Housing Costs, Zoning and Access to High-Scoring Schools* (Washington, DC: Brookings Institution, April 2012).

11. Paul Owers and John Maines, "School Grades Can Have Impact on Local Economies," *South Florida Sun-Sentinel*, July 11, 2012.

12. *Crime Analysis Report: Say Yes Analysis Request* (New York: Syracuse Police Department, Criminal Intelligence Section, February 18, 2013).

Chapter 14

1. Mary Anne Schmitt-Carey, statement to the Committee on Education and the Workforce of the U.S. House of Representatives, Arlington, VA, July 17, 2001.

2. *Resources for Children: Findings and Recommendations for Better Integration and Capacity Development* (internal report to Say Yes, Turnaround for Children Inc., New York, June 4, 2010), 9.
3. Bill Gates, "Bill Gates—A Forum on Education in America," speech transcript, Bill and Melinda Gates Foundation, November 11, 2008, http://www.gatesfoundation.org/media-center/speeches/2008/11/bill-gates-forum-on-education-in-america.
4. David Tyack and Larry Cuban, *Tinkering toward Utopia: A Century of Public School Reform* (Cambridge, MA: Harvard University Press, 1995), 7.
5. Mark A. Smylie et al., *The Chicago Annenberg Challenge: Successes, Failure, and Lessons for the Future* (Chicago: Chicago Annenberg Research Project, August 2003), 85–86.
6. Bill Gates, "A Forum on Education in America."
7. *Kick-Starting Reform: Three City-Based Organizations Showing How to Transform Public Education* (Indianapolis, IN: Cities for Education Entrepreneurship Trust, August 2012).
8. Mary B. Pasciak and Harold McNeil, "City, Schools Due for a Big Boost," *Buffalo News*, December 19, 2011.
9. Mary B. Pasciak, "Say Yes Too Good to Be True?," *Buffalo News*, November 26, 2012.
10. "Buffalo Public Schools-Action Plan Status Report Update," New York State Education Department, January 7, 2013, http://www.p12.nysed.gov/accountability/de/documents/BuffaloDE-1stQtrlyActionStatusReport.html.

Bibliography

"Affluent Students Have an Advantage . . . and the Gap Is Widening." Chart in *New York Times*, December 23, 2012.

Afterschool Implementation Summary Report 2012, Say Yes to Education and the Syracuse City School District. American Institutes for Research, Washington, DC.

"Afterschool Programs: Making a Difference in America's Communities by Improving Academic Achievement, Keeping Kids Safe and Helping Working Families." Afterschool Alliance, January 2013. http://www.afterschoolalliance.org/documents/outcomes_0208.pdf.

Alexander, Karl L., Doris R. Entwisle, and Linda Steffel Olson. "Summer Learning and Its Implications: Insights from the Beginning School Study." *New Directions for Youth Development* 114 (July 2, 2007): 11–32. http://onlinelibrary.wiley.com/doi/10.1002/yd.210/abstract.

Allensworth, Elaine. "How Do You Measure College Readiness?" CRIS webinar presented by the Consortium on Chicago School Research, Annenberg Institute for School Reform, Brown University, Providence, RI, Fall 2011.

"The American Freshman: National Norms Fall 2010." Research brief. Higher Education Research Institute at UCLA, Los Angeles, January 2011.

Attewell, Paul, and David Lavin. *Passing the Torch: Does Higher Education for the Disadvantaged Pay Off across the Generations?* New York: Russell Sage Foundation, 2007.

"Bachelor's Degree Attainment Tops 30 Percent for the First Time, Census Bureau Reports." News release. U.S. Census Bureau, February 23, 2012.

Barnett, Elisabeth A., et al. *Bridging the Gap: An Impact Study of Eight Developmental Summer Bridge Programs in Texas.* National Center for Postsecondary Research, Teachers College, Columbia University, New York, July 2012.

Bartik, Timothy J., and Marta Lachowska. "The Short-Term Effects of the Kalamazoo Promise Scholarship on Student Outcomes." W. E. Upjohn Institute Working Paper No. 12-186, Kalamazoo, MI, August 29, 2012.

Barton, Paul E., and Richard J. Coley. *Parsing the Achievement Gap II.* Educational Testing Service, Princeton, NJ, April 2009.

Berends, Mark, and Roberto Penaloza. "Increasing Racial Isolation and Test Score Gaps in Mathematics: A 30-Year Perspective." *Teachers College Record* 112, no. 4 (April 2010): 978–1007.

Bergh, Linda van den, et al. "The Implicit Prejudiced Attitudes of Teachers: Relations to Teacher Expectation and the Ethnic Achievement Gap." *American Educational Research Journal* 47, no. 2 (2010): 497–527.

Bernard, Michael E., Andrew Stephanou, and Daniel Urbach. *The State of Student Social and Emotional Health.* Australian Scholarship Groups, Victoria, Australia, October 2007.

Bettinger, Eric P., et al. "The Role of Simplification and Information in College Decisions: Results from the H&R Block FAFSA Experiment." NBER Working Paper No. 15361, National Bureau of Economic Research, Cambridge, MA, September 2009.

Beyond the Rhetoric: Improving College Readiness through Coherent State Policy. National Center for Public Policy and Higher Education and Southern Regional Education Board, Atlanta, June 2010.

Bridgeland, John, and Mary Bruce. *2011 National Survey of School Counselors: Counseling at a Crossroads*. College Board, New York, November 2011.

Brown, Janis, et al. *Algebra I and Geometry: Results from the 2005 High School Transcript Mathematics Curriculum Study*. National Assessment of Educational Progress, March 2013.

"Buffalo Public Schools-Action Plan Status Report Update." New York State Education Department, January 7, 2013. http://www.p12.nysed.gov/accountability/de/documents/BuffaloDE-1stQtrlyActionStatusReport.html.

Carnegie Foundation for the Advancement of Teaching. *An Imperiled Generation: Saving Urban Schools; A Report*. Princeton University Press, Princeton, NJ, 1988.

Carnevale, Anthony P., Tamara Jayasundera, and Ban Cheah. *The College Advantage: Weathering the Economic Storm*. Georgetown Public Policy Institute, Georgetown University Center on Education and the Workforce, Washington, DC, August 2012.

Carnevale, Anthony P., Jeff Strohl, and Michelle Melton. *What's It Worth?: The Economic Value of College Majors*. Georgetown Public Policy Institute, Georgetown University Center on Education and the Workforce, Washington, DC, July 2011.

Carroll, John. "A Model of School Learning." *Teachers College Record* 64 (1963): 723–33.

Carroll, Stephen J., and Ethan Scherer. *The Impact of Educational Quality on the Community*. Santa Monica, CA: RAND Corporation, 2008.

Casserly, Michael. Remarks at Common Core Publishers Criteria Event, New York City, June 28, 2012.

Catone, Keith, and Alexa LeBoeuf. *Student-Centered Education Starts with Student-Led Reform*. Annenberg Institute for School Reform, Brown University, Providence, RI, November 12, 2012.

Centers for Disease Control and Prevention, U.S. Department of Health and Human Services. "Youth Risk Behavior Surveillance: United States, 2011." *Surveillance Summaries* 61, no. 4 (June 8, 2012): 2.

The CEO Poverty Measure, 2005–2010. NYC Center for Economic Opportunity, New York, April 2010.

Chang, Hedy, and Robert Balfanz. "Let's Focus on Chronic Absenteeism." *Education Week*, January 18, 2012.

Checkoway, Amy, et al. "Evaluation of the Massachusetts Expanded Learning Time (ELT) Initiative: Year Five Final Report; 2010–11, Volume I." Executive summary, Abt Associates, Cambridge, MA.

Chetty, Raj, John N. Friedman, and Jonah Rockoff. "The Long-Term Impacts of Teachers: Teacher Value-Added and Student Outcomes." NBER Working Paper No. 17699, National Bureau of Economic Research, Cambridge, MA, December 2011.

Childress, Stacey. "Investing in Improvement: Strategy and Resource Allocation in Public School Districts." Working paper 10-057, Harvard Business School, Cambridge, MA, January 11, 2010.

Christie, Kathy, and Stephanie Rose. *A Problem Still in Search of a Solution*. Education Commission of the States, Denver, CO, September 2012.

Cohen, Dale J., Sheida White, and Steffaney B. Cohen. "Mind the Gap: The Black-White Literacy Gap in the Assessment of Adult Literacy and Its Implications." *Journal of Literacy Research* 44, no. 2 (June 2012): 123–48.

Cole, Susan F. "Overcoming Hurdles to a Child's Success." Letter to the editor. *New York Times*, October 3, 2012.

College Completion Must Be Our Priority. National Commission on Higher Education Attainment, American Council of Education, Washington, DC, January 2013.

College Readiness: A Guide to the Field. Annenberg Institute for School Reform, Brown University, Providence, RI, April 2012.

Condron, Dennis J. "Social Class, School and Non-School Environments, and Black/White Inequalities in Children's Learning." *American Sociological Review* 74, no. 5 (October 2009): 685–708.

Connecticut Mastery Test, Fourth Generation, Percent Meeting State Goal. Connecticut Department of Education, Hartford, CT, 2010–11.

Contreras, Sharon. *Great Expectations: Syracuse City School District Strategic Plan 2012–2017.* Syracuse City School District, NY, August 24, 2012.

Cooper, Harris. "Summer Learning Loss: The Problems and Some Solutions." ERIC Clearinghouse on Elementary and Early Childhood Education, *ERIC Digest*, EDO-PS-03-5, 2003.

Cooper, Harris, et al. "Does Homework Improve Academic Achievement? A Synthesis of Research, 1987–2003." *Review of Educational Research* 76, no. 1 (Spring 2007): 1–62.

Crime Analysis Report: Say Yes Analysis Request. Syracuse Police Department, Criminal Intelligence Section, New York, February 18, 2013.

The Critical Connection between Student Health and Achievement: How Schools and Policymakers Can Achieve a Positive Impact. WestEd and the Philip P. Lee Institute for Health Policy Studies, University of California, San Francisco, April 2009.

Denver Summit Schools Network. Far Northeast Regional Information, Denver Public Schools. http://fne.dpsk12.org/dssn.

Desimone, Laura M., and Daniel Long. "Teacher Effects and the Achievement Gap: Do Teacher and Teaching Quality Influence the Achievement Gap between Black and White and High- and Low-SES Students in the Early Grades?" *Teachers College Record* 112, no. 2 (December 2010): 3061.

Duncan, Greg J., and Richard J. Murnane, eds. *Whither Opportunity: Rising Inequality, Schools, and Children's Life Chances.* New York: Russell Sage Foundation, 2011.

Durlak, Joseph A., et al. "The Impact of Enhancing Students' Social and Emotional Learning: A Meta-Analysis of School-Based Universal Interventions." *Child Development* 82, no. 1 (January/February 2011): 405–32.

Easton, Billy. "Albany's Unkindest Cut of All." *New York Times*, May 26, 2012, A21.

The Economic Benefits from Halving the Dropout Rate: A Boon to Business in the Nation's Largest Metropolitan Areas. Alliance for Excellent Education, Washington, DC, January 12, 2010.

The Economic Impact of Communities in Schools. Economic Modeling Specialists Inc., Moscow, ID, May 2012.

Education at a Glance 2011. Organization for Economic Cooperation and Development, Washington, DC, September 2011.

Edwards, Finley. "Do Schools Begin Too Early?" *Education Next* 12, no. 3 (Summer 2012) 53–57.

Elmore, Richard. "The (Only) Three Ways to Improve Performance in Schools." Harvard Graduate School of Education: Usable Knowledge, 2009. http://www.uknow.gse.harvard.edu/leadership/leadership001a.html.

Emanuel, Rahm. "Chicago's Plan to Match Education with Jobs." *Wall Street Journal*, December 19, 2011.

England, Mary Jane, and Leslie J. Sim. *Depression in Parents, Parenting, and Children: Opportunities to Improve Identification, Treatment and Prevention*. The National Academies Press, Washington, DC, 2009.

Epstein, Joseph. "Striking Teachers, Divided Antipathies." *Wall Street Journal*, September 13, 2012.

Fantuzzo, John, et al. "Academic Achievement of African American Boys: A City-Wide, Community-Based Investigation of Risk and Resilience." *Journal of School Psychology* 50, no. 5 (June 2012): 573.

Ferguson, Ronald F. "Teachers' Perceptions and Expectations and the Black-White Test Score Gap." *Urban Education* 38 (July 2003): 460–507.

Fertick, Laini. "Say Yes to Education Perceptual Study Report." *CRITICALMASSMEDIA*, Spring/Summer 2011.

Fleming, Nora. "Push Is On to Add Time to School Day, Year." *Education Week*, October 26, 2011.

"French Teachers Strike over Having to Work Five-Day Week." *AsiaOne*, Singapore Holdings, January 22, 2013.

Fullan, Michael. *Choosing the Wrong Drivers for Whole System Reform*. Centre for Strategic Education, East Melbourne Victoria, Australia, April 2011.

Fulop, Steven. "Turning Around Jersey City's Schools." *Star-Ledger* (Newark, NJ), September 12, 2012.

Gates, Bill. "Bill Gates—A Forum on Education in America." Speech transcript. Bill and Melinda Gates Foundation, November 11, 2008. http://www.gatesfoundation.org/media -center/speeches/2008/11/bill-gates-forum-on-education-in-america.

Gershman, Jacob. "Governor Feels Squeeze." *Wall Street Journal*, April 14, 2012.

Ginsburg, Alan, and Naomi Chudowsky. *Time for Learning: An Exploratory Analysis of NAEP Data*. National Assessment Governing Board, Washington, DC, December 2012.

Goldberg, Kenneth. "The Homework Trap and What to Do about It." *Washington Post*, April 6, 2012.

"Gov. Malloy Rolls Out Education Reform Package to Improve Low-Achieving Schools." News release. Office of the Governor, February 6, 2012.

Grant, Gerald. *Hope and Despair in the American City: Why There Are No Bad Schools in Raleigh*. Cambridge, MA: Harvard University Press, 2009.

Grier, Terry B. "A Healthy Partnership Makes a Visible Impact in Houston." *American School Board Journal*, June 2012.

Grossman, Jean, Margo Campbell, and Becca Raley. *Quality Time after School: What Instructors Can Do to Enhance Learning*. Private/Public Ventures, Philadelphia, 2007.

Hahnel, Carrie, and Orville Jackson. *Learning Denied: The Case for Equitable Access to Effective Teaching in California's Largest School District*. Education Trust–West, 2012, January 12, 2012.

Hartford Public Schools 2012 CMT and CAPT Scores: What Do the Results Tell Us? Achieve Hartford, August 16, 2012.

Heitin, Liana. "Gallup Poll: Student Success Linked to Positive Outlook." *Education Week*, August 29, 2012.

Hemphill, F. Cadelle, et al. *Achievement Gaps: How Hispanic and White Students in Public Schools Perform in Mathematics and Reading on the National Assessment of Educational Progress*. National Center for Education Statistics, Institute of Education Statistics, June 2011.

Henig, Jeffrey R., and S. Paul Reville. "Why Attention Will Return to Nonschool Factors." *Education Week*, May 25, 2011.

Heyns, Barbara. *Summer Learning and the Effects of Schooling.* New York: Academic Press, 1978.

"High Performing School Systems to Close Achievement Gaps in NEA Foundation-Funded Communities." Issue brief. NEA Foundation, November 2012.

High School and Youth Trends. National Institute on Drug Abuse, National Institutes of Health, U.S. Department of Health and Human Services, March 2011.

How America Pays for College 2012: Sallie Mae National Study of College Students and Parents. Sallie Mae, Washington, DC.

How Much Protection Does a College Degree Afford? Pew Charitable Trusts, Washington, DC, January 2013.

How the World's Most Improved School Systems Keep Getting Better. McKinsey & Company, New York, November 2010.

Hoxby, Caroline M., and Christopher Avery. "The Missing 'One-Offs': The Hidden Supply of High-Achieving Low-Income Students." NBER Working Paper No. 18586, National Bureau of Economic Research, Washington, DC, March 19, 2013.

Iceberg Ahead: The Hidden Cost of Public Sector Retiree Health Benefits in New York. Empire Center for New York State Policy, Albany, September 5, 2012.

Improving the Children's Mental Health System. Children's Law Center, Washington, DC, May 2012.

Jeffries, Shaver. "After-School Programs Save Kids (Including Me)." *Star-Ledger* (Newark, NJ), July 8, 2012.

Johnson, Jean, and Jon Rochkind. "Can I Get a Little Advice Here?" *Public Agenda*, March 3, 2010.

Kania, John, and Mark Kramer. "Collective Impact." *Stanford Social Innovation Review*, Winter 2011.

Kaplan, Thomas. "Experts Warn of Budget Ills for the State Lasting Years." *New York Times*, December 19, 2012.

Kelly, Andrew P., and Patrick McGuinn. "Mobilizing Parent Power for School Reform." *Education Week*, September 25, 2012.

Kendziora, Kimberly, and David Osher. *Say Yes to Education Research Report: Student Assessment System.* American Institutes for Research, August 21, 2007.

"Key Facts on Developmental Education." Bill and Melinda Gates Foundation. http://gatesfoundation.org/postsecondaryeducation/Pages/key-facts-on-developmental-education.

Kick-Starting Reform: Three City-Based Organizations Showing How to Transform Public Education. Cities for Education Entrepreneurship Trust, August 2012.

Knocking at the Door: Projections of High School Graduates. Western Interstate Commission for Higher Education, December 2012.

Krell, Kristen, and Alma Rivera. *Challenges and Solutions to Closing the Achievement Gap.* Santa Fe Community College, July 2010.

Letters to the Editor. *Post-Standard*, October 30, 2011.

Levy, Francesca. "America's Best Places to Raise a Family 2010." *Forbes*, June 7, 2010, http://www.forbes.com/2010/06/04/best-places-family-lifestyle-real-estate-cities-kids.html.

Luppescu, Stuart, et al. *Trends in Chicago's Schools across Three Eras of Reform: Summary of Key Findings.* Consortium on Chicago School Research, September 2011.

Maeroff, Gene I. *Altered Destinies: Making Life Better for Schoolchildren in Need.* New York: St. Martin's Griffin, 1998.

————. *School Boards in America: A Flawed Exercise in Democracy.* New York: Palgrave Macmillan, 2010.

Maltese, Adam V., Robert H. Tai, and Xitao Fan. "When Is Homework Worth the Time?: Evaluating the Association between Homework and Achievement in High School Science and Math." *High School Journal* 96, no. 1 (Fall 2012): 52–72.

McCombs, Jennifer S., et al. *Making Summer Count: How Summer Programs Can Boost Children's Learning.* RAND Education, Arlington, VA, 2011.

McKown, Clark, and Rhona Weinstein. "Teacher Expectations, Classroom Context, and the Achievement Gap." *Journal of School Psychology* 46, no. 3 (2008): 235–61.

Miller, Raegen. *Teacher Absence as a Leading Indicator of Student Achievement.* Center for American Progress, November 2012.

Miner, Stephanie. "Cuomo to Cities: Just Borrow." *New York Times,* February 14, 2013.

Mishook, Jacob, Elsa Dure, and Norm Fruchter. *Districts Play a Critical Role in School Turnaround—but They Need to Do It Right.* Related commentary, Annenberg Institute for School Reform, Brown University, Providence, RI, August 23, 2012.

Moore, Stephen. "From the Fab Five to the Three Rs." *Wall Street Journal,* December 31, 2011.

Murdock, Steve H. "Population Change in Texas and San Antonio: Implications for Economic Development, the Labor Force and Education." Presentation to San Antonio Manufacturers Association, Hobby Center for Study of Texas at Rice University, October 18, 2012.

Mussa, Martha Philbeck. *Taking Attendance Seriously: How School Absences Undermine Student and School Performance in New York City.* Campaign for Fiscal Equity, May 2001.

The Nation's Report Card: Civics 2010. National Assessment of Educational Progress, National Center for Education Statistics, Washington, DC, May 2011.

The Nation's Report Card: Mathematics 2011. National Assessment of Educational Progress, National Center for Education Statistics, Washington, DC, November 2011.

The Nation's Report Card: Vocabulary Results from the 2009 and 2011 NAEP Reading Assessments. National Assessment of Educational Progress, National Center for Education Statistics, Washington, DC, December 2012.

Nauer, Kim, Andrew White, and Rajeev Yerneni. *Strengthening Schools by Strengthening Families.* Center for New York City Affairs, The New School, New York, 2008.

Needs Analysis: Camden City Public Schools. UPD and Cross & Joftus, August 21, 2012.

Nixon, Carol. "Keeping Students Learning: School Climate and Student Support Systems." Edvantia, Inc., 2010 Tennessee Lead Conference, Nashville, TN, September 20–22, 2010.

Oates, Gary L. St. C. "An Empirical Test of Five Prominent Explanations for the Black-White Academic Performance Gap." *Social Psychology of Education* 12, no. 4 (December 2009): 415–41.

Osher, David, et al. *Syracuse City School District: Academic, Social Emotional, and Behavioral Indicators.* American Institutes for Research, August 15, 2011.

Owers, Paul, and John Maines. "School Grades Can Have Impact on Local Economies." *South Florida Sun-Sentinel,* July 11, 2012.

Pasciak, Mary B. "Say Yes Too Good to Be True?" *Buffalo News,* November 26, 2012.

Pasciak, Mary B., and Harold McNeil. "City, Schools Due for a Big Boost." *Buffalo News,* December 19, 2011.

Peterson, Paul E. "Neither Broad nor Bold." *Education Next,* Summer 2012, http://education next.org/neither-broad-nor-bold.

Peterson, Paul E., et al. *Globally Challenged: Are U.S. Students Ready to Compete?* Harvard Kennedy School, 2012.

Private Student Loans. A report to congressional committees by the U.S. Department of Education and the Consumer Protection Financial Bureau, Washington, DC, August 29, 2012.

Public School District Total Cohort Graduation Rate and Enrollment Outcome Summary, 2010–11 School Year. New York State Education Department, Albany.

Pursuing the American Dream: Economic Mobility across the Generations. Pew Charitable Trusts, Philadelphia, July 2012.

"Quality Counts 2008: Tapping into Teaching." *Education Week*, January 10, 2008.

Realizing the Promise of the Whole-School Approach to Children's Mental Health: A Practical Guide. SAMHSA-funded National Center for Mental Health Promotion and Youth Violence Prevention, Educational Development Center Inc., Health and Human Development Division, Waltham, MA, 2011.

Reardon, Sean F. "The Widening Achievement Gap between the Rich and the Poor: New Evidence and Possible Explanations." In *Whither Opportunity: Rising Inequality, Schools, and Children's Life Chances*, edited by Greg J. Duncan and Richard J. Murnane, 91–116. New York: Russell Sage Foundation, 2011.

Rebell, Michael A. *Attempting to Do Better with Less.* Campaign for Educational Equity, Teachers College, Columbia University, New York, August 24, 2012.

Rebell, Michael A., Jessica R. Wolff, and Joseph R. Rogers Jr. *Deficient Resources: An Analysis of the Availability of Bare Educational Resources in High-Needs Schools in Eight New York State School Districts.* Campaign for Educational Equity, Teachers College, Columbia University, New York, December 2012.

Remediation: Higher Education's Bridge to Nowhere. Complete College America, Washington, DC, April 2012.

Report of the State Budget Crisis Task Force: New York Report. State Budget Crisis Task Force, 2012.

Report on Student Cohort Growth in Hartford. Achieve Hartford, October 11, 2012.

Resources for Children: Findings and Recommendations for Better Integration and Capacity Development. An internal report to Say Yes, Turnaround for Children Inc., New York, June 4, 2010.

Rosenthal, Robert, and Lenore Jacobson. "Pygmalion in the Classroom." *The Urban Review* 3, no. 1 (September 1968): 16–20.

Ross, Steven M., et al. *First-Year Evaluation of the Say Yes Summer Success Academy.* Say Yes to Education, October 2011.

Ross, Steven M., and Laura Rodriguez. *Student Achievement in Syracuse City School District.* Paper commissioned by Say Yes to Education, Syracuse, NY, October 2012.

Rothwell, Jonathan. *Housing Costs, Zoning and Access to High-Scoring Schools.* Brookings Institution, Washington, DC, April 2012.

Rubie-Davies, Christine, John Hattie, and Richard Hamilton. "Expecting the Best for Students: Teacher Expectations and Academic Outcomes." *British Journal of Educational Psychology* 76, no. 3 (September 2006): 429–44.

Santos, Fernanda. "Regents Chancellor Minces Few Words on the City's Schools." *New York Times*, December 7, 2011.

SAT Report on College and Career Readiness. College Board, New York, September 2012.

Say Yes Leadership Planning Retreat. Constellation Advancement, August 6–7, 2012.

"Say Yes to Education Organizational Planning Discussion." Schoolhouse Partners and American Institutes for Research, November 13, 2006. Unpublished.

Schmitt, Mary Anne. Statement to the Committee on Education and the Workforce of the U.S. House of Representatives, Arlington, VA, July 17, 2001.

Schneider, Keith. "An Ohio River City Comes Back to Its Shoreline." *New York Times*, June 6, 2012.

"SCSD Budget Analysis: Board Summary Presentation." Schoolhouse Partners, Alexandria, VA, December 8, 2011.

Silva, Elena, and Susan Headden. *Reimagining the School Day: More Time for Learning*. Wallace Foundation, New York, November 2011.

Sinclair, Beth, et al. *Approaches for Integrating Skill-Based Activities in Out-of-School Time Programs*. Policy Studies Associates, Washington, DC, February 2012.

Smylie, Mark A., et al. *The Chicago Annenberg Challenge: Successes, Failure, and Lessons for the Future*. Chicago Annenberg Research Project, University of Chicago, Consortium on Chicago School Research, Chicago, August 2003.

Sparks, Sarah D. "Gaps Found in Access to Qualified Math Teachers." *Education Week*, April 3, 2013.

Stallings, Jane. "Allocated Academic Learning Time Revisited, or Beyond Time on Task." *Educational Researcher* 9, no. 11 (December 1980): 11–16.

Stillwell, Robert, and Jennifer Sable. *Public School Graduates and Dropouts from the Common Core of Data: School Year 2009–10*. National Center for Education Statistics, Institute of Education Sciences, Washington, DC, January 2013.

Stone, Charley, Carl Van Horn, and Cliff Zukin. *Chasing the American Dream: Recent College Graduates and the Great Recession*. John J. Heldrich Center for Workforce Development, Rutgers University, New Brunswick, NJ, May 2012.

Student Debt and the Class of 2011. Institute for College Access & Success, Washington, DC, 2012.

Syracuse City School District: Talent Management Assessment and Review. Cross & Joftus, Bethesda, MD, December 5, 2011.

Thompson, Jacquelyn, et al. "Executive Summary: Syracuse City School District; Special Education System Review." Cross & Joftus, November 30, 2011.

Tough, Paul. "The Birthplace of Obama the Politician." *New York Times Magazine*, August 19, 2012.

Trends in College Pricing 2012. College Board, New York, October 24, 2012.

True, Charlene, Kyle Butler, and Rachel Sefton. "Substitute Teachers: Making Lost Days Count." *International Journal of Educational Leadership Preparation* 6, no. 1 (January–March 2011).

True North: Charting the Course to College and Career Readiness. 2012 National Survey of School Counselors, College Board, New York, October 2012.

2009–2012 SCSD Student Performance Comparison AVID vs. Non-AVID. Data Analysis, Evaluation & Research Team, Office of Shared Accountability, Syracuse City School District, January 18, 2013.

2011 Annual Report. Huntington Family Centers, Syracuse, NY.

2013 CASEL Guide: Effective Social and Emotional Learning Programs, Preschool and Elementary School Edition. Collaborative for Academic, Social, and Emotional Learning, 2012. http://www.casel.org/guide.

Tyack, David, and Larry Cuban. *Tinkering toward Utopia: A Century of Public School Reform*. Cambridge, MA: Harvard University Press, 1995.

"Urban School Superintendents: Characteristics, Tenure, and Salary." Council of the Great City Schools, *Urban Indicator*, Fall 2010.

Usdan, Michael D. "Mayoral Leadership in Education: Current Trends and Future Directions." *Harvard Educational Review* 76, no. 2 (Summer 2006): 147–52.

U.S. Education Reform and National Security. Independent Task Force Report No. 68, Council on Foreign Relations, New York, 2012.

Vanneman, Alan, et al. *Achievement Gaps: How Black and White Students in Public Schools Perform in Mathematics and Reading on the National Assessment of Educational Progress.* National Center for Education Statistics, Institute of Education Statistics, July 2009.

Vargas, Claudia. "Metal Thieves Ravage Camden School Buildings." *Philadelphia Inquirer,* August 18, 2012.

Vaznis, James. "Absenteeism Rife at Boston High Schools." *Boston Globe,* January 15, 2012.

"View of Climate." *Education Week: Quality Counts,* January 10, 2013.

Wathington, Heather D., et al. *Getting Ready for College: An Implementation and Early Impacts Study of Eight Texas Developmental Summer Bridge Programs.* National Center for Postsecondary Research, Teachers College, Columbia University, New York, November 2011.

Weiss, George. "A Passion for Learning and Helping the Underserved Succeed." *Central New York Magazine,* October 10–November 10, 2010.

Wilson, Robin. "Syracuse's Slide: As Chancellor Focuses on the 'Public Good,' Syracuse's Reputation Slides." *Chronicle of Higher Education,* October 2, 2011.

Winerip, Michael. "Trying to Keep Students' Mental Health Care out of the E.R." *New York Times,* April 9, 2012.

Zinth, Jennifer Dounay. "Defining College Readiness: Where Are We Now and Where Do We Need to Be?" *The Progress of Education Reform* 13, no. 2 (April 2012): 1–7.

Index

Printed in the United States of America